FIFTY KEY BRITISH FILMS

This book, the latest in the successful Key Guides series, provides a chance to delve into 50 British films considered a true reflection of the times. With case studies from the 1930s heyday of cinema right up to the present day, this chronologically ordered volume includes coverage of:

- *The Ladykillers*
- *The 39 Steps*
- *A Hard Day's Night*
- *The Full Monty*
- *A Clockwork Orange*
- *The Wicker Man*

In *Fifty Key British Films*, Britain's best known talents, such as Loach, Hitchcock, Powell, Reed and Kubrick are scrutinised for their outstanding ability to articulate the issues of the time from key standpoints. This is essential reading for anyone interested in film and the increasing relevance of the British film industry on the international scene.

Dr Sarah Barrow is Senior Lecturer and Pathway Leader for Film Studies at Anglia Ruskin University, Cambridge, formerly Education Manager at Cambridge Arts Cinema and Cambridge Film Festival. She has published and presented widely on British and Peruvian cinema and is currently developing a project on cinema and political violence. She is a board member of the Cambridgeshire Film Consortium and advisor on Hispanic cinema for various film festivals.

John White teaches Film and Media Studies at Parkside Community College and Anglia Ruskin University in Cambridge. He is an examiner in A-level Film Studies for the Welsh Joint Education Committee and co-author of *AS Film Studies: the Essential Introduction* and *A2 Film Studies: the Essential Introduction*.

ALSO AVAILABLE FROM ROUTLEDGE

Cinema Studies: the Key Concepts (third edition)
Susan Hayward
978-0-415-36782-0

Communication, Cultural and Media Studies: the Key Concepts (third edition)
John Hartley
978-0-415-26889-9

Cultural Theory: the Key Concepts 2 (Second edition)
Edited by Andrew Edgar and Peter Sedgwick
978-0-415-28426-4

Cultural Theory: the Key Thinkers
Andrew Edgar and Peter Sedgwick
978-0-415-23281-4

Television Studies: the Key Concepts (second edition)
Neil Casey, Bernadette Casey, Justin Lewis, Ben Calvert and Liam French
978-0-415-17237-0

Fifty Contemporary Filmmakers
Edited by Yvonne Tasker
978-0-415-18974-3

Fifty Key Theatre Directors
Edited by Shomit Mitter and Maria Shevtsova
978-0-415-18732-9

The Routledge Companion to Theatre and Performance
Paul Allain and Jen Harvie
978-0-415-25721-3

FIFTY KEY BRITISH FILMS

Sarah Barrow and John White

Routledge
Taylor & Francis Group

LONDON AND NEW YORK

First published 2008
by Routledge
2 Park Square, Milton Park, Oxfordshire OX14 4RN

Simultaneously published in the USA and Canada
by Routledge
270 Madison Avenue, New York, NY 10016

Routledge is an imprint of the Taylor & Francis group, an informa business

Typeset in Bembo by
Taylor & Francis Books
Printed and bound in Great Britain by
TJ International Ltd, Padstow, Cornwall

British Library Cataloguing in Publication Data
A catalogue record for this book is available from the British Library

Library of Congress Cataloging in Publication Data
White, John, 1956–
Fifty Key British Films / John White and Sarah Barrow.
p. cm.
1. Motion pictures–Great
Britain. I. Barrow, Sarah. II. Title.
PN1993.5.G7W45 2008
791.430941–dc22
2007033785

ISBN-10: 0-415-43329-0 (hbk)
ISBN-10: 0-415-43330-4 (pbk)

ISBN-13: 978-0-415-43329-7 (hbk)
ISBN-13: 978-0-415-43330-3 (pbk)

CONTENTS

CHRONOLOGICAL LIST OF CONTENTS

ALPHABETICAL LIST OF CONTENTS

CONTRIBUTORS

Dave Allen began his career as an art teacher but has been involved in teaching film and media studies for over 25 years. His doctoral research had a pedagogic focus and examined links between various forms of visual teaching. He has been at the University of Portsmouth since 1988 and is currently Head of the School of Creative Arts, Film & Media.

Sarah Barrow is Senior Lecturer and Pathway Leader for Film Studies at Anglia Ruskin University, Cambridge. She has published various book chapters on British and Latin American cinema, and is preparing a book on Peruvian cinema, identity and political violence. She is a member of the Board of Management for the Cambridgeshire Film Consortium and advises on education events and resources for a number of film festivals.

Sarah Casey Benyahia is a film and media studies teacher. She is the author of *Teaching Contemporary British Cinema* (BFI, 2005), *Teaching Film and TV Documentary* (BFI, 2007) and co-author of *AS Film Studies: The Essential Introduction* and *A2 Film Studies: The Essential Introduction* (both Routledge, 2007).

Ian Christie is a film historian, curator and broadcaster, currently Professor of Film and Media History at Birkbeck College and director of the London Screen Study Collection. In 2006 he was Slade Professor of Fine Art at Cambridge University. He has written books on Powell and Pressburger, Russian cinema, Scorsese and Gilliam; and worked on exhibitions such as Film as Film (1979), Eisenstein: His Life and Art (1988), Spellbound (1996) and Modernism: Designing a New World (2006). His interest in early cinema led to a BBC television series *The Last Machine: Early Cinema and the Birth of the Modern World* (1994), and he is working on a history of Robert Paul and the early film business in Britain.

Corinna Downing is a freelance film and event programmer for young audiences. Her work focuses on bringing the greatest variety of film to the widest audience of children, young people and educators. She is currently Film Programme Consultant for the London Children's Film Festival in addition to consultation, training and delivery of film projects for London-based and national organisations including the UK Film Council, British Film Institute, Human Rights Watch International Film Festival, Lambeth City Learning Centre and Film Club.

Freddie Gaffney is Course Leader for Broadcasting at Ravensbourne College of Design and Communication. A practising screenwriter and cinematographer, he has worked in both film and television. He is Principal Examiner for WJEC AS/A Level Film Studies, and has consulted for industry lead bodies. He is co-author of *AS Film Studies: The Essential Introduction* and *A2 Film Studies: The Essential Introduction* (both Routledge, 2007).

Lincoln Geraghty is Principal Lecturer in Film Studies and Subject Leader in Media Studies in the School of Creative Arts, Film and Media at the University of Portsmouth. He is author of *Living with Star Trek: American Culture and the Star Trek Universe* (IB Tauris, 2007) and *American Science Fiction Film and Television* (Berg, forthcoming) and the editor of *The Influence of Star Trek on Television, Film and Culture* (McFarland, 2007), *The Shifting Definitions of Genre: Essays on Labelling Films, Television Shows and Media* co-edited with Mark Jancovich (McFarland, forthcoming), and *Future Visions: Key Science Fiction and Fantasy Television Texts* (Scarecrow, forthcoming).

Steven Gerrard is a film lecturer at the University of Wales, Lampeter. He is currently engaged in researching the *Carry On* films as part of his PhD thesis. He has taught modules on *Introduction to Film*, *The Western*, *Film Genre*, and *Film Stars*. When he is not too busy he dreams of being the next *Doctor Who*.

Nigel Herwin is Course Director of Film and Television Studies for Continuing Education at the University of East Anglia. He also gives guest lectures on various aspects of Film and TV at sixth form colleges and regional film theatres. Special interests include silent cinema, European cinema, comedy, *Doctor Who* and depictions of bipolar affective disorder.

Isabelle McNeill is Affiliated Lecturer in the Department of French at the University of Cambridge and a Fellow of Trinity Hall. She specialises in film theory as well as French and Francophone film. She has published articles on various topics, including memory, media and the city in recent French film, and decadent cinema. She is a founding member of the Cambridge Film Trust and contributes to the programming of the Cambridge Film Festival.

Cathy Poole is Director of Lifelong Learning at Bristol University, and lectures on the Bristol MA in Screen Studies. She was previously Head of Learning at Watershed Media Centre, then Education Advisor at South West Screen. She has published materials about film for teachers and students at primary, GCSE and A Level, and contributed the chapter 'How to introduce Media Literacy to Schools' to a compilation produced as a result of the 'Media Skills and Competence' conference in Finland (2005). She was a member of the BFI's Associate Tutor panel, and is convener of the MovIES group (Moving Image Education Specialists).

Robert Shail lectures in Film Studies at the University of Wales, Lampeter. He has published articles and essays on film stardom, gender, and British cinema history. His most recent publications include *British Directors: A Critical Guide* (Edinburgh University Press, 2007) and *Stanley Baker: A Life in Film* (University of Wales Press, 2007).

Trish Sheil is Education Officer for the Cambridgeshire Film Consortium, and guest lecturer in Film Studies at Anglia Ruskin University. Before this, she taught English and Drama in schools and colleges in England and Wales. Her principal research interests are performance codes, melodrama and silent cinema, and the theatrical heritage of the post-war films of Powell and Pressburger. She has written on film for the Welsh Academy.

Neil Sinyard is Professor and Head of Film Studies at the University of Hull. He is the author of more than twenty books on film, including monographs of directors such as Billy Wilder, Alfred Hitchcock, Woody Allen, Steven Spielberg, Richard Lester, Nicolas Roeg and Jack Clayton. He is also co-editor of the series of monographs of British Film Makers for Manchester University Press, and of a volume of essays on 1950s British Cinema. He has been teaching Film Studies for over thirty years.

Justin Smith is Principal Lecturer and Subject Leader in Film Studies at the University of Portsmouth, UK. A cultural historian with a specialism in British cinema, his research interests and writing cover film fandom, reception and exhibition cultures, and issues of identity and memory. He has published articles in *The Journal of British Cinema and Television* and *Fashion Theory* and has recently contributed a chapter on web ethnography to *The New Film History* (Palgrave-Macmillan, 2007). He is currently writing a book based on his PhD entitled *Cult Films and Film Cults in British Cinema, 1968–86.*

Lynda Townsend teaches film and English and in recent years has been working with the Open University and the Institute of Continuing Education at Cambridge University. She is a freelance writer on film and art, and has made contributions to *frieze* magazine. She has a particular interest in filmic representations of gender and contemporary expressions of modernity in world cinema.

Simon Ward is Head of Programming & Development at the Independent Cinema Office. His obsession with cinema began after sneaking into Romero's *Dawn of the Dead* in a Dublin fleapit at the tender age of eleven. He took a degree in Film Studies at the University of Kent, and after graduating spent several years working at the London Film Festival before becoming Deputy Director of Cinema at the Institute of Contemporary Arts (ICA) in London.

Jean Welsh is Head of Media Studies and Film Studies at Hills Road Sixth Form College, Cambridge and teaches A-levels in these subjects. She has run INSET sessions on various aspects of film and media for both the BFI and the WJEC and contributed to the *In the Picture* Film Reader on British Cinema.

Nigel Wheale includes amongst his publications *The Postmodern Arts* (Routledge 1995), *Writing and Society: Literacy, Print and Politics in Britain 1590–1660* (Routledge 1999) and *Remaking Shakespeare: Performance across Media, Genres and Cultures* (edited with Pascale Aebischer and Edward J. Esche, Palgrave, 2003). His most recent publication is *Raw Skies: New and Selected Poems* (Shearsman Books, 2005).

John White is a teacher of film, English and media currently working at Parkside Community College and Anglia Ruskin University in Cambridge. He is a co-author of *AS Film Studies: the Essential Introduction* and *A2 Film Studies: the Essential Introduction* (both Routledge, 2007) and an A-level examiner for Film Studies with the Welsh Joint Education Committee. He is a co-editor of both *Fifty Key British Films* and its forthcoming companion volume, *Fifty Key US Films* (both Routledge).

Melanie Williams is a Lecturer in Film Studies at the University of Hull. She has written on British cinema for various journals including *Screen*, *Cinema Journal*, *Sight and Sound* and *Film Quarterly*. She is currently working on a co-edited collection of essays on Ealing Studios (I.B. Tauris) and a monograph on the films of David Lean (Manchester University Press).

INTRODUCTION

This book is not an attempt to assert that the 50 films discussed here are the 'greatest' or 'best' British films ever made. The suggestion is more simply that this selection of films operates to provide an initial appreciation of British cinema over the past 100 years. As an introductory survey focusing on individual texts, several other '50s' would serve equally as well. There is neither effort, nor wish, to promote a particular canon of British films. The very nature of a 'canon' is that it is exclusive and this list is not designed to be that (other than in the sense that we only have room for 50 essays in this book). Nor is this list ranked in order of merit; there are two contents lists, one in date order and the other in alphabetical order, and both of these structures leave a virtually infinite space for your own additions.

It is true, however, that compiling lists of films according to various criteria has always been a favourite pastime of both cinephiles and movie-goers. It is fun; and film, like all storytelling and art-forms, is built around different types of pleasure. Therefore, beyond the theoretical seriousness of discussions about the potential elitism, exclusivity and political manoeuvrings associated with the notion of canons, hopefully you will also simply enjoy agreeing and disagreeing with the inclusions and exclusions you find here.

What were our benchmarks for deciding on these particular 50 films? We wanted to include a spread that extended from the period known as 'early cinema' (roughly 1895–1910) to the present. We wanted to have a range of mainstream genres but also a few titles that took us beyond commercial cinema. We wanted readers to see that certain titles that have reached 'classic' status had been included and were present for their consideration, but we also wanted other films to be included that might encourage the adoption of a wider viewing experience. We wanted the selection to be useful to both students and the general reader looking for an introductory range of material.

We cannot speak for each of our contributors,[1] but for ourselves in the writing we wanted to stress that film form, narrative structure, genre, authorship and other technical approaches to film analysis only have significance within the social experience of making and reading film; that the crucial context of film and film studies is that of producers and audiences making films and making sense of films within a social context. We wished to stress the historical and cultural, as well as the cinematic contexts. Films are clearly not created in isolation from what is happening in society during the period in which they come into being. They are products of particular societies and each is made at a particular moment in that society's history. In viewing them, for us, it is crucial to see them as determinedly exploring, purposefully commenting upon, or unwittingly reflecting issues relevant to their particular socio-historical moment, but also to see them as being continually re-framed and re-constituted by their reception at different times. Films do not exist, cut off from the world in splendid isolation within the cinema auditorium, or behind the drawn curtains of the home cinema experience or blackout facilities of the university or college screening room. In their conception, their production, their distribution, their exhibition and their reception, they take their place within the social sphere; and to be properly understood they need to be seen within this context. Although it is the case that films are re-created in every act of viewing by the individual spectator, and although any social action and historical moment can be seen and understood in a plurality of ways, still invalid and incorrect readings are possible and the validity or otherwise of any particular reading is a vital matter for discussion. Equally, every reading that has been argued clearly from the evidence of the social and historical context remains contestable. The contesting of readings is, after all, the testing of readings and this process is at the heart of both academic debate and everyday political engagement.

To finally be truthful, as our emphasis on social context suggests, as editors we cannot escape charges of 'canon building'.

> That canons exist in film studies and that canon formation is involved with the political sphere is evident. Much less evident is the shifting politics, past and present, of the factors contributing to canon formation.[2]

However lacking in political 'malice aforethought' we assure you the process has been, we have ultimately chosen this list of 50 films over all other possibilities and in doing so we are displaying vested interests; but that is merely in the nature of all social exchange. What matters is that as viewers of film we should engage in this social exchange with critical awareness. As Barbara Klinger has suggested, there are 'competing voices involved in a particular film's public signification'.[3] We should not attempt to stand apart from this creation of 'public signification', detached from this discussion, aware of each of these 'competing voices' but never entering into the fray; rather we should 'get our hands dirty', become involved in discussing the implications of these voices and through this action arrive at our own voice and political position.

Despite our strong initial focus on the films themselves we agree with Janet Staiger when she suggests that:

> interpreting texts or films is a historical reality determined by context, not an inherent or automatic act due to some essential human process . . .

and would emphasise with her that it is at this point that the critical debate can begin, because:

> once interpretation becomes historical rather than universal, then claims for privileging some interpretations can be refuted. Interpretations-in-history become politicized since they relate to historical social struggles, not to essences.[4]

In discussing her concept of a 'totalised view', Staiger talks of achieving an approach to texts in which the discovery of meaning and significance has been displaced from text to context. More accurately for us, in an alert reading, context is recognised as being fully sutured into text.

With essays of this length, the number of questions raised is always going to be greater than the number successfully answered, but that is as it should be. Hopefully, these short essays will encourage you to return to, or seek out for the first time, at least some of these films with the enthusiasm to explore further and with one or two questions for which you are determined to seek answers. Each entry aims to be suggestive rather than exhaustive, attempting to introduce selected aspects of film form and thematic content in relation to the focus text, as well as considering historical and cultural contexts. A synopsis is not given since it is assumed the reader is familiar with plot and storyline, or can become so very easily. Similarly, details of a film's production history are not supplied unless this is in some way relevant to ideas at the core of the film. There is, as we have emphasised, a strong underlying concern throughout to place these films within social, historical and political contexts, and not simply to analyse the 'look' of a film. Concepts and debates relevant to film studies as an academic subject are considered within individual entries, where appropriate. So, ideas relating to genre, narrative structure, auteur theory, representation, spectatorship and performance, for example, are dealt with at various points.

In summary, this book offers brief introductions to a range of films, many of which have gained 'classic' status through critical and/or popular acclaim. The contents pages provided give both date-ordered and alphabetical listings, allowing both students and the general reader to use it as a reference work, and the index of key names, institutions and topics has been designed to help with more specific research activities. The effort throughout is to offer entries that are accessible to the well-informed general reader but also sufficiently exploratory and analytical to be useful as models for students of film.

Notes

1 The central feature of a book structured around individual contributions from colleagues working in film education and the film industry is that it allows for a diversity of approaches, and is likely to absorb within itself something of this core aspect of Film Studies.
2 Janet Staiger, 'The Politics of Film Canons', *Cinema Journal* 24, (3), Spring 1985, pp. 4–23.
3 Barbara Klinger, 'Film History Terminable and Interminable: Recovering the Past in Reception Studies', *Screen* 38 (2), 1997, pp. 107–128.
4 Janet Staiger, *Interpreting Films: Studies in the Historical Reception of American Cinema*, Princeton, NJ, Princeton University Press, 1992, p. 18.

FIFTY KEY BRITISH FILMS

RESCUED BY ROVER (1905)

[Production Company: Hepworth. Director: Lewin Fitzhamon. Producer: Cecil Hepworth (also as 'the Father').]

THE ? MOTORIST (1906)

[Production Company: Paul's Animatograph Works. Director: Walter Booth. Producer: Robert Paul.]

If there are any familiar images of early British cinema to match the workers filmed leaving the Lumière factory in 1895 or the Western gunman of *The Great Train Robbery* (1903), they may well be either the sheepdog star of Cecil Hepworth's *Rescued by Rover* (1904), or a vintage jalopy circling Saturn's rings in Robert Paul's *The ? Motorist* (1906). Both of these films were considerable successes in their own day, and testify to a thriving British industry, before American cinema became the universal diet of filmgoers in most countries.

During the mid-twentieth century, early films were usually considered 'primitive' examples of what cinema would eventually become; it is not too hard to imagine *Rescued by Rover* being described as an early version of the family adventure, or *The ? Motorist* as a shape-shifting fantasy anticipating the flying car of *Chitty-Chitty Bang Bang* (1968). The very terms once used to describe early film – 'silent', 'flickering', 'black and white' – all suggest something missing, not yet achieved. Such attitudes persist, but early film is now more widely seen in good conditions, thanks to presentations of 'live silents' and high-quality DVD restorations.[1]

More recently, historians of early media have also argued that early films need to be seen as part of the world that created and consumed them, since their themes and stories are often 'intermedial', or shared across different media.[2] Another key concept is the idea of a 'cinema of attractions', rather than one of narrative efficiency.[3] From this standpoint, such films used devices and strategies to give exhibitors the material to attract audiences and hold their attention. Their aim may be to surprise, amuse, or shock – and only incidentally to tell a story. Straightforward storytelling as the main function of cinema would come later, after 1907, and it would involve losses as well as gains – especially loss of the variety in a mixed programme of short film that early audiences expected.

To place these two landmarks of early British cinema, then, we need to realise that they belong to the second decade of moving picture entertainment, coming after the early years of brief comedies and 'actualities'. This is also just before the time of specialised cinema buildings, when films are being shown as part of music hall programmes, at fairgrounds, and in every kind of hall imaginable, from town halls and assembly rooms to church halls. Some of these programmes were long – up to two hours in the case of Mitchell and Kenyon's shows of local films.[4] They could also be highly topical, covering national and international events, such as the Anglo–Boer War, or the comings and goings of royalty. But with films such as *Rescued by Rover* and *The ? Motorist*, experienced producers were reaching beyond simple attractions and anecdotes towards a more ambitious kind of story film with something of the complexity of the short fiction that was then common in newspapers and magazines.

Rescued by Rover manages to combine a number of familiar motifs in what would prove to be a winning formula. One of these, a maid's rendezvous with her soldier beau in the park, had already been filmed twice by Paul, in 1896 and 1898.[5] In Hepworth's film, a nursemaid is taking baby for an outing in the pram near a park, but is more interested in the soldier she meets ('every afternoon', we learn from Hepworth's catalogue). Her distraction allows a beggar–woman, whom she has just snubbed, to take the infant from the pram, which would have chimed with the widespread belief that gypsies commonly stole babies.[6] These two components, the careless maid and the callous kidnapper, lay the groundwork for the film's main 'attraction': the family's faithful dog discovering the child and alerting the father.

Stories about dogs' powers of detection and extraordinary devotion had been popular for decades, especially in dog-loving Britain. In Conan Doyle's second Sherlock Holmes novel, *The Sign of Four* (1890), it is Toby, 'a queer mongrel with the most amazing power of scent', that leads Holmes and Watson to the heart of the mystery. As for stories of canine devotion to children, the most recent example would have been Nana, a Newfoundland who acts as the Darling family's nursemaid in J. M. Barrie's play *Peter Pan and Wendy*, which had its premiere in December 1904. These stories, together with countless more anonymous ones on similar themes, would have made *Rescued by Rover* an up-to-date version of the ever-popular rescue narrative – as featured in a film like James Williamson's *Fire!* (1901), where a fireman rescues a baby from a burning house.

Here it is the family's collie, Rover, and no fewer than 16 of the 22 shots that make up this fast-moving film show Rover's mission: setting off from his master's suburban house, swimming across a river, and searching a terrace of mean hovels, before he finds the baby in the old woman's garret, then makes the return journey to bring his master. We see the same journey three times – although when the husband uses a convenient boat to cross the river, we catch sight of a bridge that both dog and man could have taken, but with less dramatic effect. For drama is what *Rescued by Rover* concentrates on delivering, by means of showing motive and generating narrative momentum. After an appealing close-up of the baby at the centre of the story, the first scene shows how the nursemaid's refusal of the beggar's appeal leads to an opportunistic kidnapping. And after Rover intuits the reason for the distress of the nursemaid and his mistress, a series of five varied shots show him moving constantly towards us in his search.

The garret scene offers a sharp contrast with the comfortable family home of the baby and its parents with roof timbers and bare brick exposed and a jumble of rags on which both baby and beggar sleep. But the action is also purposeful, establishing motive, as the kidnapper first removes the baby's plentiful clothes, and takes a swig from a bottle of something undoubtedly alcoholic. After the father has rescued the baby, the old woman will content herself with still having the clothes to sell, no doubt funding another bottle. But it is the handling of the three legs of the rescue journey that has been best remembered about this film, essentially because Hepworth's 'director' (although the term was not yet in use), Lewin Fitzhamon, uses a highly fluent grammar of narrative, with Rover seen consistently moving away from the camera in his journey back, and the third leg, as he leads his master, following the same route, suitably varied and accelerated by means of shorter shots.

Rover indeed proved to be a runaway success leading to so many orders that Hepworth had to re-shoot the film twice to make new negatives. Rover would also return, two years later, to co-star with a horse in *Dumb Sagacity*, another film celebrating animal instinct. This might suggest that Hepworth had turned his back on modern subjects of the kind that British film-makers needed to make to remain internationally competitive; and indeed he would be increasingly identified with traditional English stories. But it might be more accurate to say that he failed to realise the full potential of animal-centred adventure films, in view of the enormous success enjoyed by the Rin-Tin-Tin series, produced in Hollywood between 1923 and 1931, and the later Lassie films.

Hepworth had actually made several early motoring comedies, but it was another pioneer British film-maker and motorist, Robert Paul, who would produce an eccentric manifesto for the freedom offered by the new horseless carriage. *The ? Motorist* begins as if anticipating an adventure serial, with a speeding motorist and his female companion running over a policeman who tried to stop them. But it quickly turns fantastic when they escape by driving straight up the side of a building and off into space, orbiting the moon and Saturn. They crash land through the roof of 'Handover Court', scattering the lawyers, and make another fantastic escape from the law by turning briefly into a horse and cart, before triumphantly driving away. The car used in the film was Paul's own, a 1903 model, and his own experience of the law's hostility towards 'horseless carriage' drivers may have inspired the film as a kind of fantasy revenge.[7] Another inspiration was probably Georges Méliès, Paul's one-time client and now competitor.[8] Méliès' *The Impossible Journey / Voyage à travers l'impossible* (1904) similarly transported its travellers through a nursery-style solar system, while his 1905 version of a madcap road race from Paris to Monte Carlo may have prompted Paul's own motoring fantasy.

This may be primarily a 'trick film' showing off what Paul and his ex-magician collaborator Walter Booth could achieve with a combination of live-action shooting and model work in Paul's Muswell Hill studio. But it's also a film inspired by the new freedom of motoring and the friction this caused in Edwardian society, as would be reflected in the ambiguous treatment of Mr Toad's reckless driving in *The Wind in the Willows* (1908). And at a time when English producers still enjoyed worldwide export markets, it made a strong impression on at least one distinguished spectator – the Russian Symbolist writer Andrei Bely, best known for his modernist novel *Petersburg*. In a 1907 essay, Bely wrote of a car that crashes through a wall, rushes up another wall, 'defying the laws of gravity', and 'zooms up into the sky', dodging meteors, then rather bizarrely described the driver as 'death in a top hat, baring his teeth and rushing towards us'.[9] Here Bely seems to be linking the imagery of the film with his own apocalyptic view of modernity. And set alongside the conservative social world of *Rescued by Rover*, Paul's *Motorist* is a reminder of how anarchic, even avant-garde, early film-making could be, before feature-length storytelling dictated a more sober realism.

Notes

1 Abel Gance's *Napoleon* was shown in London with an orchestral score in 1979. Many festivals now show silent-era films in this way, including the annual 'Giornate del Cinema Muto' in Sacile, Italy, and 'Bristol Silents', specialising in comedy film. The two films discussed here are available on the DVD, *Early Cinema: Primitives and Pioneers* (BFIVD643).

2 On 'intermediality', see the introduction and various essays in Rick Altman and Richard Abel (eds) *The Sounds of Early Cinema*, Bloomington, Indiana University Press, 2001.

3 A term coined by André Gaudreault and Tom Gunning. See Gunning, 'The Cinema of Attractions: Early Film, Its Spectator and the Avant-Garde', in Thomas Elsaesser and Adam Barker (eds) *Early Cinema: Space, Frame, Narrative*, London, BFI, 1989.

4 See Vanessa Toulmin et al. (eds) *The Lost World of Mitchell & Kenyon: Edwardian Britain on Film*, London, BFI, 2004.

5 The second of these is included on a DVD, *R.W. Paul: the Collected Films 1895–1908*, BFI (BFIVD642).

6 The kidnapper here is not strictly a gypsy, since we see her attic lair, but this would not prevent her being associated with supposed gypsy behaviour. On the persistent belief that gypsies abduct babies see, for instance, A. T. Sinclair, 'Notes on the Gypsies', *The Journal of American Folklore*, Vol. 19, No. 74, Jul.–Sep., 1906, pp. 212–213.

7 Paul's conviction for speeding in the same car used in the film appeared in *The Barnet Press*, 10 August 1907, p. 8. He admitted he had been to a 'club meet' – presumably a motoring club – in Hatfield, and knew that 'the police were timing cars', but claimed his car could not exceed the speed limit.

8 Méliès bought a batch of projectors from Paul in 1896, and converted one of these into his first camera. By 1901 both were leading producers of elaborate trick films.

9 On Bely's reaction to this film, see Yuri Tsivian, *Early Cinema in Russia and its Cultural Reception*, London and New York, Routledge, 1994, pp. 150–151.

Further reading

Ian Christie, *The Last Machine: Early Cinema and the Birth of the Modern World*, London, BFI/BBC, 1994.

Thomas Elsaesser and Adam Barker (eds) *Early Cinema: Space, Frame, Narrative*, London, BFI, 1989.

Simon Popple and Joe Kember, *Early Cinema: From Factory Gate to Dream Factory*, London, Wallflower, 2003.

IAN CHRISTIE

THE LIFE STORY OF DAVID LLOYD GEORGE (1918)

[Production company: Ideal Film Company. Director: Maurice Elvey. Screenwriter: Sir Sidney Low. Producer: Simon Rowson. Cast: Norman Page (David Lloyd-George), Ernest Thesiger (Joseph Chamberlain), Alma Reville (Megan Lloyd-George), Douglas Munro (Benjamin Disraeli).]

How can a film that doesn't appear in any history of British cinema be a 'key British film'? The story behind *The Life Story of David Lloyd George* is as remarkable as the film itself, and helps to explain why British film history now needs to take account of its biggest discovery from the silent era. If this ambitious film had been released at the end of 1918, it might have changed the reputation of film-making in Britain. Instead it lay forgotten in an attic, until Lord Tenby, grandson of its subject, brought it to the attention of the Wales Film and Television Archive, which led to its restoration and a premiere in 1996, delayed by nearly 80 years.

Why then was it not released in 1918? During the First World War, film had come to play an increasingly important role in public life. It delivered propaganda of different kinds, against the enemy and on behalf of the war effort. It communicated news of major events; and with the official film *The Battle of Somme* (1916), it contributed to boosting national morale after the huge losses in this battle. Film also provided welcome distraction from the war, for civilians and service personnel alike, with films ranging from the 'Ultus' adventure serials to Charlie Chaplin's knockabout comedies.[1] With the end of the war widely anticipated, there were various plans to make major commemorative films, one of which was D. W. Griffith's *Hearts of the World* (1918), following America's entry into the war in 1917. The British company Ideal, led by Harry and Simon Rowson, had already enjoyed success with several speciality films, such as *Masks and Faces* (1917), featuring an all-star cast of famous stage actors, and decided to make a biography of Britain's war leader, the Prime Minister David Lloyd George.

The working title for the film was *The Man Who Saved the Empire*, and the film press carried increasingly impressive advertisements for the film during late 1918. In December, these stopped abruptly and the film that was to mark the climax of Ideal's ambitions disappeared. What had happened was that a blustering journalist, MP and convicted swindler, Horatio Bottomley, had attacked the Rowsons in his influential paper *John Bull*, suggesting that because they had changed their name from 'Rosenbaum' and had employed some foreign-born extras to play the parts of soldiers in the film's war scenes, their motives in making the film were less than patriotic.[2] The Rowsons retaliated with a writ for libel, but in the meantime were informed that Lloyd George now wanted the film suppressed. According to Harry Rowson, an agent called at Ideal's offices with £20,000 in cash to cover the production costs – a high figure for this period in Britain – and took away the negative and a print, which were never seen again.

Many questions remain unanswered, even after the film's discovery and restoration. Lloyd George appears to have supported the production initially. With war over, was he advised that appearing in a film might harm his chances in the forthcoming general election? Was he afraid of the slur in Bottomley's scurrilous article, implying that the Rowsons had not only concealed their German background but their Jewishness? Or even, as Lloyd George's biographer suggested, might his mistress have influenced him by objecting to the film's conventional portrayal of his domestic life?[3]

Although none of these speculations can be confirmed, the simple fact that a prestige production could be made to disappear on the eve of release indicates how potentially powerful film was seen to be in the Britain of 1918. But now that we have *The Life Story of David Lloyd George* resurrected and, unusually for a film of this period, complete and in excellent condition, what can we make of it today?[4] For a modern audience, it offers a curious mixture of what seems almost Victorian along with episodes that are startlingly modern in their staging. In this respect, it can usefully be compared with one of the few models that could have guided the producers and director Maurice Elvey as they tackled an epic of modern history: *Birth of a Nation* (1915). Griffith's film is largely fictional, although set against the background of the American Civil War and featuring the historical figures of Abraham Lincoln and the Civil War generals. For all its fame as the film that gave cinema a new status – quite apart from its notoriety in legitimising the Ku Klux Klan – *Birth of a Nation* also combines sentimentality and pantomime antics with a sometimes astonishing sense of historical presence and real epic sweep. The war that occupies the last third of *Lloyd George* offered no such opportunities for visual display, with Lloyd George's direct contact with the actual conflict limited to his visit to the Western Front, accompanied by his French allies. But the sense of accurate historical reconstruction throughout is, if anything, even greater than in Griffith.

As the original title indicated, the film makes no bones about wholehearted praise for its subject, ignoring all of the controversy that surrounded Lloyd George. Although the script was written by a respected historian,[5] it follows the traditional pattern of biography of a 'great man', showing how the experiences of Lloyd George's childhood and youth shaped – or foreshadowed – his adult qualities. When the family is forced to leave their house after the early death of his father, young David is shown fiercely resisting those who have bought the furniture, with a title spelling out the moral that this is the future Liberal politician's 'first revolt against authority'. Similarly, a children's mock battle based on the still-recent Franco-Prussian War of 1870–71, in which David leads the French against the Germans, pointedly anticipates his role as national leader in the Great War. The idea that 'the child is father of the man' was a staple of inspirational biographies in the nineteenth century,[6] and it continued to play an important role in biographical films, even while new styles of psychological and subjective biography were appearing, notably from Bloomsbury group writers and followers of Sigmund Freud.[7]

The film's most unexpected aspect, at once archaic yet also highly filmic, is its use of 'supernatural' devices to lend extra weight to Lloyd George's actions. The first of these follows the children's mock battle, which turns into a duel between a youngster and a giant figure in ancient armour. The future prime minister has become David battling Goliath in the Biblical story, with his adult image and that of Kaiser Wilhelm of Germany briefly superimposed on the two figures to make clear the allegorical significance of the scene. This might have been suggested by the name 'David', leading by association to 'David and Goliath', but it also recalls the tradition of political caricature in such journals as *Punch*, in which the Kaiser, always portrayed in his spiked helmet, could be cast as a heavily armed warrior destined to be defeated by a weaker but more resourceful enemy. Such boldly metaphorical insertions would continue to play a part in films during the silent era, easily incorporated into the film's flow, but would quickly disappear in the sound era, when similar effects would be achieved by more realist means.

Other non-realist effects include the gradual appearance of a row of elderly figures against a long wall to illustrate dramatically how 'the workhouse doors opened' as a result of Lloyd George introducing old age pensions as Chancellor of the Exchequer; and his being surrounded by the ghosts of past politicians, both British and American, as he takes responsibility for leading the war against Germany. The effect here is not unlike Griffith's allegorical use of a woman rocking a cradle, as a kind of muse of history, in his *Intolerance* (1916).

But if such episodes link the film with traditional forms of representation that pre-date cinema, Elvey also clearly wanted to situate it in the modern world of press photography and cinema newsreels. Two of the most impressive sequences in the film are crowd scenes, filmed in recognisable public locations and with many hundreds of extras. In the first, Lloyd George escapes from an unruly mob besieging Birmingham Town Hall in 1900, when he has taken a stand against Joseph Chamberlain and the war against the Boers; while in the second, he is pursued outside the Queen's Hall in London by militant

Suffragettes during the long campaign for women's right to vote. Both sequences have an immediacy that looks forward to Eisenstein's handling of crowds in his revolutionary epics *The Battleship Potemkin* (1926) and *October* (1928), or even to more modern films that aim to reproduce the feel of newsreel, such as *The Battle of Algiers* (1966). Yet with its combination of different styles and its sense of a mysterious, overriding destiny at work, it might also be compared to Oliver Stone's controversial *JFK*.

Opinions differ among the relatively few who have so far seen *The Life Story of David Lloyd George* as to whether it is a lost masterpiece, or a curiosity. Yet it has a confidence in its subject and a boldness of execution that are disarming and undeniably impressive. This may not convince sceptics that Maurice Elvey, one of the most prolific of all British directors, is a neglected British auteur, but it certainly challenges received opinion that British film-making in the 1910s was uniformly lacking in ambition. Had the film been released in early 1919, and no doubt generated controversy by making an intervention into post-war politics, might cinema have had a higher profile in British history? Could 'Elvey's *Lloyd George*' have been mentioned in the same breath as Griffith's and Eisenstein's now famous films about recent American and Russian history? We shall never know, but now at least we can speculate.

Notes

1 After the success of *Ultus and the Grey Lady* in 1916 George Pearson made three further adventures in the series for British Gaumont, developing a home-grown version of the popular French and American serials. Chaplin made 20 films in 1914 alone, becoming the most popular film star in Britain, as elsewhere.

2 For details of the legal and political manoeuvring that led to the film's withdrawal, see Sarah Street's introduction to and extracts from 'The Memoir of Harry Rowson' in David Berry and Simon Horrocks (eds) *David Lloyd George: The Movie Mystery*, Cardiff, University of Wales Press, 1998, pp. 33–49.

3 John Grigg, 'Speculating on the Projections of History', *David Lloyd George: The Movie Mystery*, pp. 60–61. Grigg is also the author of the most authoritative biography of Lloyd George.

4 The film material found by Lord Tenby left archivists with a number of choices in selecting what to include in the restoration, and how to tint it in the authentic style of the time. The resulting film is almost certainly longer than it would have been, at over two and a half hours, but is also of higher quality than any other surviving British film of the silent era (indeed it is one of the best preserved of *all* silent films). On the restoration, see chapter 5 of *David Lloyd George: The Movie Mystery*.

5 Sidney Low was lecturer in imperial history at King's College, London, and knighted in 1918, probably for his services in wartime propaganda and as chairman of the Ministry of Information's Wireless Service. But when his central European origins were exposed he was forced to resign, paralleling the scandal that led to the film's suppression. See Appendix D, *David Lloyd George: The Movie Mystery*, pp. 199–200.

6 From Wordsworth's poem 'My Heart Leaps Up When I Behold', 1802.

7 On early twentieth-century trends in biography, see Laura Marcus, 'The Newness of the "New Biography"', and Malcolm Bowie, 'Freud and the Art of Biography', both in Peter France and William St Clair (eds) *Mapping Lives: The Uses of Biography*, Oxford, Oxford University Press, 2002, pp. 193–218 and pp. 97–122.

Further reading

David Berry and Simon Horrocks (eds) *David Lloyd George: The Movie Mystery*, Cardiff, University of Wales Press, 1998.

Ian Christie, 'Mystery Men: two recent archival rediscoveries', *Film Studies* No. 1, 1999.

——, 'A Life on Film', in Peter France and William St Clair (eds) *Mapping Lives: The Uses of Biography*, Oxford, Oxford University Press, 2002, pp. 283–302.

IAN CHRISTIE

THE LODGER (1926)

[Production Company: Piccadilly Productions. Director: Alfred Hitchcock. Screenwriter: Elliot Stannard. Cinematographer: Gaetano di Ventimiglia. Editor: Ivor Montagu. Cast: Marie Ault (Mrs Bunting), Arthur Chesny (Mr Bunting), June (Daisy Bunting), Malcolm Keen (Joe Betts), Ivor Novello (The Lodger).]

Although officially Hitchcock's third feature, the director himself preferred to refer to *The Lodger* as his first proper film. Indeed, it was his first suspense thriller, a genre he went on to make his own with more world-famous films such as *Vertigo* (1958 US) and *Psycho* (1960 US). It also stands out as the film that drew attention to him as a prominent film-maker whose approach was for a long time difficult to categorise. In fact, with films like *The Lodger*, Hitchcock began to shape new categories and drew on a wide range of cinematic and broader cultural influences, from German expressionism to the psychoanalytical work of Sigmund Freud. Moreover, *The Lodger* was responsible for introducing a range of what were quickly to become classic Hitchcockian themes, for as Robert Murphy has pointed out:

'What makes the film so fascinating is the way it dissolves into pre-echoes of Hitchcock's later work' (in Murphy 2003: 691). Issues of gender struggle and questions about guilt, suspicion and redemption are all wrapped up in an engrossing yarn that encompasses violence, romance, chase scenes and moments of raw emotional intimacy.

Adapted from a successful novel by Marie Belloc, the film re-interprets and offers a solution to the story of infamous serial killer Jack the Ripper and re-imagines the seedier parts of London in the nineteenth century.[1] After an initial sequence that makes clear that the killer known by his calling card as 'The Avenger' has just committed another murder, and that his victims are all blonde young women, the film then introduces the working-class Bunting family who run a typical lodging house in a grimy impoverished part of the city. This family centres around Mr and Mrs Bunting (Arthur Chesny and Marie Ault), the elderly and devoted parents of aspiring model Daisy (played by an actress known only as 'June'), but also includes Daisy's would-be suitor, police detective Joe Betts (Malcolm Keen). A little later, the detectives who have been assigned to work on the notorious case deduce that the pattern of murders appears to be moving towards the very same lodging house, and the mysterious lodger (Ivor Novello) who arrived there a day after the seventh murder and who was absent from the house at exactly the time the eighth was committed nearby, is held under suspicion. Meanwhile, Daisy and The Lodger fall in love, much to the concern of her parents and the great discontent of Joe, who then turns the murder case into a personal vendetta and a quest to reclaim his damaged masculine pride.

The compelling story of *The Lodger* benefits from a carefully crafted plot, in which twists and turns keep audiences guessing about the identity and motivation of the protagonist until the very end. It does so with very few intertitles, relying deliberately instead on the power of the cinematic image and the melodramatic performance style of its actors.[2] Such suspicion of dialogue (intertitled or otherwise), was part of a general concern Hitchcock shared with film-makers like F.W. Murnau and Fritz Lang, around the introduction of synchronised sound to what had until then primarily been a visual medium. There was a logic to their resistance to change in that they, like Chaplin and Eisenstein, feared that sound would adversely affect the possibilities of film-making and make audiences lazier in their consumption of films. As Duguid notes, 'the limitations of silent cinema meant that directors were forced to be imaginative in using images to convey dialogue and effects',[3] and many were afraid that such creativity would be lost if the addition of sound were made possible.

In any case, *The Lodger* shows Hitchcock's mastery of (silent) film technique in his use of a wide variety of camera techniques and props to communicate the emotions of the various characters. He also deploys a frugal yet strategic placement of intertitles to announce characters, break up the narrative, and to add to the sense of mystery. Perhaps an even greater sign of cinematic sophistication is the staging of much of the plot in the narrow, multi-level boarding house which allows characters on different storeys to be seen interacting with the plot simultaneously. On a narrative level, the film is also quite complex. It moves towards a memorable finale, in which quick cuts between frames from different angles follow The Lodger as he is chased by a bloodthirsty mob. Just before this, a short but effective flashback sequence from The Lodger's tragic past allows Daisy and the audience privileged access to the motivation for his strange behaviour and his air of melancholy.

The opening sequence, using an almost expressionistic style with quirky tilt angles and shadows, sets the mood of a city terrorised by a mysterious killer. Indeed, as Geoffrey Macnab points out, 'the pleasure of the film lies less in its being about a serial killer per se than in its manipulation of audiences' expectations and its evocation of mist-shrouded London streets' (2007: 11). This section incorporates frantic scenes in a newspaper office, printing office, and out on the streets as people clamour with a mix of fear and anticipation to read about the latest murder in their neighbourhood. Such images are intercut with others featuring catwalk models preparing themselves for work, and the transition from one activity to another is set up by the delivery of a note from the killer to the show that states he is on the lookout for a girl with golden curls. At first all seem to be blonde and hence all ideal targets for the killer, but as their peroxide wigs are removed, it is quickly revealed that only very few possess the features that might attract The Avenger.

Such features, the 'golden' hair and translucent fair skin in particular, are exactly those that are on display again three decades later via *Rear Window*'s Lisa (Grace Kelly 1954), *Vertigo*'s Madeleine/Judy (Kim Novak), *Psycho*'s Marion (Janet Leigh) and *The Birds*' Melanie (Tippi Hedren 1963). In fact, the idea of a constructed and idealised, yet threatening female identity that is so clearly explored by those later films is pre-echoed in *The Lodger* by the reference to wigs, make-up and costume, the display of young models, and the playful use of fake dark hair by one of the fair-haired girls to try to outwit the killer. Indeed, while critics continue to debate whether Hitchcock was uncomfortable with and hostile to women, or whether he admired them, it is clear that, as Mark Duguid points out, 'Hitchcock saw female sexual vulnerability as a powerful dramatic device, which he exploited ruthlessly'.[4]

The supposed villain of the piece is portrayed with some ambivalence: the initial careful framing of The Lodger's face makes him appear menacing and mysterious, while later on he looks vulnerable and victimised. The direct, frontal angle which shows only part of his head as the rest is sheltered from the cold by a thick scarf, adds to the piercing and mesmeric nature of his eyes, his ghostly, translucent skin and sharply contrasting dark hair, all of which make him appear quite monstrous at first. Moreover, his unexpected arrival at the Buntings' lodging house is prefigured by a flickering and inexplicable extinction of the kitchen gas lamp, and a frenzied malfunction of the family's cuckoo clock. As Mrs Bunting opens the door, The Lodger seems to appear from the fog itself, creating a memorably chilling moment that sets the tone for the assumptions that are made about this tragic stranger, until it is almost too late. In fact, The Lodger's eccentric appearance and behaviour have more to do with his upper-class background, but are misunderstood by the Buntings and Joe as evidence of his deviance.

All this helps generate the tone of suspense by which Hitchcock's work was later defined. The sinister way in which The Lodger turns round all the paintings of women on the walls of his room and then insists that they are removed sets up questions about who he is, where he has come from and what his intentions might be, which are left unanswered for the majority of the film. The shaking of the kitchen lamp as he paces above, and the use of a transparent ceiling/floor to allow the audience to see his feet as they walk up and down, heighten the effect of anxiety. Moreover, the very timing of his arrival to coincide with the hysterical reporting of the seventh murder, and his absence from the boarding house while the eighth is committed only deepens the effect of suspicion within the diegesis and for the audience. Could this man really be the Avenger lurking within their very midst? And yet, his tenderness towards Daisy and her absolute faith in his integrity lead to further uncertainty.

On another level, this is also a film about patriarchy and Joe's assumed ownership of Daisy as his fiancée-to-be. While he appears to assume a right to become her husband, he also seems to realise that he needs to prove himself to her. She seems less than impressed by his early attempts to woo her, and downright insulted when he sadistically handcuffs her to the staircase while The Lodger watches. He appears to have the approval of Daisy's parents but has not won her heart. Will his attempts to apprehend the Avenger impress her suffi-ciently? Her rebuttal of his advances and rejection of his proposal send him into a jealous rage, especially when he catches her playing chess with The Lodger in his room, and later finds them locked in amorous embrace. His determination to win her back becomes entangled with a parallel obsessive quest to capture the murderer and to remove or destroy the threat to his macho sense of self.

All the classic Hitchcockian issues of gender and class difference, fetishistic sexuality, misunderstanding and mistaken identity surface in this gripping silent drama that shows a maturity of style and tone. It oscillates between suspense and humour, fear and tenderness, and demonstrates the young director's growing confidence in using cinema to connect emotionally with an audience. At this stage, however, Hitchcock did not have as much control over his work as he would later enjoy. It has been reported that he would have pre-ferred to construct a more ambiguous ending to *The Lodger*'s narrative, but the British studio involved wouldn't allow the suggestion that The Lodger might actually be the murderer to be confirmed.[5] Nevertheless, the film, like its originating story, caught the public imagination and marked the start of the career of one of the British film industry's greatest directors.

Notes

1 The film was also known as *The Case of Jonathon Drew and The Lodger: A Story of the London Fog*. It was supposedly based on an anecdote told by a landlady who was sure that one of her tenants had been Jack the Ripper.
2 Even the intertitles are visually attractive with their 'explicitly graphic quality' (Sergeant 2005: 89) thanks to the deco-style designs of McKnight Kauffer.
3 Mark Duguid, 'Hitchock's Style', www.screenonline.org.uk/tours/hitch/tour3.html (2003–2006), accessed 14 July 2006.
4 Ibid.
5 Novello (1893–1951) was a box office draw in the 1920s: he was praised for his acting ability as well as his good looks.

Further Reading

Geoffrey Macnab, 'Still making a killing', *Independent*, 4 May 2007, pp. 10–11.
Robert Murphy, 'The Lodger', in John Pym, *Time Out Film Guide 2004*, London, Penguin, 2003, p. 691.
Amy Sergeant, *British Cinema: A Critical History*, London, BFI, 2005.
François Truffaut, *Hitchcock*, London, Simon & Schuster, 1985.

SARAH BARROW

PICCADILLY (1929)

[Production Company: British International Pictures. Director/ producer: E. A. Dupont. Screenwriter: Arnold Bennett. Cinematographer: Werner Brandes. Music: Neil Brand (for DVD). Editor: J. W. McConaughty. Art Director: Alfred Junge. Cast: Anna May Wong (Shosho), King Ho-Chang (Jim), Gilda Gray (Mabel), Jameson Thomas (Valentine), Cyril Ritchard (Victor).]

> I'd never have left China if it hadn't been for Piccadilly.
> I don't think I'd ever have left Piccadilly if it hadn't been for China.

This exchange of middle-aged male reminiscence appears not in E. A. Dupont's original silent film, but in the prologue to the later sound version. A studio-inspired plot leader, it is designed to introduce some modernity by 'beefing up' verbally the narrative of the original, an essentially stereotypical tale of eternal triangles, centred on a Chinese scullery maid turned exotic dancer, whose charms seduce both the audience of the Piccadilly nightclub, and the European club owner. But the perfunctory nature of this dialogue trail, coupled with its ambiguous re-establishment of the safer comforts of a rural British retreat – 'I've got my flowers, dog, fishing, plenty of sleep' – serves only to point up the seductions attached to the peril of stepping out with China, and so out of assigned colonial role in race, class, and gender.

Dupont's silent *Piccadilly* so powerfully represents such seductions and perils that its impact has never been lukewarm. Its initial reception in 1929 had audiences entranced by the new star, and was critically acclaimed as a potential saviour of the British film industry from over-Americanisation. But this was tempered by suggestions that the sparkling cinematography over-shadowed the plot, and by some still familiar questioning whether such a 'Europudding' production, with its German director, could be considered 'British', or whether, on the contrary, its American-Asian stars constituted brave internationalism, a canny following of Hollywood's lucrative world inclusiveness. A period of obscurity for the film followed, with American product seemingly unassailable and an often poor critical opinion of British film. The film's present revival has, ironically, re-asserted its status as saviour of the national reputation, as a re-discovered gem of early British cinema.[1]

Piccadilly's release in 1929 is significant, at the end of more than a decade of silent film, grown confident in its use of light and camerawork, but facing the coming of the 'talkie' and of colour. Critics such as Robert Keser point to the extraordinary bunching of masterworks of European cinema in that last year of silents,[2] and *Piccadilly* belongs to this crucial moment: still firmly rooted in the visually imaginative, it is, like others in the second half of the 1920s, taken by its German émigré director towards a more realist mode, bringing social commentary to the narrative.

The storyline concentrates on the eruption of China into Piccadilly in the form of Chinese-American Anna May Wong, playing a scullery maid whose Oriental dancing eclipses that of the old-style European bill-toppers, and who also supplants the female lead in the club owner's affections; a clash between youth and age as well as East and West. The role thrust Wong to celebrity, launching a career that vacillated between success in Europe, and returns to Hollywood and disappointment at Paramount's cautious use of her 'problematic' status. Karen Leong,[3] outlining this negotiation of her dual identity in dual geographies and cultures, has commented that European and United States audiences both cast an 'essentialising' gaze on Wong's Chinese identity. Leong has traced Wong's use of the British film industry to replace the more racist limitations of her efforts in America, maintaining a negotiation of British press and industry attitudes that insisted on her outer 'Chineseness' yet simultaneously expressed surprise at her American 'flapper' modernity. Anna May Wong's own perception of her racial identity and her performance of it was shifting and complex. While making use of a more open European industry, she viewed with increasing frustration her stereo-typical roles as instrumental in maintaining the Asian status quo. Leong points out that in most of her starring appearances she is a killer and/or is killed, or her suicide makes way for the happiness of white heroines. Nevertheless, in Europe visiting 'exotic' celebrities, such as Anna May Wong became, were linked not with low-status workers but with exotic entertainers, often ones who as part of their act per-formed their own 'otherness' for the fascination of white Europeans.

This performance of 'orientalness' for white consumption forms a key element of Wong's role as Shosho in *Piccadilly*. Yiman Wang[4] argues that her performance here, and in all the various Asian ethni-cities she portrayed in the 20s and 30s, can be compared to the Negro practice of 'black blackface' performance, in which mixed-race performers 'black-up' to become indistinguishable from fully Negro actors, succeeding in both underlining and undermining the racial content of their appearance and roles. Wang points to a continual critical underrating of the extent of Anna May Wong's performance, describing it as 'yellow yellowface', a deliberate performed excess of the racial stereotype, designed to both play to the desires for exotic 'other' of the white audience, and, in its ironic excess, to expose the oriental-ised nature of both her image and its narrative role, often as seductress, betrayer and ultimately violent destroyer; all of which can be seen in *Piccadilly.*

Wang identifies a crucial moment when Shosho takes club owner Valentine into oriental Limehouse to buy her dance costume. She manoeuvres her Chinese lover, Jim, into modelling the scanty dress, a role he undercuts by looks and gestures, while Shosho displays her power, challenging 'I dance in this or not at all'. Anna May Wong's 'screen passing', in her 'yellow yellowface' performance, ironises her Asian vamp, while Jim's demeanour both recognises and deprecates the de-powering feminisation of his Asian and male role.[5] Such gendered and racial ironies are further complicated by Wong's appearance and dress, orientalising both a Louise Brookesesque hair-style and an androgynous flapper-look redolent of the 'new woman' emancipation overtaking European womanhood and already gen-erating, through the vamp figure, the kind of male anxieties which would later emerge as the femme fatales of film noir.

The overlapping triangles of desire centre on the two women's conflict, and are expressed visually and bodily, often through their dance scenes which allow the diegetic and the cinema audience a vaudeville spectacle. While Anna May Wong's presence has always gripped public and critical attention, the spectacular aspects of Dupont's filming, for which he was celebrated in the 1920s, are crucial to these dynamics and to *Piccadilly*'s effects. Dupont's earlier work in Germany, especially in his 1925 hit, *Varietie,* had been well received and was critically twinned with Murnau's *The Last Laugh* for its technical skill and modernity in virtuoso camerawork and spark-ling *mise-en-scène.* This can be found in *Piccadilly,* as in the opening interior Club scene full of myriad lights, twinkling glasses in mirrored reflections and refractions. But *Piccadilly* also displays a more muted realism: critics such as Richard McCormack[6] see in Dupont's work an early example of a social critique being fully integrated into the narrative, with visual excess and realism working together.

This mix can be seen in the key dance scenes. Star attractions Mabel and Vic make synchronised sweeps down dual staircases while the camera cuts between their somewhat dated hoofing[7] to track round their audience in a swirl of concentrated eyes and looking positions, which are both visually arresting, but also fully contained within the realism of their audience viewing role.

Significantly for Mabel's later eclipse this first dance is interrupted by emanations from Shosho's scullery, taking Club owner Valentine downstairs to be enthralled by his, and our, first glimpse of the spectacle of Shosho's mesmerising languorous dance. The camera mirrors its earlier tracking of the Club audience, but now lingering on the faces of scullery staff, puts focus on this lowest social order. Through her seduction of Valentine, Shosho gains access to both worlds, becoming our, and (briefly) Valentine's, entry into a double underclass in the Limehouse society, which she pointedly sets against his upper class status and location, stating 'This is our Piccadilly'.

In the last dance scene the emphasis is more fully on Limehouse. Valentine is taken by Shosho for his final visit, to a pub, where the shot introducing the bar forms a clear mirroring of the introductory one in the 'Piccadilly' Club: a spectacular tracking shot of hands lining up glasses ready for more hands to take them. But in Limehouse this is allowed an erotic outcome as Valentine's hand covers Shosho's.[8] The now familiar track around the audience follows, but here they are not viewing a specific spectacle; instead this shot is deliberately focused in a lingering close-up on the faces of the Limehouse workers with an almost Vertovian sense of record. Attention shifts to a drunken white woman whose subsequent dancing with a Negro leads to alarm, and her ejection, to the discomfort of Shosho and Valentine, a similarly mixed-race couple. Limehouse functions as the darker side of Piccadilly; a reminder that, when genders are disturbed and there is some looking back at the gaze on otherness, violence can follow.

Dupont's emphasis on audience and looking displays a self-consciousness made more intense by his use of modernist techniques which critics such as Peter J. Hutchings have described in relation to Hitchcock's films.[9] Dupont's film, too, shows an intense modernist interest in the relations between visuals, and the use of words as visual display as well as givers of information. Newspapers, in particular, feature constantly as headlines or used as props. When Shosho wakes to find herself famous, the newspaper report is conveyed by her lover Jim in a scene of naturalness which contrasts and complicates her 'fiendish vamp' act with Europeans. Covering Jim's head with the newspaper, she bends to kiss his hidden lips, and then moves away; the paper slips to reveal his rapture, focused again on eyes, this time closed. In a combination of word and image it economically conveys her gain as his potential loss, and a slipping away of innocence which undercuts the later stereotypical outcomes.

The same use of words for both information and visual objects closes the film once the triangles have been resolved through a double eradication of the disruptions of China. Newspaper headlines reveal the plot's bluff in announcing the trial's outcome; in a circular return, the modernity of the city re-asserts itself, focusing ironically on a passing billboard proclaiming 'Life Goes On'. So the technologies of modernity both produce stylistic excess and cover over it, word images not quite suturing the unresolved ruptures which would not have been raised 'if it hadn't been for China'.

Notes

1 See Matthew Sweet, *Shepperton Babylon: The Lost Worlds of British Cinema*, London, Faber and Faber, 2005.
2 Notably G.W. Pabst's *Diary of a Lost Girl* and *Pandora's Box* (Robert Keser, 'Lust in Translation: The Women That Men Yearn For', *Bright Lights Film Journal*, No. 44, May 2004.)
3 Karen Leong, 'Anna May Wong and the British Film Industry', *Quarterly Review of Film and Video*, London, Routledge, 2006.
4 Yiman Wang, 'The Art of Screen Passing: Anna May Wong's Yellow Yellowface Performance in the Art Deco Era', *Camera Obscura*, Vol. 120, No. 3, Durham, NC, Duke University Press, 2006.
5 Ian Christie has pointed out that the geographic mobility of Shosho between these two worlds is in contrast to Jim, who is more fully ghettoised in Limehouse. (Lecture, Centre for Research in the Arts, Social Sciences and Humanities, University of Cambridge, 2006.)
6 Richard M. McCormack, 'From Caligari to Dietrich: Sexual, Social and Cinematic Discourses in Weimar Film', *Signs*, Vol. 18, No. 3, Chicago, University of Chicago, Spring 1993.
7 Neil Brand, rather harshly, likens Mabel and Victor's turn to parents at a school dance. (Neil Brand on 'Composing for *Piccadilly*', DVD extra, BFI Video Publishing.)
8 Ian Christie comments that few British films offer 'anything approaching this virtuoso tracking shot' (DVD Notes on *Piccadilly*).
9 Peter J. Hutchings, 'Modernity: A Film by Alfred Hitchcock', www.sensesofcinema.com/contents/00/6/modernity.html, accessed 15 April 2007.

Hitchcock's *The Ring* (1925) is a re-make of Dupont's *Varietie* of two years earlier.

Further Reading

Gina Marchetti, *Romance and the 'Yellow Peril': Race, Sex and Discursive Strategies in Hollywood Fiction*, Berkeley, University of California Press, 1993.
Amy Sargeant, *British Cinema: A Critical History*, London, BFI, 2005.

LYNDA TOWNSEND

DRIFTERS (1929)

[Production Company: Empire Marketing Board. Director and editor: John Grierson. Cinematographer: Basil Emmott. Music: Mike Nolan.]

Drifters, widely credited as the founding film of the British Documentary Film movement, draws cinematic attention to hitherto overlooked aspects of British society while drawing on creative film techniques to distinguish it from the more functional and recognisable newsreel form. It takes the form of a 'day–in–the–life' of the North Sea herring fleets, following the fishermen as they go in search of the creature that has become their livelihood. With this film, John Grierson established a new approach to cinema, combining a deliberately creative treatment of reality with a strong ethical belief in the role film should play in building a democratic and unified society. This was the style that came to characterise the emerging British school of documentary film production, and which marked a new phase for film-making in the UK. According to Ian Aitken, Grierson in fact envisaged this approach as a new genre comprising 'films of thirty to forty minutes which through creative editing of actuality footage would enable stories to be "orchestrated into cinematic sequences of enormous vitality"' (in Aitken 2001: 61). Indeed, as Aitken also points out, 'its combination of naturalistic images and formative editing has influenced traditions of documentary film-making in Britain ever since' (2001: 60).

Drifters was the first and indeed only film directed by Grierson himself and as such the only film that can truly be said to be indicative of his personal vision, although he went on to nurture the work of a range of other documentary film-makers. His approach was much influenced by the work of Irish-American Robert Flaherty, especially his silent film *Nanook of the North* (about an Inuit community in Canada, made in 1921 for a fur trading company) and *Man of Aran* (Flaherty's impression of Ireland, made in 1934), with whom he would later collaborate.[1] It was originally planned that *Drifters* would be the first in a series of publicity films for the Empire Marketing Board, promoting trade links between Britain and the countries of the Empire. However, it quickly became a far more ambitious project and was well received critically, far exceeding its official brief. Amongst the multitude of accolades bestowed upon it at the time of its release, *Drifters* was hailed by Paul Rotha, a writer who later became another of the great British documentary film-makers, as one of the very few examples of authentic British film-making at that time. Rotha praised it in particular for seeking a new creative form, for revealing what he called 'a sense of cinema' and for not imitating the American or German models of expression that were popular and critically acclaimed at the time.[2]

An hour in length, *Drifters* follows the daily rituals of a group of herring fishermen, starting with their early morning preparations and ending with the eventual sale of their catch at market. Various approaches are taken to represent these potentially unexciting activities which combine to make for a visually appealing, hypnotically compelling film that brings together concrete information with abstract contemplation. Filmed mainly on location, at sea in all weathers, *Drifters* constructs a straightforward linear narrative that allows the audience to get really close to the fishermen in order to observe their largely unseen activities. Only the most basic information is provided via intertitles; the images are largely left to speak for themselves. A certain amount of drama is suggested by the news of an incoming storm that will make the job of hauling in the heavy nets even more challenging. However, it is also implied by the resigned acceptance on the faces of the fishermen, shown in unflinching close-up, that bad weather is an everyday hazard. Nothing remarkable happens. The fish are eventually hauled in and the boat sets off back to the dock.

The pleasure and excitement of the film lies less in the 'narrative' and more in the images themselves, in the sublime quality of many of the shots, and the careful juxtaposition of them, which together reinforce the potential of the 'documentary' as a creative form. For example, the opening images reveal an idyllic rural landscape, while others linger on the flock of seagulls that follow the boat in the hope of food. Sometimes those birds are followed in flight; at other moments they are shown grabbing at dead fish on the sea. The patterns they create, caught in the light against sky or water, offer a different kind of visual pleasure that reveals the director's commitment to experimentation with form. Close-ups of the herring as they are gathered in the nets are lit so as to show every glinting detail of their scales, and the underwater attack on them by the dogfish while the fishermen sleep is constructed as the real moment of heightened dramatic tension. One critic remarked upon the importance of such shots that place the herring themselves at the centre of the drama, suggesting that 'this prosaic and even slightly comic fish has provided the excuse for camera-work at once satisfying to the eye and emotions' (Peter Fleming 1929 cited in Sargeant 2005: 133–134). Meanwhile, other approaches are included that do not involve the shooting of 'actuality footage', the most striking example being the insertion of scenes shot in studio to capture below-deck activities of the fishermen and tending to the fire.

Drifters is ultimately shaped and defined by its skilful editing. As Nield points out, 'particular attention has been paid to the pacing of the piece, its rhythms matching the gentle rocking of the waves, an effect enhanced by the superb, but never over-emphatic, use of superimpositions plus Mike Nolan's delicate piano score' (2005: 1). The sense of repetition and rhythm is especially noticeable in the shots of the machinery that enables the boats to move swiftly out to sea. The steam rising from chimneys and steel engines pounding away below deck add a sense of modernity to the otherwise time-lessness of the work of the herring fishermen. Moreover, the influence of the montage experiments of the Soviets is clear as *Drifters* makes effective use of quick editing and suggestive juxtapositions.[3]

By emphasising the fundamental qualities of mankind, by reifying the value of hard physical labour, and by emphasising the heroic figure of the working man, the film's individual characters become 'representatives of a nation rather than of a specific class or other restricted social group' (Higson 1995: 199) Nevertheless, this is achieved through a focus on one specific fishing crew, with which the audience is invited to become familiar and with whom we are asked to empathise. None of the crew is named, but 'types' are clearly marked out: the bearded captain is shown lying awake at night, clearly anxious about the catch; the young lad is sympathetically observed as he learns to cook and carry out other basic but essential tasks; and in one really memorable shot, the engine stoker deftly lights his pipe from the coal fire that keeps the boat in operation. Somehow, the ordinary is made to appear extraordinary in that it sheds light on those things that are important to this tight-knit group of men, brought together by their sense of purpose. Moreover, *Drifters* succeeds in placing the work of the crew within the context of the fishing industry more generally. This is especially evident in the final section back at quayside, in which each frame bustles with life as auctioneers call buyers together as the fleet arrive with their catch, and the townspeople gather to contribute to the business of preparing the fish.

The gently rolling rhythm (evocative of the movement of the boat) and mesmerising, hypnotic images that make subtle yet effective use of soft focus, dissolves and super-impositions, give *Drifters* a quality that has been described by many as poetic. This idea of visual poetry in documentary would continue to emerge throughout the following decade in work such as *Night Mail* (Harry Watt and Basil Wright 1936), which Grierson helped to produce and for which he provided the voice-over commentary. Such an approach helps to evoke an impression of life for the fishermen at work at that time, and for the fishing town generally, rather than informing through facts in the style of a newsreel, and as such *Drifters* helped to mark the documentary out as a distinctive form.

John Grierson, who is credited with having coined the term 'documentary' when reviewing Flaherty's second film, *Moana: A Romance of the Golden Age* (1926 US), went on to become the founder and leading figure in the British Documentary film movement. This influential group is now widely regarded as one of the main reference points for the approach of realism that is recognised as central to British cinema – fiction as well as documentary. He continued to believe passionately that 'cinema was unable to perform an educational or public service role in the private sector' (Enticknap 2000: 209). In fact, he was hostile to the ethos of entertainment cinema and sought to use film instead for more austere social purposes.

Concerned to reveal and explore the social role documentary film could play, as well as with its distinct aesthetic qualities as a cinematic form, Grierson argued that documentary film-makers within the genre should 'devote themselves to the social duty of revealing and describing social interconnection' (Aitken 2001: 61). His views emerged largely as a response to the economic difficulties and insecurities of the inter-war period, and were rooted in a firm belief that film, as a relatively new form of mass communication, could play a key role in strengthening a sense of national unity and stability.

Having made *Drifters* and established his reputation as a socially committed film-maker with a concern for invigorating the artistic potential of cinema, Grierson then went on to collaborate with and support the careers of other film-makers such as Jennings, Alberto Cavalcanti, Henry Watt, Len Lye and Basil Wright. He also employed the likes of Benjamin Britten and W. H. Auden to provide evocative soundtracks on his later documentary collaborations. When the Empire Marketing Board was disbanded, Grierson helped set up and became head of the General Post Office film unit in the 1930s, a Government-run production and distribution organisation for non-commercial cinema, later renamed the Crown Film Unit. Within all these institutions, he continued and developed the strategy that he had begun with the making of *Drifters*, that of using government money to make films with clear social intent, but which also had ambitious aesthetic aims. Such a strategy was continued throughout the 1930s and ensured the development of the much respected film-making tradition of social realism that still influences fiction and documentary production in the UK and beyond today.

Notes

1 Flaherty, like Grierson, was interested in the ongoing struggle with the forces of modernity. They first worked together on *Industrial Britain* (1931), also sponsored by the Empire Marketing Board's Film Unit.
2 Paul Rotha's seminal book, *The Film Till Now*, was first published in 1930.
3 This aspect of the rhythm of modern machinery has led to comparisons with the work of Soviet documentary film-maker Dziga Vertov, in particular his *Man with a Movie Camera* (1929). The montage style more generally is indebted to the work of other famous Soviet film-makers, Eisenstein and Pudovkin, with *Drifters* sharing a programme with Eisenstein's banned *Battleship Potemkin* (1925) at a Film Society event in London in 1929.

Further Reading

Ian Aitken, 'The British Documentary Film Movement', in Robert Murphy (ed.), *The British Cinema Book,* 2nd edn, London, BFI, 2001.
Geoff Brown, 'Paradise Found and Lost: The Course of British Realism', in Robert Murphy (ed.), *The British Cinema Book,* 2nd edn, London, BFI, 2001.
Leo Enticknap, '*This Modern Age* and the British Non-Fiction Film', in Justine Ashby and Andrew Higson, *British Cinema, Past and Present*, London and New York, Routledge, 2000.
Andrew Higson, *Waving the Flag: Constructing a National Cinema in Britain*, Oxford, Clarendon Press, 1995.
Anthony Nield, '*Drifters*' in *DVD Times*, http://dvdtimes.co.uk/content.php?contentid = 56120, 11 February 2005.
Paul Rotha, *The Film Till Now* (revised edition), London, Spring Books, 1967.
Amy Sargeant, *British Cinema: A Critical and Interpretative History*, London, BFI, 2005.
Dean Williams, 'Robert Flaherty', in http://www.sensesofcinema.com/contents/directors/02/flaherty.html, October 2002.

SARAH BARROW

THE 39 STEPS (1935)

[Production Company: Gaumont-British Picture Corporation. Director: Alfred Hitchcock. Screenwriters: Charles Bennett and Ian

Hay (from novel by John Buchan). Cinematographer: Bernard
Knowles. Music: Louis Levy. Editor: Derek Twist. Cast: Robert
Donat (Robert Hannay), Madeleine Carroll (Pamela), Lucie Mannheim
(Annabella Smith), Geoffrey Teale (Professor Jordan), Peggy Ashcroft
(Margaret Crofter), John Laurie (John Crofter).]

[it is a] perfect example of the thriller plot in its natural state.

(Rohmer and Chabrol 1957: 42)

At nearly every stop on its cross country journey we find com-
placency and venality. It is a country without confidence, unity
or purpose.

(Glancy 2002: 18)

For Hitchcock, all these shifting identities [in the film] are
emblematic of the disparity between appearance and reality, of
the unpredictable basis of relationships and the precarious necessity
of trust – a complex of ideas made clear in each sequence of the
picture.

(Spoto 1992: 43)

These quotations suggest that *The 39 Steps* is a genre film – a thriller –
made to excite and entertain an audience. It also apparently deals
with significant themes such as the nature of identity and the state of
a nation. If this is so then *The 39 Steps* illustrates one of the central
arguments for film studies as an academic subject – that popular,
genre films can be as thoughtful and stimulating as more obviously
'serious' films (or even works of literature, fine art etc.).

This idea is part of a much wider theoretical context – the perceived
divide between high art and popular culture. These two groups can
be defined through certain attributes. In high art the producer is
characterised as a uniquely gifted individual driven by the desire to
create, whose work is received by an elite audience whose specialist
knowledge provides intellectual pleasures. In opposition to this,
popular culture is often produced in collaboration within the context
of a commercial institution, for a global audience for the purpose of
entertainment.

While these categories are probably recognisable there are clear
contradictions. Not every text fits neatly into one side or the other;
arias from opera have become sporting anthems and chart hits. Texts
shift between the categories; Shakespeare's plays were originally performed for a popular audience, later becoming part of elite theatre

and the focus of academic study, more recently translated into contemporary television drama using popular stars. Initially it would seem cinema fits firmly into the popular culture category but within film there are further divides, most clearly between Hollywood genre and art house cinema. Traditionally, high art with its appeal to an elite, educated audience was judged as more worthwhile than popular culture's seemingly easy pleasures.

Some theorists (e.g. Bourdieu[1] and Hall[2]) have argued that this divide is another example of the way that powerful groups categorise people to create hierarchical societies. In this analysis the 'great divide' works in a similar way to the class system, with some types of knowledge worth more than others. This has been referred to as an individual's cultural capital (knowledge of opera is more highly rated than knowledge of soap opera) which signifies social status. According to this model the divide between high art and popular culture is another form of conflict between groups in society; the culture which is consumed by the masses – including genre film – is seen as less important than the high art consumed by elite groups. If mass culture is frivolous, superficial and merely entertaining then it is easier to characterise the groups in society which enjoy it as also being less important.

In the late twentieth century a philosophical and cultural movement – postmodernism – explicitly challenged this idea, arguing that this division within the arts was a false one. The increase in academic courses in film, media and cultural studies is an indication of the influence of this movement. *The 39 Steps* illustrates the constructed nature of the divide; it is a popular genre film which provides thrills, excitement and humour as well as complex themes about identity and human behaviour. It isn't that these themes are 'bolted on'; they are an integral part of the genre form.

The 39 Steps raises questions about human experience from the first scenes. What motivates people to act in the way they do? What is the difference between acting for good and acting for evil? How do we define ourselves? How fixed is identity when it can change, slip away or be disguised so easily?

The film opens with an establishing shot of the illuminated sign for a music hall followed by a low angled, asymmetrical shot of a man (Hannay) buying a ticket. The audience hears the man's voice but does not see his face; instead the camera follows the man to his seat in the audience. These first moments introduce several ideas that are relevant to the main themes. Throughout the film Hannay has to pretend to be different people in order to escape his captors. Even in the opening he isn't introduced; he isn't given a name or face. The first setting, the music hall, is a type of theatre, a place for performance, for assumed identities – such as Mr. Memory. The audience is working class, signified by costume, props (beer glasses) and the noisy atmosphere. Hannay doesn't belong in this milieu; this is made clear to the audience when we are finally introduced to the central character. Rather than the full close up that often indicates the appearance of a star, Hannay is part of a crowd, but his difference is denoted in the clean lines of his coat and the stylish cut of his hair. (Hannay's difference is also later emphasised by the fact that he is Canadian – in the novel he's English – which also affects the representation of Britishness in the film.) Hannay is introduced in this way – a face in the crowd – because it emphasises the random nature of events which is found across Hitchcock's films. Why should it be Hannay rather than anyone else who is caught up in murder?

The opening of the film therefore establishes some crucial ideas. Hannay is the hero of the film but an insubstantial one who doesn't seem to fit into his surroundings. We discover very little about him throughout the film – subverting audience expectations about identification and the development of character.[3] Life seems to be directed by seemingly random events which can have catastrophic consequences – whether we behave well or badly. People are motivated to act for all kinds of reasons – without having any idea of the consequences.

These themes construct a chaotic view of the world; one at odds with a belief in order and control and denying the comfort that these can bring. The precariousness of existence is signified in the second shot of the film, an off-kilter composition influenced by German Expressionism, an art movement which represented the irrationality of everyday life. The film therefore sets up Hannay's quest for the truth about the 39 Steps within a framework of chance and chaos. In the foreground the search itself, the desire for knowledge which is probably always going to be elusive. (In this context, the MacGuffin, the plot device which has no meaning in itself, makes perfect sense.)

Introduced in the first shots, these ideas are developed consistently throughout the film within the connected themes of patriotism, politics and sexual desire. These in turn are linked to the concept of performance. The ease of assuming – and discarding – different identities suggests that ideological positions (the good versus evil of the thriller genre) are simply costumes to be worn at different times. For example – why does Hannay take Annabella, the spy, home with him? What motivates the spy? Not the ideal of patriotism but money. Britain is represented as a repressed, parochial country where the landowners, travelling salesmen, academics, politicians — even milkmen — are hypocrites, liars and murderers. Religion is a cover for cruelty and misogyny in the character of the Scottish crofter; the hymn book which stops a bullet aimed at Hannay has a practical rather than spiritual use.

The thriller is often interpreted as an allegory — the shadowy organisation against the hero who defeats it — but *The 39 Steps* removes these certainties through the constant undermining of audience expectations. The pleasures of the thriller form — visceral excitement, suspense etc. — are often derided as purely transitory and superficial but in *The 39 Steps* they can be understood as an attempt to jolt the viewer out of conventional attitudes — an integral part of the meaning of the film.

The influence of the themes and style of *The 39 Steps* can be seen most explicitly in Hitchcock's later Hollywood films. In *North by Northwest* (1959) there is a similar use of narrative structure, genre and character, while *Notorious* (1946) returns to the themes of patriotism and betrayal.

The motif of the innocent man forced on the run is a popular one in contemporary thrillers. *Enemy of the State* (Scott, 1997) can be read as a homage to *The 39 Steps* (and *North by Northwest*), *Arlington Road* (Pellington, 1998) places the innocent man in the setting of a paranoid conspiracy thriller. *The Bourne Identity* (Liman, 2002), while having a spy as the central character, also uses a similar plot and atmosphere of cynicism about government action and motivation.

Notes

1 Pierre Bourdieu, *Distinction: A Social Critique of the Judgement of Taste*, London, Routledge, 1984.
2 Stuart Hall, 'Notes on Deconstructing the Popular' in R. Samuel (ed.) *People's History and Socialist Theory*, London, Routledge, 1981.
3 This is very similar to Roger O. Thornhill (Cary Grant) in *North by Northwest* — when asked what his middle initial stands for, he replies 'nothing'.

Further Reading

Mark Glancy, *The 39 Steps*, London, I. B. Tauris, 2002.
Pauline Kael, 'Three Films' in Albert Lavalley (ed.) *Focus on Hitchcock*, New Jersey, Prentice Hall, 1972.
Albert Lavalley (ed.) 'Introduction' in *Focus on Hitchcock*, New Jersey, Prentice Hall, 1972.

Tania Modleski, *The Women who Knew Too Much*, London, Routledge, 1989.
John Orr, *Hitchcock and Twentieth Century Cinema*, London, Wallflower, 2005.
Eric Rohmer and Claude Chabrol, 'The English Period' in *Hitchcock: the First Forty-Four Films*, Northam, Roundhouse, 1957/1992.
Donald Spoto, 'The 39 Steps' in his *The Art of Alfred Hitchcock*, London, Fourth Estate, 1992.
Robin Wood, *Hitchcock's Films Revisited*, London, Faber, 1989.

SARAH CASEY BENYAHIA

THINGS TO COME (1936)

[Production Company: Alexander Korda Film Productions. Director: William Cameron Menzies. Screenwriter: H.G. Wells. Cinematographer: Georges Perinal. Music: Arthur Bliss. Editors: Charles Crichton and Francis Lyon. Art director: Vincent Korda. Cast: Raymond Massey (John Cabal/Oswald Cabal), Edward Chapman (Pippa Passworthy/Raymond Passworthy), Ralph Richardson (The Boss), Margaretta Scott (Roxana/Rowena), Cedric Hardwicke (Theotocopulos).]

If science fiction is about creating a sense of wonder and imagining the future while reflecting on the past then *Things to Come* should certainly be considered one of the key films of the twentieth century; the fact that it is a British film, depicting a future Britain at the cutting edge of scientific innovation and cultural rebirth, makes it all the more significant in the face of Hollywood dominance of the science fiction genre. Describing the film's cultural and artistic impact, Christopher Frayling (1995: 12) declared '*Things to Come* is to Modernism as *Blade Runner* is to Post-Modernism'. Its vision of human survival after years of war is an unflinching depiction of what technology and science can offer in a free society. Yet, deep at the heart of the film, there is an unerring sense of caution, a warning to those who would rebel against progress that democracy comes at a price: stand together and the future will be bright, stand alone and society will crumble.

Adapted from his novel, *The Shape of Things to Come* (1933), H. G. Wells wanted *Things to Come* to endure as a measurable marker for the world's potentials and a solution to its great ills, yet both the book and film's 'most memorable achievement was [their] prediction of the outbreak of the Second World War' (Wager 2004: 209). Wells felt that it was his duty to make *Things to Come* a true depiction of what a future utopia could be like. Themes such as pacifism, scientific planning, egalitarianism, and freedom imbue the film with a sense of purpose. W. Warren Wager (2004: 199) sees *Things to Come* as a 'full-blooded "romance of revolution," a tale of how humankind faced and met the grave challenges to its survival in the twentieth century and persevered to build an integrated world civilization'. Such a revolution would take years to come about perhaps, but the sheer scope was not beyond the producers of the film who strove to combine Wells's literary vision with the very latest in film-making techniques and set design.

Before discussing the generic qualities of the film it is important to recognise the critical and cultural contexts in which the film was produced. Clearly Wells felt that it was his film, after all it was his story, yet the contributions made by the likes of Korda and Menzies help to truly make this a 'key British film' and therefore must be addressed. It is interesting to note that Alexander Korda was best known for producing historical films 'which addressed questions of class and gender from different stylistic and ideological perspectives' (Street 1997: 40). Films produced by Korda in this period, for example *The Private Life of Henry VIII* (1933), emphasised the relationship between the proletariat and aristocracy, showing working-class British audiences that they 'enjoyed a special bond with upper social echelons' (ibid: 41). *Things to Come* can be considered alongside Korda's other works since it is undoubtedly a historical film – the outbreak of the Second World War, the bandit era and the arrival of the airmen, and the future city of 2036 make up the three historical periods of Wells's future – but also the film's concentration in the last act on the conflict between technocrat Oswald Cabal and artisan Theotocopulos reflects both Korda's desire to show sympathy for the working class and support for the role of educated scientists in modern society. Jeffrey Richards believes this part of the film 'is replete with irony' for the present-day audience since it is the artisan rather than the scientist who acts as the 'identification figure for many' (Richards 1999: 21). The former represents the 'back to basics' ideal that counteracts the damaging effects of technological expansion promoted by the latter. Of course, for Wells, Korda, and Menzies the positives offered by the modernist attitude toward technological progress and the values of science far outweighed any negatives that such a battle between technocrat and artisan could bring about – World War Two, after all, was just around the corner and it was up to the British public to look beyond petty squabbles:

> For all the artificiality of some of the special effects, the 'period' awfulness of some of the dialogue, the cut-glass accents and

impeccable upper-class English manner of the juveniles and the hamminess of some of the acting, it remains a visionary film of compelling power, awesome imagination and uplifting optimism.

(Richards 1984: 280)

If Alexander Korda offered Wells's vision a home on the British cinema screen then it was William Cameron Menzies and Vincent Korda who gave it life. Both were well respected for their artistic and design talents, Menzies being influenced by F. W. Murnau and Sergei Eisenstein (Frayling 1995: 28), and Korda by the modernist designs of Oliver Hill's furniture, Le Corbusier's garden landscapes, and Norman Bel Geddes's futuristic aircraft (Richards 1999: 18–19). Such visual inspiration places *Things to Come*'s visioning of 'Everytown' alongside science fiction's other great futuristic city, 'Metropolis'. Fritz Lang's New York-inspired *Metropolis* (1926) has become the prototype for modern depictions of the urban landscape (see for example *Blade Runner*, 1982), with the consequence that the city in science fiction is now largely the signifier of a dystopian future since *Metropolis* blamed technology, bureaucrats, scientists, and machinery for humanity's moral failures and the continued subjugation of the working class.

Some might contend that the prevailing theme at the heart of science fiction is not a sense of wonder, as suggested earlier in this essay, but instead an uncompromising belief in the battle between man and machine, technology and society. To see scientists and the futurist city held up as an example of what might be our best possible utopia in *Things to Come* stands in stark contrast to the vision offered by Lang in *Metropolis*; where the city and its despotic rulers hold workers at the mercy of the monstrous machine, humans being merely fodder for the production and consumption driving the capitalist system. H. G. Wells and Vincent Korda were at pains to point out the potentials for 'Everytown' of the future; it was a completely new start after the ravages of war had taken their toll on the population: people would be able to retreat below ground, to live as one in a pristine world of white. 'Metropolis', according to Wells, was a dystopian city based on the skyline of a contemporary cityscape, New York, and offered nothing new; skyscrapers were already, by the time of the film's release, visions of the past rather than the future. For Janet Staiger (1999: 110), 'If *Metropolis* accepts divided labour as a prerequisite for a successful future, in *Things to Come* the final narrative crisis ironically ... asserts its necessity'; the division of society into tech-nocrats and artisans is both inevitable and integral to the pursuit of utopia and Wells's original dream. Both films contend that the city's sprawling urban space holds the key to achieving utopia, yet the subtle differences between their artistic inspirations and iconic visual imagery help to endorse *Things to Come*'s claim for being a key film, not only in a British context but also within the context of the entire science fiction genre.

Contemporary critics' fondness for claiming *Metropolis* as progenitor of the archetypal science fiction cityscape is not unwarranted, nevertheless, *Things to Come* offers viewers more than just a futuristic city. Certainly, its iconographic imagery can be seen as inspiration for other key films of the genre, for example the enclosed cities of *THX-1138* (1971) or *Logan's Run* (1976), but equally its philosophical message, of technology as saviour, stands out as unique amongst science fiction films.[1] For David Desser (1999: 87), 'More than in *Metropolis*, and more than in most science-fiction films, technology is imaged as humanity's positive side', and is a recurrent motif in other adaptations of H. G. Wells stories such as *The Time Machine* (1960). In a genre that frequently hails postmodern dystopian cities as humanity's inevitable habitat – British examples include *A Clockwork Orange* (1971), *1984* (1984), and *Brazil* (1985) – *Things to Come* challenges this negative attitude and in fact speculates that through cooperation and the recognition of common goals the modern city is only the launch pad to a wider, brighter world; science, and those who can master it, will take humans to the stars. The final act of the film sees Oswald Cabal send two young 'astronauts', his daughter and Passworthy's son, into space using a rocket fired from the giant Space Gun. While a large crowd attempts to stop the launch, roused by the individualist Theotocopulos, Cabal tells Passworthy why the peace and tranquillity of 'Everytown' had to be sacrificed:

> Rest enough for the individual man. Too much, too soon, and we call it death. But for Man: no rest and no ending. He must go on – conquest beyond conquest – first this little planet with its winds and ways, and then all the laws of mind and matter that restrain him; then the planets about him, and at last, out across immensity to the stars. And when he has conquered all the deeps of space and all the mysteries of time, still he will be beginning.

Such belief in the possibilities and wonders of space travel is a largely American trope in science fiction, an extension of the national obsession with the frontier, yet we can also see it played out here in the climax of *Things to Come*. Not only is the film progressive in its representation of technology but it is also pre-empting the surplus of British and American science fiction films that would be released in the 1950s where spaceflight, spaceships, and interplanetary conquest were central themes that made the genre even more popular with audiences. The Space Gun, its rocket projectile, and the influx of cinematic spacecraft that were to follow, symbolise both the genre's fascination for technical gadgetry and special effects and also Western culture's fetishisation of technological consumption: 'Spaceships are the emblems of the technology that produces them; a technology of cultural reproduction, rather than science' (Roberts 2000: 154).

Things to Come was not popular with audiences in 1936, however, soon after war had broken out people realised H. G. Wells's vision of the future was an accurate one. The film's lack of impact at the box-office should in no way detract from its overall cultural significance: as a science fiction film it laid the foundations for countless others to borrow and reproduce its iconographic set designs, flying ships, and themes of space travel and technological utopianism; yet, more importantly, as a key British film *Things to Come* even today still challenges the generic dominance of Hollywood, having set out to imagine a future world of progress and peace almost 20 years before America had turned its attention to space.

Note

1 One could argue that the American television series *Star Trek* (1966–1969) followed in the footsteps of *Things to Come* by presenting science and technology as pivotal agents in humans overcoming social problems such as war, poverty, hunger, and racism. Humanity's faith in technology and its mastery over it were hallmarks of creator Gene Roddenberry's utopian, multicultural future.

Further Reading

David Desser, 'Race, Space and Class: The Politics of Cityscapes in Science-Fiction Films' in Annette Kuhn (ed.) *Alien Zone II: The Spaces of Science Fiction Cinema*, London, Verso, 1999.

Christopher Frayling, *Things to Come*, London, British Film Institute, 1995.

Jeffrey Richards, *The Age of the Dream Palace: Cinema and Society in Britain, 1930–1939*, London, Routledge & Kegan Paul, 1984.

——, '*Things to Come* and Science Fiction in the 1930s' in I.Q. Hunter (ed.) *British Science Fiction Cinema*, London, Routledge, 1999.

Adam Roberts, *Science Fiction*, London, Routledge, 2000.

Janet Staiger, 'Future Noir: Contemporary Representations of Visionary Cities', in Annette Kuhn (ed.) *Alien Zone II: The Spaces of Science Fiction Cinema*. London, Verso, 1999.

Sarah Street, *British National Cinema*, London, Routledge, 1997.

W. Warren Wager, *H.G.Wells: Traversing Time*, Middletown, Wesleyan University Press, 2004.

LINCOLN GERAGHTY

LOVE ON THE DOLE (1941)

[Production Company: British National Films. Director and producer: John Baxter. Screenwriters: Walter Greenwood, Barbara Emery, Rollo Gamble. Cinematographer: James Wilson. Music: Richard Addinsell. Editor: Michael Chorlton. Cast: Deborah Kerr (Sally Hardcastle), Clifford Evans (Larry Meath), Geoffrey Hibbert (Harry Hardcastle), Joyce Howard (Helen Hawkins), Mary Merrall (Mrs Hardcastle), George Carney (Mr Hardcastle), Frank Cellier (Sam Grundy), Martin Walker (Ned Narkey).]

Love on the Dole, following the novel and play of the same name, focuses upon the working-class experience of the Depression of the 1930s. The idea for the film was initially proposed in 1936 but it was not seen as suitable subject material for cinema audiences until 1940 when the project was given the go-ahead. It is frequently cited as an example of censorship in British cinema, reflecting the changing concerns and priorities of 'the Establishment' in Britain between the late 1930s and early 1940s. It was initially vetoed by the censors for showing 'too much of the tragic and sordid side of poverty' (Mathews 1994: 53) but by its release in 1941 it was felt the film would enable audiences to see themselves as fighting for a better future without the unemployment of the 1930s.

The film examines the feeling of entrapment and longing for escape felt by a working class alienated first by the unremitting grind of their work and later by mass unemployment. Set in fictional Hankey Park during the economic depression that hit Britain after the Wall Street Crash of 1929, *Love on the Dole* appears to have a clear left-wing, socialist agenda. The social analysis offered is not simplistic: the tension between the generations within the working class (most obviously between Mr Hardcastle and his son and daughter, Harry and Sally) is revealed and characters are not shown as 'good' simply by virtue of being members of the working class. Those who drink too much (Ned Narky) are portrayed as abusive 'wasters'. The possessive and violent male is exposed in the character of Helen's father, heard off-screen beating his wife. Mrs Nattle runs her 'clothing club' for nobody's benefit other than her own. Sam Grundy, the bookmaker, in addition to his cold manipulation of Sally is shown exploiting the way the men dream of escaping their lot through a win on 'the horses'.

However, these negative images are counter-balanced by the potential for a better future embodied in the heroic, if rather idolised, Larry (Clifford Evans), the innocent Sally (Deborah Kerr), and the simple, hard-working Mr and Mrs Hardcastle.[1] Larry attempts to prevent violence and hold to democratic principles even in the struggle against what is clearly an oppressive system, and despite his passionate hatred of that system.

The extent to which this use of what could be called 'character types' is successful is debatable. Certainly, some characters might be seen as too one-dimensional and the 'lessons' they embody for the audience might be said to be too obvious, perhaps even patronisingly didactic. This could also be seen as a feature of devices within the film's construction. In the opening minutes there is a shot of a headline proclaiming an economic upturn (on a newspaper being used to encourage the fire to draw) only for this to symbolically 'go up in flames'.

Just as off-putting for the audience, and perhaps contributing to its lack of box-office success (Aldgate and Richards 1994: 342), there is no sign of a conventional comforting resolution; Larry is killed, Sally has her innocence taken away and, to achieve an escape from poverty for herself and her family, abandons her ideals, and Mr and Mrs Hardcastle are left with little other than the knowledge that they did their best in impossible circumstances.

So, does the film show a socialist future as envisioned by Larry as an impossible dream or do his ideals remain the essential 'message' of the film? How should we ultimately read the film? Do Sally's final actions represent defeat or the emergence of a strong, independent woman? Certainly the position of women in society is raised as an issue; Sally, for instance, says, 'You marry for love and find you've let yourself in for a seven day a week job with no pay.' The words of Labour MP and member of the wartime coalition government, A.V. Alexander, given at the end make the wartime message and peacetime promise clear:

> Our working men and women have responded magnificently to any and every call made upon them. Their reward must be a new Britain. Never again must the unemployed become the forgotten men of peace.

Is this a fine liberal message, or a condescending attitude to take towards a working-class audience that suffered unemployment in the 1930s and is now sending its young men to war just 20 years after the last major conflict in Europe?

The film does present positive images of working-class figures and does offer a socialist challenge to the status quo; Baxter films Larry, for example, making a strongly socialist speech almost directly to camera. But it is also an attempt to negotiate a potential crisis in capitalism by seeking a compromise that does not involve the overthrow of that system. The real political message is that improved social conditions for the working class are a necessity if the capitalism is to be maintained.[2]

There are strong elements of social realism (the smoke from the industrial chimneys and the drab greyness of the back-to-back terraced houses in the opening) but this is also a melodrama. Emphasising censorship and socialist politics can mean this aspect of the film is not given due attention. Essentially this is Sally's story rather than Larry's; any character development that occurs takes place within her character, and the central action within the film is her decision to become Grundy's mistress. American censors did not pass the film until 1945 and then only on condition that it was implied Grundy would marry Sally (Slide 1998: 99), suggesting they saw the moral implications of the central female character's actions as vital to any reading of the film. Deborah Kerr's opinion was that the film was more appreciated in America than Britain.[3] Was this because for British audiences the drama of the woman's position was lost within an overriding experience of being preached at?

Love on the Dole has, justifiably perhaps (although this is essential to melodrama), been accused of being overly sentimental[4] but is generally recognised as also showing real understanding of the working-class experience. The realities of working-class life are closely observed; see, for example, how Grundy turns Harry's win on 'the horses' into a publicity coup that ensures more people will willingly lock themselves into the dream that he sells (the concept behind the national lottery is nothing new!). Unemployment and the accompanying hardships including the millstone of debt are all examined; yet people are also shown as having a certain dignity and even humour. What they all share is a desire to escape the harsh conditions of their existence. The women do this through a drink (at home) and a séance, and the men through a drink (in the pub) and betting. The young all hope to escape the place itself; although for Larry, personal escape is not enough, he wants freedom from poverty for all. But, Larry's vision of the future is trampled not simply by the police as agents of the status quo but also by the violence of his own side, the working class. And Sally is reduced to selling out on the moral, principled stance she and Larry believed in. As Larry says, 'It's this place. . . . it gets everybody in the end.'

To begin with Sally believes, 'They can take away our jobs but they can't take away our love, can they?' (Although even here she phrases it as a rather desperate question.) With Larry dead she pragmatically takes the only way out with Sam Grundy. Has she sold out or is this straightforward commonsense? Or are such judgements out of place, can we only observe and not presume to judge? What would be the range of responses from an audience in the 1940s? Despite the fact it was unusual to see sexual matters dealt with within a contemporary context rather than being transposed into Regency or Restoration settings in order to bypass the censors (Aldgate and Richards 1994: 164), would the majority simply see Sally's actions as part and parcel of the reality of life?

Baxter was clear about how he saw this film and film-making during the war. *Love on the Dole* could be seen to contain a radical message and yet it was also clearly in his view propaganda for the war effort. As a producer at British National he was interested in films that promised better times and showed audiences why they were fighting. He felt audiences should be given:

> pictures that will show them just what they are fighting for, pictures with a glimpse of the better world we all envisage after the sacrifices and hardships are through
>
> (Taylor 1988: 37)

> I felt that the successful outcome of the war depended in no small measure on the loyalty and hard work of, for want of a better term, 'the working man'
>
> (Brown and Aldgate 1989: 78)

Before the war this film was seen by the censors as advocating unacceptable socialist change; despite the male hero's advocacy of peaceful protest one scene shows striking workers not only marching through the streets but fighting the police. Putting such material before readers of a novel or an audience attending a play was one thing but 'the Establishment' was unlikely to allow a film like this to be made for a mass audience at a time of continued economic depression. But by 1940 the war had ensured almost full employment. And, as James Park suggests in *British Cinema: The Lights That Failed*, in some ways film-makers enjoyed more freedom during the war than before since a nation that was in its propaganda so strongly in favour of freedom of speech could hardly argue British institutions should be exempt from criticism (Park 1990: 67).

Notes

1 'Simple people joining together in some kind of decent human endeavour, was a common theme in Baxter's films' (Shafer 1997: 184).
2 Baxter's *The Common Touch* (1941), *Let the People Sing* (1942) and *The Shipbuilders* (1944) make similar pleas for a changed post-war society without unemployment, poverty, class conflict and injustice (Murphy 2001: 312).
3 'Strangely enough it was much more appreciated in America than in Britain.' Kerr in Brian McFarlane, *An Autobiography of British Cinema by the actors and filmmakers who made it*, London, Methuen, 1997.
4 John Grierson described Baxter's films as 'sentimental to the point of embarrassment; but at least about real people's sentimentalities' (Murphy 2001: 251).

Further Reading

Anthony Aldgate and Jeffrey Richards, *Britain Can Take It: The British Cinema in the Second World War*, Edinburgh, Edinburgh University Press, 1994.
Geoff Brown and Anthony Aldgate, *The Common Touch: the Films of John Baxter*, London, BFI, 1989.
Andrew Higson, 'Space, Place, Spectacle: Landscape and Townscape in the "Kitchen Sink" Film' in Andrew Higson (ed.) *Dissolving Views: Key Writings on British Cinema*, London and New York, Cassell, 1996.
Tom Dewe Mathews, *Censored*, London, Chatto and Windus, 1994.
Robert Murphy (ed.) *The British Cinema Book*, London, BFI, 2001.
James Park, *British Cinema: The Lights That Failed*, London, Batsford, 1990.
Stephen C. Shafer, *British Popular Films 1929–39: the Cinema of Reassurance*, London and New York, Routledge, 1997.
Anthony Slide, *Banned in the USA: British films in the US and their Censorship, 1935–60*, London, I.B. Tauris, 1998.
Sarah Street, *British Cinema in Documents*, London and New York, Routledge, 2000.
Philip M. Taylor, *Britain and the Cinema in the Second World War*, London, Macmillan, 1988.

JOHN WHITE

LISTEN TO BRITAIN (1942)

[Production Company: Crown Film Unit. Directors and editors: Humphrey Jennings and Stewart McAllister. Cinematographer: H. E.

Fowle. Sound: Ken Cameron. Cast: Chesney Allen (himself), Bud Flanagan (himself), Myra Hess (herself, pianist), Queen Elizabeth, the Queen's mother (herself, uncredited).]

Humphrey Jennings (1907–50), the main creative force behind this short yet powerful documentary film, was an established poet and painter as well as a sublime film-maker, who was much influenced by the European Surrealist movement of the 1920s and 1930s.[1] With those artists, he shared a desire to explore the symbolic in the everyday and, as can be seen throughout *Listen to Britain*, chose to use 'an impressionistic style dependent on juxtapositions and association' (Aitken 1998: 216). He was certainly a careful observer and recorder of his nation at a time of crisis, but he was also very much an artist who created images and sounds that were laden with meaning and open to various interpretations simultaneously. If his subject matter was often quite ordinary, his expressive mode was quite unique and it is the distinctive visual poetry inherent in his films that has been lauded by subsequent generations of British film-makers and critics. In his extensive biography of this most extraordinary of film-makers, Kevin Jackson describes the film as 'a total work of art [with an] intense visual beauty' (2004: 252).

Jennings began directing films in 1939, on the eve of the Second World War. Rather than hinder him, the war in fact gave impetus to his ideas and created the conditions for his best work to be produced. In particular, they allowed him to bring to the screen images of ordinary people, sharply glimpsed as they go about their everyday business during wartime, whether farming in East Anglia (*Spring Offensive* 1940) or contributing to the war effort in the industrialised north (*Heart of Britain* 1941). These early pictures, and others like them, were in many respects pieces of crude propaganda accompanied by didactic commentaries, and yet they already revealed the poetic tendencies of a director for whom the associative possibilities of the image were crucial.

Listen to Britain was one of several films made by Jennings between 1941 and 1945 that show the development of a coherent, personal style and a very individual approach to the depiction of a nation at war. As director and writer Lindsay Anderson points out, 'They are all films of Britain at war, and yet their feeling is never, or almost never, war-like'.[2] Instead of aggression, they are inspired by nationalistic pride in the spirit of the ordinary people of Britain facing up to great adversity, and by a sharp sense of the importance of tradition and community.

With *Listen to Britain*, Jennings abandoned the strategies of commentary voiceover and linear narrative altogether and focused attention on the technique of associative editing, building up and synthesising oppositions and connections through a careful layering of image and sound. The overarching theme he thus develops is the evocation of a strong and deep sense of national unity, linking places and people from across the country, all walks of life, and as they are involved in many different activities. As Aitken points out, 'films such as *Listen to Britain* are an intense reflection on this belief in the underlying unity of the nation [. . .] and could only have been made during the war, when there was a focus on the issue of national identity' (1998: 216). After the war, the political and social divisions which had been concealed for the sake of the war effort were again exposed, and the unity of experience evoked by *Listen to Britain* was no longer as sharply relevant.

Jennings also shared with the Surrealists a desire to urge people to awaken from a complacent stupor, to reject preconceived beliefs, and to produce more spontaneous cultural forms. He was concerned with the capturing of small moments that might shed light on the meaning of broader experiences, and called for the central role of the artist to be reclaimed, and redefined if necessary, given the twentieth-century priorities of industrialisation and capitalism. Perhaps more importantly in the context of this film, Jennings appeared to hold an unshakeable admiration for what he felt were the distinctively irritating qualities of the English, stating in an essay of 1948 that:

> The English are in fact a violent, savage race; passionately artistic, enormously addicted to pattern, with a faculty beyond all other people of ignoring their neighbours, their surroundings, or in the last resort, themselves. They have a power of poetry which is the despair of all the rest of the world. They produce from time to time personalities transcending ordinary human limitations. Then they drive other nations to a frenzy by patronising these archangels who have come among them, and by indicating that any ordinary Englishman could do better if he liked to take the trouble.
>
> (Aitken 1998: 222–223)[3]

Such thoughts appear to have acted as the motivating force behind *Listen to Britain*, made by Jennings in collaboration with the editor Stewart McAllister, for the Ministry of Information at the Crown Film Unit as part of a propaganda campaign. Drawing on an already established montage tradition in British documentary, the film offers, as Higson describes, 'apparently discrete fragments of sounds and images of the home front at work and leisure, juxtaposed with images from the traditional iconography of pastoral England and the new iconography of the war period' (1995: 201). The apparent fragmentation, however, is overridden by a powerful sense of ideological unity that results from the associations between images which are implied rather than stated.

The idyllic opening images and sounds of a rustling, brightly lit cornfield followed by a peaceful coastal scene at sunset are sharply interrupted by those of people listening in their blacked-out homes to radio warnings of imminent attacks, with the buzzing of planes overhead. The overarching sense of communal spirit and shared experience is then quickly conveyed by the next lengthy shot of a dance hall, with a static high-angle camera watching as couples hold each other tightly and move in unison and harmony across the wide space of the frame. Moreover, there is a neat coming together, sometimes almost a collision, of the contemporary with the traditional (shots of tanks charging through a rural village), the rural with the urban, the low with high art. The various scenes of different musical occasions help develop these contrasts while also reinforcing the idea of communality and shared experience: factory canteen sing-a-longs with music-hall double-act Flanagan and Allen are joyfully presented, while moments later classical pianist Dame Myra Hess is shown playing Mozart in the National Gallery before a diverse audience that includes the Queen. In this way, the idea of harmony between classes is reinforced and, as Higson notes, 'national identity is proposed as the sum of this productive variety' (1995: 202).

The iconography is remarkable for its blend of image types familiar from 1930s social documentaries by the likes of John Grierson with those that revealed sights that were less common on the cinema screen. While the former showed the worker in his or her place of toil, with an emphasis on both the splendour of the machine age, and the determined spark of humanity within the industrialised workplace, the latter provided opportunity for new sets of pictures of leisure and communal activity outside work. Alongside evocative images, sound is lovingly crafted into one great symphony that conveys mood, creates dramatic emphasis, and flags up connections between people and places. Whistles are blown and steam hisses to signal the arrival of a train at its destination; birds twitter amongst the cornfields; Big Ben tolls; horses' hooves clip-clop along the cobbles; leaves shimmer on the trees; spitfires roar overhead; machinery clanks incessantly. All provide, as Leonard Brockington points out in his introduction, 'the trumpet call of freedom, the war song of a great people, the first sure notes of the march of victory'.[4]

The shared experience of music-making is reinforced in many scenes, and the music that is made serves to link the various elements of a film that rejects conventional linear narrative strategies and places emphasis instead on evoking nostalgia. Canadian soldiers sing as they reminisce on the train; women whistle along to the radio as they work; piano music is heard as schoolchildren play outside; the muffled sound of the dance hall music is still heard as the camera moves outside to observe the home brigade as they put on their helmets and prepare to report for duty.

Not everyone is impressed by the film's poetic charm, instead claiming to find it scarily manipulative in a way that is reminiscent of critiques of Leni Riefenstahl's seminal but controversial documentary work in support of the Nazi regime, *Triumph of the Will* (1935 Germany). Indeed, one response on the Internet Movie Database comments that the film's great efforts to convey the idea of shared community seems to leave it horrifyingly devoid of any sense of individual identity. 'After all,' claims the amateur reviewer, 'if you can make something as light as wheat flowing in the wind look like rows of well-organized troops with bayonets, you can certainly sell the idea of a perfect society as a strict, organized conglomerate of so-called "superior people" in all of their blank-faced homogeneity.'[5] The explicitly and unashamedly romanticised celebration of all things British, with the masses singing 'Rule Britannia' as the images return to timeless ones of cornfields and clouds, has also been greeted with some inevitable irritation.

Nevertheless, *Listen to Britain*'s main purpose was to develop a sense of purpose and unity, however illusory, for its primary audience during wartime, while also serving to remind those British audiences that saw it what they were fighting to protect. More than that, it went beyond the standard informational expectations of documentary film-making at that time and offered 19 minutes of what Mike Leigh describes as 'exemplary storytelling'.[6] For audiences today, it continues to offer indelible images and sounds that convey an impression of what Britain might have been like for those living during World War Two, and which have become part of the imagined sense of that war.

Notes

1 Jennings was part of the organising committee of the 1936 Surrealist Exhibition in London.

2 Lindsay Anderson, 'Only Connect: Some Aspects on the Work of Humphrey Jennings', *Sight and Sound*, Spring 1954, reproduced in the

booklet accompanying the special DVD Collection of Jennings's work by Film First, 2005.

3 Jennings's essay 'The English' (1948) is reproduced in full in Aitken's text, pp. 220–228.

4 The Ministry of Information insisted that a spoken introduction be added to the film to help the audience make sense of its images and sounds. This was presented in the form of a foreword read by a Canadian; Leonard Brockington K.C. Jennings and McAllister were reportedly outraged.

5 Polaris_DiB (US), 'Terrifyingly ordered', 24 January 2007, IMDb, http://www.imdb.com/title/tt0034978/usercomments, accessed 5 February 2007.

6 Mike Leigh was speaking as part of Kevin MacDonald's documentary *Humphrey Jennings: The Man who Listened to Britain*, included in the special DVD collection (2005).

Further Reading

Ian Aitken (ed.) *The Documentary Film Movement: An Anthology*, Edinburgh, Edinburgh University Press, 1998.

Andrew Higson, *Waving the Flag: Constructing a National Cinema in Britain*, Oxford, Clarendon, 1995.

Kevin Jackson, *Humphrey Jennings: The Definitive Biography of One of Britain's Most Important Film-makers*, London, Picador, 2004.

Robert Murphy, *British Cinema and the Second World War*, London, Continuum, 2000.

SARAH BARROW

THE LIFE AND DEATH OF COLONEL BLIMP (1943)

[Production Company: Archers Film Productions. Directors, screen-writers and producers: Michael Powell and Emeric Pressburger. Cinematographer: Georges Perinal. Music: Allan Gray. Editor: John Seabourne. Production designer: Alfred Junge. Cast: Roger Livesey (Clive Wynne-Candy), Anton Walbrook (Theo Kretschmar-Schuldorff), Deborah Kerr (Edith Hunter/Angela Cannon), Roland Culver (Colonel Betteridge), Harry Welchman (Major Davies).]

Martin Scorsese, Francis Coppola – and Stephen Fry – are among many directors and writer-actors who consider *The Life and Death of Colonel Blimp* to be a great British film, and beyond that, one of the finest works in world cinema. But then why is this national epic not better known? *Blimp* is, at every level, a wonderfully paradoxical piece: a war film that refuses to show violent conflict; a moving love story without much passion, in the generally accepted sense; an anti-Nazi propaganda tract with, at its centre, a touching friendship between two officers, one very English, the other profoundly German. Finally, the narrative is spread over a 40-year period and recounted in one sustained and complex flashback. On one estimate, *Blimp* was the second most successful British film of 1943, after the Hollywood melodrama *Random Harvest*, Noel Coward's *In Which We Serve*, and Michael Curtiz's *Casablanca*. Powell and Pressburger's film also bene-fited from a degree of notoriety due to a government campaign to have it banned, driven with particular vehemence by Churchill himself (Chapman 1995: 43). *Blimp* has since drawn admiring com-parisons with *Citizen Kane* and *Gone with the Wind*, films that its makers were perhaps striving to surpass. But at nearly three hours' running time, *Blimp* fell victim to drastic cuts when shown in the post-war years, and it was only with its final restoration by the BFI in 1983 that the film's unique qualities could be fully appreciated. Yet the 'meaning' of *The Life and Death of Colonel Blimp* remains elusive. 'It is a handsome piece. It is frequently a moving piece. But what is it about?' wrote C. A. Lejeune, the most respected film critic of the time, for the *Observer*. We should acknowledge this complexity that undoubtedly limited the film's circulation but which is also a mark of its subtlety and true achievement.

Michael Powell (1904–1990), a 'Man of Kent' (Powell 1987: 6), and Emeric (Imre) Pressburger (1902–1987), born into the Jewish middle class of Miskolc, Hungary, together created the single most impressive group of films in British cinema. As 'The Archers', between 1942 and 1957 the pair led a superbly gifted team whose key members were often European émigrés – art director Alfred Junge, composer Josef Zmigrod ('Allan Gray'), cinematographer Georges Périnal. Pressburger had been one of the most valued screenwriters in the German film industry before Hitler's rise to power, and he was intimately familiar with European cinema. *Blimp*'s moving evocation of 'Englishness', like Hollywood's projection of American values, was very much the creation of foreigners in exile. To properly appreciate the scale of the Archers' achievement, *Blimp* should be considered together with *A Canterbury Tale* (1944), *I Know Where I'm Going* (1945), *A Matter of Life and Death* (1946), *Black Narcissus* (1947) – 'that rare thing, an erotic English film' (Thomson 2003: 696) – and *The Red Shoes* (1947), as a superb sequence which portrays a complex vision of national identity and Britain's post-war dilemmas (Wheale 1997: 107–115). *Blimp* remains the most ambi-tious and elusive of these films, their unique qualities best celebrated by the Scottish novelist, A. L. Kennedy:

Within those celluloid worlds, film was allowed to be fully itself: articulate beyond any limits other than those of its own nature. Light and colour were manipulated to produce images as delicate as painting or still photography; which could enunciate subtexts, atmospheres and tones of emotion ... It has always hurt, just a little, to watch things so beautiful and so resonant in so many parts of my mind.

(Kennedy 1997: 14)

The film's paradoxes begin with its title. 'Colonel Blimp' was a despicable, reactionary figure created by the cartoonist David Low for the *Evening Standard* in 1934. Low's Blimp possessed no redeeming qualities, but stood for the failure to adapt to changing circumstances that characterised so much of British institutional life at the time, in the colonies and ruling institutions as much as in the armed forces. Winston Churchill's unreasoning and, eventually, illegal opposition to the film may have stemmed from his fear of being identified with Blimp, just when his conduct of the war was under severe question. More than this, the agitation at Cabinet level shows how much wartime administrations valued the vital contribution of feature films to morale on the home front (just as true in Moscow and Berlin as London).

Clive 'Sugar' Candy VC, CB, DSO, possesses none of the original Blimp's vicious stupidity, though he looks exactly like Low's character, and we first meet him in a Turkish bath, which was the cartoon Blimp's preferred recreation. By contrast, Roger Livesey's Candy is an endearing old fellow, a true national hero of the Boer War campaigns, yet he is also someone who has become stranded in time. Candy's defining trauma occurred back in 1902 at the moment he unwittingly fell in love with Miss Edith Hunter, and after he had lost her to his duelling antagonist, Oberleutnant Theo Kretschmar-Schuldorff. Clive Candy has become frozen at the point of his love that can never be fulfilled. He is condemned to a vain repetition in his search for the simulacrum of his lost beloved, Edith. Partly as a consequence of this personal tragedy, he also feels the need to create and defend an increasingly anachronistic ideal of England and the English soldier. This identification of Edith Hunter with Englishness is also powerfully endorsed by Theo during his questioning under the Enemy Aliens Order when he arrives in London as a political refugee. His speech, written specifically for Adolf Wohlbrück, is profoundly moving, and must have drawn deeply on Emeric Pressburger's own experiences (double brackets indicate a cut, single brackets an addition to the final screenplay):

And very foolishly I remembered the [[English]] countryside, [the gardens,] the green lawns [[where I spent the long months of captivity]] ... [And] a great desire came over me to come back [[here]] to my wife's country.

(Christie 1994: 250)

Clive Candy's notion of soldiering is brutally dismissed by the two American officers he encounters in Flanders. As he is driven away by 'Armstrong' (a regrettably stereotyped black soldier, played by the uncredited Norris Smith, and the only false note in the film), one remarks to the other that Candy's campaigns 'weren't wars. Those were just summer manoeuvres' (Christie 1994: 201). But time after time, the film also seems to endorse Candy's values and perspective, either emotionally, or in stronger, pragmatic terms. When Candy receives a despatch announcing the Armistice cease-fire the *mise-en-scène* is frankly theatrical, providing an ironic frame for Candy's question to Murdoch: ' ... do you know what this means? *Murdoch*: I do, sir. Peace. We can go home. Everybody can go home!' Murdoch has 'the common soldier' view, and John Laurie delivers his lines with great feeling. But Candy takes an elevated tone: 'For me, Murdoch, it means more than that. It means that Right is Might after all ... Clean fighting, honest soldiering, have won!' (Christie 1994: 211) Immediately we hear the song of a skylark rising into the sky, and celebratory music fades up. The lark song on cue is simultaneously ridiculous and poignant, both affirming and mocking of Candy's naïve credo.

A notorious propaganda poster, current when the film was being made, proclaimed, '*Your* courage, *your* cheerfulness, *your* resolution, will bring *us* victory'. This was widely seen to be a divisive appeal, in which the mass of the population would make sacrifices so that the British establishment could be preserved. If the pronoun had been 'Our' rather than 'Your' then the call would have immediately become more inclusive. The confrontation between James McKechnie's 'Spud' Wilson and Roger Livesey's elderly Candy presents a stark opposition between Blimpish values and the pragmatic, even brutal new spirit that is required to oppose and destroy the Nazi threat – 'Moderation in war is Imbecility', read an advert from August, 1942 sponsored by the Co-op, and quoting Lord Macaulay. Ambitious young Second Lieutenant Wilson, who has progressed rapidly through the ranks by pure merit, will use 'any means at my disposal' to defend the country, including breaking agreed rules. Ian Christie's edition of the screenplay shows some crucial revisions. Asked early in the film what H.Q. means by making Exercise Beer-Mug 'like the real thing', the original text has Wilson reply, 'obviously [[prisoners must be bayoneted to death, women must be raped,]] (Wow!) our losses divided by ten and the enemy's multiplied by twenty!' (Christie 1994: 80) The double-bracketed section was cut in production, and given the sensitivities already inflamed by the film one can see why Spud's severe ironies had to go. Yet there remains a threatening brutality in the contrast between young men in battle dress waving their rifles around in the steam room and the naked flesh of vulnerable elderly men, a scenario that summons images of the Fascist massacres even then taking place in Europe.

'*Blimp* is a film dominated by women' (Macdonald 1994: 210). While Candy's hopeless love for Edith Hunter is the reason for his belatedness in a rapidly changing world, each of Edith's incarnations frankly opposes Candy's anachronistic views on the conduct of war and the nature of the enemy. 'Hunter', 'Wynne', and 'Cannon' are names that suggest masculine aggression, and Deborah Kerr succeeded in creating three very distinct, yet linked characters out of the minimal number of lines given to her roles. Paradoxically, Edith is the most directly outspoken of the three, even though she is the most severely restricted by an hourglass figure and the conventions of her time. She is accused of being a 'suffragette', four years before the first recorded use of the word, and she adroitly manoeuvres Candy into confronting Kaunitz in the Berlin café. Barbara Wynne is the most enigmatic of Candy's three loves, and her denunciation of German atrocities during the failed visit to Theo in the prisoner of war camp is all the more striking, delivered as it is by her apparently reserved character.

Angela 'Johnny' Cannon and her boyfriend Spud embody the new, youthful Britain that increasing numbers of people yearned for in the midst of war, a genuine meritocracy that would finally shake off the burdens of class and established privilege. Yet the liberation from the repressive conventions of gender enjoyed by Angela/Johnny is also compromised. She has to adopt male values and attributes in order to operate in the brave new world of 1943, even as she is still characterised as 'Mata Hari', the seductive vamp who knocks her boyfriend out at the beginning of the action. The couple chase each other around the roadhouse tearoom to the music of Glenn Miller on the juke-box ('War has become/Like a juke-box tune that we dare not stop' – Auden, *For the Time Being*, 1944), an American soundtrack that has forever blown away the elegant lilt of *Mignon*'s aria and the Café Hohenzollern of 1902.

A. L. Kennedy notes that just one of *Blimp*'s small but telling tragedies is an absence of children. The two sons of Edith and Theo have become Nazis and so are lost to their parents; Clive and Barbara were not blessed with a child – did Barbara die during childbirth in Jamaica? – and when Clive jokes before his duel that he has learned the outlandish name 'Oberleutnant Theo Kretschmar-Schuldorff' so that he can tell his grandchildren whose ear he cut off, we know that this will never come to be. Candy himself becomes the child of his time, 'a kind of holy fool, walking the battlegrounds of his century, underestimated and overlooked' (Kennedy 1997: 51).

Further Reading

James Chapman, '*The Life and Death of Colonel Blimp* (1943) Reconsidered', *Historical Journal of Film, Radio and Television*, Vol. 15, No. 1, 1995, pp. 19–36.

Ian Christie (ed.) *The Life and Death of Colonel Blimp*, London, Faber, 1994.

A. L. Kennedy, *The Life and Death of Colonel Blimp*, London, BFI, 1997.

Kevin Macdonald, *Emeric Pressburger. The Life and Death of a Screenwriter*, London, Faber, 1994.

Michael Powell, *A Life in Movies. An Autobiography*, London, Methuen, 1987.

David Thomson, *The New Biographical Dictionary of Film*, 4th edition, London, Little Brown, 2002.

Nigel Wheale, 'Beyond the Trauma Stratus: Lynette Roberts' *Gods with Stainless Ears* and the Post-War Cultural Landscape', *Welsh Writing in English*, Vol. 3, 1997, pp. 98–117.

NIGEL WHEALE

MILLIONS LIKE US (1943)

[Production Company: Gainsborough Pictures. Directors and screenwriters: Frank Launder & Sidney Gilliat. Cinematographer: Jack Cox, Roy Fogwell. Editor: R. E. Dearing. Music: Louis Levy. Cast: Eric Portman (Charlie Forbes), Patricia Roc (Celia Crowson), Gordon Jackson (Fred Blake), Anne Crawford (Jennifer Knowles).

Your husband is dead. You're far from home, with a monotonous job you never wanted. All your romantic dreams have been shattered. And there's a war on. Still, never mind, join in with a good old sing-along and everything will be better ... So ends *Millions Like Us*, a testament to the courage, cheerfulness and resolution of the British people on the home front during World War Two. It is also British cinema's most sublime piece of propaganda.

The part played by ordinary men and women during the Second World War led to the idea of it being a 'people's war'. With encouragement from the government via the Ministry of Information (MOI), British wartime films presented an ideology of national unity and social cohesion. Everyone had a part to play in the war effort, no matter what class or gender. What emerges is a democratic sense of community and comradeship, where the country's interests are greater than that of the individual. The government needed all these powers of persuasion when it came to the difficult issue of the conscription of women.

Voluntary appeals had failed to find enough recruits and female conscription was introduced with the National Service (No 2) Act of December 1941. All single women between 19 and 30 had the option of either the non-combatant Auxiliary Territorial Service (ATS) or working full-time in essential industries. Two months later, the Employment of Women Order of February 1942 allowed the government to direct the movement of female workers aged 18 to 40. Consternation and resentment about such powers had to be assuaged. Women had to be reassured that mobilisation was vital to the war effort and that they were capable of performing their assigned tasks well. Men, concerned about their future livelihood, just had to be reassured that this was a temporary state of affairs brought about by the war. Anxieties such as these are articulated in *Millions Like Us*.

Originally planned as a documentary about the home front, *Millions Like Us* changed form when the MOI approached Frank Launder and Sidney Gilliat to write a script. Launder and Gilliat were established in the British film industry having scripted such successes as Hitchcock's *The Lady Vanishes* (1938) and *Night Train to Munich* (Carol Reed, 1940). Both films feature the comic double-act of upper-class officers, Charters and Caldicott (played by Basil Radford and Naunton Wayne, respectively, who also appear in *Millions Like Us*). However, Launder empathised with the MOI, and wanted to create a socially responsible, realist cinema showing 'people we know – people that live next door to us – that travel with us on the bus' (Brown 1977: 9).

In preparation for their script, Launder and Gilliat toured the country, visiting various places of work all over Britain, including munitions factories. They came to the conclusion, with commercial interests in mind, that the best way to provide what the Ministry wanted was 'to cloak it in a simple fictional story' (Brown 1977: 108). According to Gilliat they were 'greatly impressed with the fate ... of the conscripted woman, the mobile woman. And that's what we would have liked to call the thing if it hadn't been such a silly title!' (Brown 1977: 108) Silly title or not, 'The Mobile Woman' would have been far less appropriate for a film that directly addresses its intended mass audience: 'and millions like you' run the credits after listing the stars and just before the title, *Millions Like Us*. It is also one of the first British films to place working-class women at the heart of its narrative as serious fictional characters without recourse to comedy or cliché. Furthermore, the original documentary approach is still present in the film, providing a context within which the propaganda is embedded.

Millions Like Us opens with the masses: documentary footage of working people purposefully marching to and from work underlined by the strident tones of Beethoven's Fifth Symphony. These are the 'millions like you' addressed in the credits. It is interesting that the address is initially aimed at the working classes. As the film progresses, other classes are encompassed, principally through the cameos of Charters and Caldicott and also by the character of Jennifer Knowles (Anne Crawford), the upper-class socialite; all have difficulty adapting to wartime changes. Furthermore, the casting of Patricia Roc, with her received pronunciation (RP) tones, turns the character of Celia into a classless 'everywoman'.

There then follows a montage sequence of the masses at the seaside accompanied by an ironic-nostalgic voice-over: 'Remember that summer before the war?' It appeals to the collective memory of those days before the war and rationing, before powdered eggs, when you could still slip up on a piece of orange peel. The non-diegetic onscreen reminder as to what an orange is provides a nod and a wink to a knowing audience. It's a cheap, throwaway gag but humour helps to sugar-coat the pill of propaganda. However, there's now a war on, priorities are different and things have changed, as the film later makes clear: Charters and Caldicott have mined the beaches and the Eastgate that Celia revisits on her honeymoon with Fred (Gordon Jackson) is very different from the one she visited on her family holidays.

Once this opening montage is over, the film dissolves to a barrel organ (the film does allow space for some working-class clichés) and the camera tracks to the Crowford family preparing for their summer vacation. The story of how the war affects a typical working-class family has begun. However, this does not signal an end to the documentary aspects of the film. For the first half hour, the film adopts a panoramic approach, interweaving the characters (the 'private'), with the 'public' sphere of the history of the war so far, detailed in documentary style. The latter validates the former, as Andrew Higson observes:

> The film seems to declare that the individual dramas only make sense within the real historical space already established in the initially unnarrativised diegesis. This more objective (because documentary) sense of history orders and situates, and therefore validates what would otherwise be the mere discourse of the film's little dramas.
>
> (1995: 240)

Therefore, the narrative is rendered authentic and realistic by the documentary techniques. But as the film progresses, those aspects become contained within the narrative. The most notable instance of this is when Celia boards the bus to the factory (to the familiar jaunty strains of the theme from the radio programme, *Worker's Playtime*) and between this and her arrival, there is a montage sequence showing the construction of a bomber. Celia will become part of this important chain. However, the realism continues with many scenes beginning or ending by dwelling on an authentic detail: pamphlets, posters or productivity charts.

Although the film begins with a panoramic overview of how people are reacting to the war, the narrative eventually focuses on the experiences of Celia, recounting her coming-of-age. Shy, naïve and dreaming of Charles Boyer, Celia does display a practical side by being the surrogate mother-figure of the family. The antithesis is her good-time sister, Phyllis (Joy Shelton), who, despite initial impressions, enlists in the ATS, placing country above her father's wishes, and makes a success of it. Celia also dreams of joining the ATS upon conscription. In contrast to the objective documentary realism of the film to this point, Celia's daydream at the labour exchange is depicted: a subjective reverie of the romantic possibilities while working for the ATS. However, reality intrudes at the interview when her options are limited and factory work is assigned. 'There's nothing to be afraid of in a factory,' the civil servant tells her, 'Mr Bevin needs another million women.' The film's central propaganda message is thus cleverly incorporated into the narrative. It is reiterated upon arrival at the factory. Greeted by the no-nonsense northern foreman, Charlie Forbes (Eric Portman), the women are welcomed with the words: 'Now you'd better understand there's not much glamour in a machine shop. You'll be working with small component parts you'll never hear of again. But you'll be indispensable, remember that.'

While Celia has fears, like all the women, about her new life, it is Gwen Price (Megs Jenkins) who articulates them to the negative extreme: they are now part of a 'chain-gang' and she imagines the dormitories as 'a cross between a house of correction and a home for illegitimate children'. The reality is somewhat different. They are met by a caring matron, the work is hard but there is regular entertainment in the form of communal meals, dances and concerts (strangely, cinema is not included!). The new community presents a cross-section of classes and parts of the country: Celia (working class, London), Jennifer (upper class), Gwen (working class, Wales), and Annie Earnshaw (working class, the North). Annie (Terry Randall) presents a more 'common' version of the working class in comparison to Celia, and her scenes are mainly played for humour, particularly regarding the culture-clash with Jennifer. What they all share are the circumstances that have brought them together and they cohere into community for the benefit of the country.

Yet Celia threatens to disrupt this with her romance and marriage to Fred. Unlike Jennifer, who merely has dalliances, Celia still has romantic dreams and sees a future with a husband and children – or rejection and suicide as revealed in another dream sequence. Despite his own naivety and shyness, Fred takes a more realistic view: he worries about how they will afford to live in the future. *Millions Like Us* is thus notable because it acknowledges a time when the war will be over.[1] However, despite placing private interests above those of the country, the institution of marriage is not questioned; neither are Jennifer's dalliances condoned. Her burgeoning romance with Charlie is a counterpoint: how war can cause an unlikely attraction across the classes and regions. Charlie, ever the realist, realises this and makes the point in the penultimate scene.[2] He wonders if this classless society will continue after the war, or whether they will slide back into old ways. 'That's what I want to know. I'm not marrying you, Jenny, till I'm sure.'

The film ends with another communal dinner and concert. The band is ironically playing 'Waiting at the Church' much to Celia's discomfort. Then there's the sound of bombers flying overhead.

So, your husband is dead: but he has been sacrificed for the greater good. You're far from home and family: but you've found a new 'family' with your community of friends who encourage you to join in and sing. The job may be monotonous but it's essential. All your romantic dreams have been shattered but now you can face the reality of the home front: after all, you're indispensable and you can hold your head high. The final dissolve from a medium close-up of Celia up to the bombers flying overhead makes this point explicit, and the 'millions like us' can also exit the cinema, heads held high.

Notes

1 It is also notable for restraint in jingoistic anti-German propaganda: apart from loss of life, the worst they can do is bomb the Queen's Arms.
2 Unlike the rest of the film, this scene is set in the countryside, reminiscent of the contemporary series of photographs in Picture Post entitled 'What We're Fighting For'.

Further Reading

Geoff Brown, *Launder and Gilliat*, London, BFI, 1977.
James Chapman, *The British at War: Cinema, State and Propaganda, 1939–1945*, London & New York, I. B. Taurus, 2000.
Christine Gledhill and Gillian Swanson, 'Gender and Sexuality in Second World War Films – A Feminist Approach', in Geoff Hurd (ed.) *National Fictions: World War Two in British Films and Television*, London, British Film Institute, 1984, pp. 56–62.
Andrew Higson, *Waving the Flag: Constructing a National Cinema in Britain*, Oxford, Clarendon Press, 1995.
Antonia Lant, *Blackout: Reinventing Women for Wartime British Cinema*, Princeton, Princeton University Press, 1991.

NIGEL HERWIN

BRIEF ENCOUNTER (1945)

[Production Company: Cineguild. Director: David Lean. Screenwriters: Noel Coward, David Lean, Anthony Havelock-Allan. Cinematographer: Robert Krasker. Editor: Jack Harris. Music: Sergei Rachmaninov. Cast: Celia Johnson (Laura Jesson), Trevor Howard (Dr. Alec Harvey), Joyce Carey (Myrtle Bagot), Stanley Holloway (Albert Godby), Cyril Raymond (Fred Jesson).]

Jeremy Paxman begins his book, *The English: A Portrait of a People*, with a detailed account of the film *Brief Encounter*: a good indicator of just how far this film has become an icon not only of British cinema but also of British national identity, particularly in terms of the behaviour of its two lead characters. Laura (Celia Johnson), a housewife, and Alec (Trevor Howard), a doctor, both happily married to other people, happen to fall in love with each other, quite by chance and apparently without calculation, after he removes a piece of grit from her eye. Friendship develops into romance, and the couple meet in town once a week before they finally call off their 'affair', which remains unconsummated. Their sense of duty towards their respective spouses and families, as well as their overwhelming need to behave in accordance with the accepted morality of the time, prevents them from taking their relationship any further. Instead, sexual passion is displaced by awkward conversation and furtive, loving glances at each other in the Milford Junction station tearoom or the Kardomah café: no wonder that Raymond Durgnat proclaimed the motto of the film to be 'Make tea not love' (1971: 181).

Durgnat further noted how the film that was critically lauded upon its 1945 release (even winning the Critics' Prize at the 1946 Cannes Film Festival) met with quite a different reception 20 years later, when its ethos of restraint no longer seemed quite so appealing to the exponents of sixties free love, and the most innocuous little details of the film provoked impatience and irritation in its viewers. He recalls that at one screening he attended 'Even the name of the town enraged a well-spoken young lady who finally cried out, "Where the hell is Milford Junction anyway?"' (1971: 180).

However, the suggestion that the film did not meet with antipathy until the 1960s is slightly misleading, since even in the 1940s the film had a mixed reception. When it was first test-screened in a cinema in Kent that had a working-class clientele, it was heckled and laughed at throughout because of the (much parodied) middle-class speech of its protagonists, not to mention its unimpeachably 'correct' morality. *Brief Encounter* may be a national icon but from the moment of its initial release onwards there have been any number of iconoclasts who have called into question its ability to speak for them and their national identity. Perhaps the critic Gavin Lambert was correct when he called the film a 'definitive document of middle-class repression', the last word on a particular kind of Britishness, specific to a time and a place and most crucially a *class*.[1] Even within the film, we see the operation of a slightly different moral code via the parallel relationship between Myrtle (Joyce Carey), the station tearoom manageress and Albert (Stanley Holloway), the stationmaster, who belong to a different social class from Alec and Laura, and are less inhibited about acting on their feelings for each other.[2]

Brief Encounter was the fourth and final collaboration between the celebrated playwright Noel Coward and director David Lean, who would go on to make two of the most highly regarded adaptations of Dickens novels, *Great Expectations* (1946) and *Oliver Twist* (1948) before moving into epic mode with later films such as *The Bridge on* the River Kwai (1957), Lawrence of Arabia (1962) and Doctor Zhivago (1965). Having risen to the status of the top British film editor by the end of the 1930s, Lean had been asked to co-direct the war film In Which We Serve (1942) with Noel Coward, providing technical expertise to complement Coward's ease with actors. The partnership proved highly successful and continued with Lean directing the family saga This Happy Breed (1944) and the supernatural comedy Blithe Spirit (1945), both adaptations of Coward's stage successes. It is a sign of Lean's growing confidence as a director that he encouraged Coward to rethink the chronological structure of his half-hour play Still Life, the source for Brief Encounter, when converting it into a screenplay. Lean told Coward that the original dramatic structure lacked intrigue and surprise. He suggested that the film version could play with audience expectation by beginning with an enigmatic scene showing the couple's final parting:

> ... and then you go back and explain that this is the last time they see each other. They were never going to see each other again. And you play the first scene in the picture – it made no sense to you at all and you didn't hear half the dialogue – again, and that's the end of the film.
>
> (Brownlow 1997: 194)

This strategy is highly effective, particularly as it comes at the film's most emotionally extreme moment: Laura's sudden suicidal impulse. In the first version, we remain in the tearoom with Myrtle and Laura's friend Dolly (Everley Gregg) vaguely wondering where Laura has got to, before she re-enters the room looking pale and shaky. In the second version, we go *with* Laura as she rushes out onto the platform determined to throw herself under the express train thundering past, and this time we understand the significance of the moment and know exactly why she has reached this abject state. She hesitates at the last moment and resists suicide, although as she admits in her voice-over narration (an imaginary confession to her husband, but also the key to the viewer's intimacy and empathy with the character) that this is not because of a sense of duty towards her family but because she 'wasn't brave enough' to go through with it.

Despite Lean's important contribution to the film, in 1945 the film was sold as a Noel Coward film, and Andy Medhurst has read the film as an oblique expression of Coward's homosexuality. The film's forbidden relationship is heterosexual, but its depiction of 'the pain and grief caused by having one's desires destroyed by the pressures of social convention' (1991: 204) could be understood as a coded reference to the tribulations of (then still illegal) homosexual relationships. Several decades on, Richard Kwietniowski's short film *Flames of Passion* (1990) paid homage to *Brief Encounter*'s queer subtext by offering a gay re-imagining of the original film. It even takes its title from the torrid melodrama that Alec and Laura go to see at the cinema, but which they leave halfway through because they find it too silly and implausible.

Brief Encounter's 'meta-cinematic' elements (characters within the film commenting on films and the focus on aspects of 1940s cinema-going like the differently priced seats, the organist who plays beforehand, the trailers and Disney cartoon prior to the main film) are important reminders of the central role that fantasy plays in our lives; every small town has its cinema where people can spend a pleasant few hours inhabiting a cinematic dream world. However, Laura seems particularly prone to the lure of fantasy. She borrows romantic novels from the library and, as her husband Fred (Cyril Raymond) remarks, she is a 'poetry addict' able to fill in the missing word from his crossword puzzle, taken from a line from Keats ('Huge cloudy symbols of a high romance' – a phrase that could apply to Laura's own romance, punctuated by clouds of steam and smoke from passing trains). Meanwhile for down-to-earth Fred, 'romance' is just 'something in seven letters' that fits in with 'delirium' and 'Baluchistan'. Laura is the one who turns on the radio broadcast of Rachmaninov when she returns home from her final terrible meeting with Alec, and who uses the pounding dramatic Russian music as a soundtrack for her remembrance of her love affair, communicating the depth of her feelings where words fail.

Indeed, the emotive power of these elements of the film belie its reputation as a realist, restrained, repressed text, and as Richard Dyer suggests, to see *Brief Encounter* 'as only cups of tea, banal conversation and guilt is not really to see or hear it at all' (1993: 66). Rather, it is precisely that interaction in the film between suburban mundanity – such as going to Boots to buy a toothbrush, eating a Banbury cake at a café – and overwhelming unexpected emotion – falling in love, wanting to die if one cannot be with one's lover – that makes *Brief Encounter* so resonant. At one point Laura says 'I'm an ordinary woman – I didn't think such violent things could happen to ordinary people'; but the film never lets us forget that beneath the surface of bland normality, unsuspected flames of passion flicker away; that in the imagination of a respectable middle-class housewife, the 'pollarded willows by the canal just before the level crossing' can be magically transformed into moonlit palm trees under which she embraces her lover. The film grants us privileged access into these suppressed dreams and brings them vividly to life while also recognising the impossibility of sustaining them in reality. 'Whatever your dream was – it wasn't a very happy one, was it?' says a newly insightful Fred to Laura in the film's final moments, and on the whole he is right, for her romantic idyll causes her more pain than pleasure. And yet Laura still wants 'to remember every minute – always – always – to the end of my days'.

One final point, although it may not be immediately apparent to today's viewer, the cinema-goer of 1945 would have recognised instantly that *Brief Encounter* was not a contemporary drama but set a few years earlier, pre-war. It carefully depicts a late-1930s milieu with pointed details like Laura and Fred being able to leave their curtains open with lights blazing (no blackout), trains running on time, and no coupons required to buy items like chocolate. But there is more to *Brief Encounter*'s temporal shift than simple nostalgia for the luxuries of the recent past. As Antonia Lant has argued, a 'contemporary audience member could view the film with a sense of historical superiority that appealed to his or her sense of place, knowing that the constructed epoch on the screen had a definite and catastrophic endpoint' (1991: 170). Neither Alec nor Laura seem to realise that their affair is taking place in the larger historical context of the final days before the beginning of the Second World War, and there is an irony implicit in their renunciation of each other in favour of stability and continuity ('One has one's roots after all, hasn't one?', Dolly states, a sentiment with which Laura agrees, albeit rather half-heartedly) when the world is about to change immeasurably, and roots are about to be ripped up, no matter what they choose to do.

Notes

1 Gavin Lambert in conversation with Stephen Frears and Alexander Mackendrick, during Frears's documentary *Typically British: A Personal History of British Cinema*, Channel Four/BFI, 1994.
2 It should be noted that the film's use of working-class characters as little more than comic counterpoint to the more dignified and 'important' middle-class love affair has also attracted much criticism.

Further Reading

Kevin Brownlow, *David Lean*, London, Faber, 1997.
Raymond Durgnat, *A Mirror for England*, London, Faber, 1971.

Richard Dyer, *Brief Encounter*, London, BFI, 1993.

Antonia Lant, *Blackout: Reinventing Women for Wartime British Cinema*, Princeton, Princeton University Press, 1991.

Andy Medhurst, 'That Special Thrill: *Brief Encounter*, Homosexuality and Authorship', *Screen*, Vol. 32, No. 2, Summer 1991, pp. 197–208.

Jeremy Paxman, *The English: A Portrait of a People*, London, Penguin, 1999.

MELANIE WILLIAMS

THE WICKED LADY (1945)

[Production Company: Gainsborough Pictures. Director and screen-writer: Leslie Arliss. Cinematographer: Jack Cox. Editor: Terence Fisher. Music: Hans May. Cast: Margaret Lockwood (Barbara Worth), James Mason (Capt. Jerry Jackson), Patricia Roc (Caroline), Griffith Jones (Sir Ralph Skelton), Michael Rennie (Kit Locksby), Felix Aylmer (Hogarth).]

The Wicked Lady is the best known example of a cycle of film-making called Gainsborough melodrama, named after the British studio that found itself specialising in racy costume dramas in the mid-1940s. This film, along with others like *The Man in Grey* (Arliss 1943), *Fanny by Gaslight* (Anthony Asquith 1944), *Madonna of the Seven Moons* (Arthur Crabtree 1944), *Caravan* (Crabtree 1946) and *Jassy* (Bernard Knowles 1947), provided a potent form of escapism for audiences in the grim years of wartime and immediate post-war austerity. They were despised by critics for their lack of historical verisimilitude – 'Perhaps because I am, by inclination at least, an historian, *The Wicked Lady* arouses in me a nausea out of proportion to the subject', fumed Simon Harcourt-Smith in *Tribune* – but British cinema-goers flocked to them nonetheless.[1] Indeed, in research conducted by the British Film Institute to ascertain which films have been most popular at the British box-office from the 1930s to the present day, *The Wicked Lady*, the most successful of the Gainsborough melodramas, ranked ninth in the top 100, with an estimated audience attendance of 18.4 million.[2] Clearly, this was a film that captured the public's imagination.

However, much as it infuriated the critical establishment, Gains-borough were less concerned with absolute historical accuracy than with using the seventeenth-, eighteenth- and nineteenth-century settings of their films as a source of visual pleasure. Indeed, they acted in part as a pretext for showcasing elaborate sets and opulent costumes (such as the low-cut gowns designed by costumier Elizabeth Haffenden for *The Wicked Lady*), a world away from the utility furniture and rationed clothes of the contemporary situation. As Harcourt-Smith was willing to admit, it was precisely the contrast with 'the tedium, the grey ruin of modern life' that made the Gainsborough style of flamboyant costume drama so popular.[3] An additional source of their appeal for female cinema-goers was their focus on heroines, sometimes virtuous but sometimes thrillingly bad, as in the case of Barbara Skelton (Margaret Lockwood) in *The Wicked Lady*. Very often, there was a doubling between good and bad women in the films, with each rivals for the same man, as in the case of sweet sincere Caroline (Patricia Roc) and sly scheming Barbara who here compete for the affections of both Ralph (Griffith Jones) and Kit (Michael Rennie).[4]

Female cinema-goers could thus enjoy a dual identification, supporting the well-behaved girl but also surreptitiously revelling in the antics of the outrageously badly behaved one. Barbara is ruthlessly ambitious and intolerant of any kind of boredom ('I like danger'), which finally leads to her career in highway robbery, as a desperate attempt to inject some excitement into her suffocating existence. Her behaviour is frequently unsympathetic: she tramples over the feelings of her supposed best friend, Caroline (after having stolen Caroline's fiancée, and hurrying him into marriage, the spurned bride-to-be kindly offers to give Barbara her wedding dress only to be told, 'Wear that? I wouldn't be buried in it') and once installed as the lady of the house, fails to conceal her impatience with the dull round of needlework and household management that her new role entails. One of the things that particularly annoys her is the genealogical chatter of the two maiden aunts of the family, hinting at Barbara's unease with discussions of ancestry, since she is from a family of a lower social class than the one she has managed to marry into, and not keen to be reminded of her inauspicious origins. Baulking at rural domesticity, instead she longs for the social whirl of London, to be admired and envied by her peers.

Wicked she may be but there is nonetheless something almost admirable about Barbara's demonic energy. Using language more characteristic of a woman of the twentieth century than one of the restoration, she complains 'I've got looks and brains and personality and I want to use them instead of rotting away in this dull hole', a sentiment with which many women watching the film, war-weary and burdened with household duties, would have been able to empathise. Indeed, the sequences in which she pretends to play a newly pious woman for the benefit of the religious elderly servant Hogarth (Felix Aylmer) who has found out about her murderous career, have a likeable black humour to them; while they kneel and pray together, Barbara is secretly poisoning him with doctored home-made fruit cordial which Hogarth had taken to be a sign of her new commitment to domesticity. When he recovers and threatens to denounce her, she finally dispatches him with a pillow over the face in one of the film's most shocking scenes.

All of this was quite a departure for Margaret Lockwood. Subsequently, she would always be associated in the public mind with her role as the errant Lady Skelton, beauty spot and heaving décolletage to the fore. Prior to this film, however, she had more often played the briskly sensible girl-next-door, most famously in Hitchcock's *The Lady Vanishes* (1938), than the ruthless vamp. The film critic Leonard Mosley found her sudden transformation rather implausible – 'I just cannot believe in Miss Margaret Lockwood as a femme fatale ... what I see is no wicked lady, but a nice ordinary girl' – but it was precisely that element of suburban middle-class ordinariness still visible through the wickedness that made Barbara such an iconic figure for young British women in the 1940s.[5]

In addition to Lockwood, *The Wicked Lady* also had the considerable advantage of a starring role for James Mason, who plays Barbara's partner-in-crime and lover, the dashing highwayman Jerry Jackson. Mason was Gainsborough's top male star (closely followed by Stewart Granger) and his trademark was a brooding Byronic manner, often intermingled with an air of brutality towards women: he had thrashed Margaret Lockwood's character to death with a riding crop in the earlier Gainsborough hit *The Man in Grey* and had smashed a walking cane onto Ann Todd's hands as she played the piano in the non-Gainsborough melodrama *The Seventh Veil* (1945). Such acts of on-screen cruelty seemed to make Mason even more attractive to female audiences, and as Peter William Evans points out, 'the popularity of an actor characterised by sadistic behaviour towards women raises important questions about spectatorship and masochistic audience identification' (2001: 113). But Mason is slightly different in *The Wicked Lady* with a performance defined less by sadism than a roistering *Merrie England* sexuality, coupled with a ready wit. The saucy badinage between Jackson and Barbara is one of the most enjoyable things about this film, at times even verging on *Carry On*-style innuendo: when Barbara pleads with her lover during one of their robberies to load up another chest of gold bullion, saying 'Oh, just one more', Jackson replies, with sardonic raised eyebrow, 'I've heard you say that in other circumstances'.

The sexual frankness of the film, notable for its time, is evident from the sequences set on Barbara's wedding night, with dialogue referring directly to the impending consummation of the marriage (to the bride: 'Aren't you scared?'; to the groom: 'Into the fray, you lucky hound'). But it was bodily display rather than bawdy dialogue that caused the film the greater problems when it was due to be released in the USA, and in order to conform to the demands of the Production Code, scenes had to be re-shot so that cleavage was far less conspicuous. Joe Breen, head of the Production Code Association (PCA) was scandalised by 'fifty scenes showing the breasts of several of the women partially and "substantially" uncovered' (Street 2002: 121).

Of course, Barbara cannot be allowed to escape punishment for her evil deeds and the penultimate sequence of the film shows her undone by her own scheming. She makes the mistake of holding up one last coach (containing her true love Kit, Ralph, and Caroline) and is shot by Kit, who fails to recognise her in her male highwayman disguise. Mortally wounded, she staggers back to her bedchamber through the secret passage that has enabled her to carry out her double life. Later, Kit visits her to tell her the good news (that Ralph will grant her a divorce so they can finally be married) but finds a dying woman. Barbara's deathbed confession ('I'm wicked. All my life I've cheated to get what I wanted. I had to have excitement. That's why I took to the road') repulses Kit and, despite Barbara pleading with him to stay with her, he leaves her to die alone. Her final isolation is underlined by the camerawork, as a crane shot takes us up and away from the dying Barbara, before cutting to an exterior view framing her final agonies through the window of her room, alone and abandoned.

Despite its remarkable success, Gainsborough melodrama fell into decline by the late 1940s, partly because of new studio head Sydney Box's preference for social realism over flamboyant fantasy, but also as a result of larger historical forces: the moment of its relevance to audiences had passed. During the Second World War, Pam Cook argues, 'short-term sexual relationships, adultery and illegitimate births flourished: sex, passion and the drama of emotional life were brought to the fore, breaking up family unity' (2005: 82) and these sea changes in British society were reflected, indirectly through the cloak of historical distance, by the taboo-breaking behaviour of the heroines of Gainsborough melodrama. Barbara Skelton, an independent woman acting upon her sexual desires and thriving on danger, may ostensibly belong to the late seventeenth century, but she is also very much a heroine of wartime Britain.

Notes

1 Simon Harcourt-Smith, 'Review of *The Wicked Lady*', *Tribune*, 23 November 1945.

2 Ryan Gilbey (ed.), *The Ultimate Film: The UK's 100 Most Popular Films*, London, BFI, 2005.
3 Simon Harcourt-Smith, 'Review of *The Wicked Lady*', *Tribune*, 23 November 1945.
4 Note that in Crabtree's *Madonna of the Seven Moons* (1943), both good and bad femininities are contained within a single character, with the heroine Maddalena (Phyllis Calvert), a demure wife and mother, suffering from a personality disorder which transforms her into Rosanna, a sexually expressive woman who runs away to be with her foreign lover.
5 Leonard Mosley, 'Margaret is my blind spot', *Daily Express*, 15 August 1947.

Further Reading

Bruce Babington, 'Queen of British Hearts: Margaret Lockwood Revisited', in Bruce Babington (ed.) *British Stars and Stardom*, Manchester, Manchester University Press, 2001.

Pam Cook, 'Melodrama and the Women's Picture', *Screening the Past: Memory and Nostalgia in Cinema*, London, Routledge, 2005.

Peter William Evans, 'James Mason: The Man Between' in Bruce Babington (ed.) *British Stars and Stardom*, Manchester, Manchester University Press, 2001.

Sue Harper, *Picturing the Past: The Rise and Fall of the British Costume Film*, London, BFI, 1994.

Sarah Street, *Transatlantic Crossings: British Feature Films in the USA*, London, Continuum, 2002.

MELANIE WILLIAMS

THE RED SHOES (1948)

[Production Company: The Archers. Directors and screenwriters: Michael Powell and Emeric Pressburger. Cinematographer: Jack Cardiff. Editor: Reginald Mills. Music: Brian Easdale. Cast: Moira Shearer (Vicky Page), Anton Walbrook (Boris Lermontov), Marius Goring (Julian Craster), Leonide Massine (Grischa Ljubov).]

The Red Shoes is a significant British film in terms of both its melodramatic aesthetic and its representation of shifting gender roles in a post-war economy. Based on Hans Christian Andersen's folk tale, the plot follows the career of Vicky Page (Moira Shearer) who rises to fame to dance the ballet of The Red Shoes. She falls in love with conductor Julian Craster (Marius Goring), but impresario Boris Lermontov (Anton Walbrook), fiercely protective of Vicky's career, forces Julian to resign. Vicky follows him in loyalty but marriage fails to fulfil her. While holidaying in Monte Carlo, she agrees once more to dance The Red Shoes ballet, but Julian arrives to persuade Vicky not to dance, making her choose between ambition and love. Lermontov dismisses Vicky: 'Go with him, be a faithful housewife, a crowd of screaming children and finish the dancing forever!' But as she tells Julian that she does love him, the camera cuts to her red shoes. His realisation that she loves dancing more than him precipitates his departure. Lermontov raises his arms in a gesture of triumph but as Vicky heads towards the stage, the shoes impel her to her death.

While today we may wonder at the extremity of Vicky's choice, it was very pertinent to British women in the late 1940s, who had been mobilised for work for the duration of the Second World War. In the post-war period, official advice for a returning serviceman was that he should resume his rightful place as breadwinner of the household and the Treasury halved its subsidies for nurseries after 1945. However, the baby boom from 1947 to 1951, the establishment of a National Heath Service and the changes in welfare and education services, created new jobs for women in administration, nursing and teaching which contradicted the official message, reinforced by filmmakers, that the real role for women still lay in 'home-making' (Braybon and Summerfield 1987: 259–277; Aspinall 1983: 291).

The Red Shoes explores these issues in terms of Vicky's conflict between career and domesticity. Narrative closure offers only death but her strength of will and artistic aspirations are celebrated in the film through an extravagance of spectacle, colour and glamour. J. B. Mayer's 1948 survey of 1940s' audiences showed that women enjoyed the colour, romance and exoticism of the melodrama films of that time.[1] Powell and Pressburger's The Red Shoes thus provided the pleasure of a sparkling romance for a strong-willed heroine set for the most part in the sunshine of glamorous Monte Carlo.

Furthermore, as rationing still continued after the war, women began to resist government-imposed utility fashion designs, and there was a hunger for romantic dressing. Christian Dior's 1947 New Look design of wasp waists and longer, fuller skirts satisfied this war-weary desire for romanticism and in The Red Shoes the modern and stylish costumes designed by French couturier Jacques Fath for Moira Shearer followed this romantic trend. As Powell recalls:

> In 1948 England was still on rationing. Austerity was the cry. We had won the war. We had lost the Empire. Now we must tighten our belts and save Europe [...] But not the Archers. We

thought the best way to save Europe was to make extravagant, romantic British films.

(1992: 23)

Powell's insistence on extravagance may have been influenced by the Rank Organisation's aspirations since 1945 to emulate Hollywood production values and fund 'prestige' rather than 'quality' British films, for export to the US market (Murphy 1986: 60–61). But in 1946, Powell also stated that he was searching for a new form of storytelling. He wanted an aesthetic that required 'visual wit, movement, pantomime, comedy, eked out with music, songs and dialogue ... only when it was needed' (Powell 1946: 109). This led him to draw inspiration instead from melodrama and silent cinema and to prioritise image over the dialogue, claiming that: 'In my films, images are everything; words are used like music to distil emotion' (1992: 168).

Powell's first experiences of silent cinema in the Nice studios of Metro Goldwyn Mayer working on Rex Ingram's 1925 silent film *Mare Nostrum* informed this aesthetic: 'This was pretty heady stuff for a first picture, and looking back I am not surprised that I never had much taste for kitchen-sink drama' (1992: 128). As in silent films, Powell wanted music, rather than dialogue, to be the master. He experimented with the composed shot in which acting is choreographed and edited to a previously composed musical score; for *Black Narcissus* (1947) he produced a five-minute composed sequence and for *The Red Shoes*, a 17-minute composed ballet. 'For me, filmmaking was never the same after this experience.' (1992: 583)

In The Red Shoes' ballet, Brian Easdale's Oscar-winning soundtrack leads the choreography of movement to music, allowing Powell and Pressburger to explore highly codified gestural language rather than dialogue, for the tension between dancing and love, ambition and domesticity and the expression of female desire. A shoemaker (Leonide Massine) presents a pair of red ballet shoes to a young girl who leaves her lover to dance downstage; in a magical jump-cut the scarlet ribbons wrap around her ankles and she is suddenly dancing in the red shoes. Her lover gradually recedes and from hereon we, like the girl, are caught in a spell of fantastical extravagance as we follow her balletic journey through Bauhaus-trained production designer Hein Heckroth's painterly and expressionist sets and compellingly grotesque masks, heightened by Jack Cardiff's Technicolor lighting. Vicky is driven relentlessly by the red shoes as she exhausts her dancing partners to the lonely heights and depths of fame. Forever lurking in shadows, dancing around her, is Massine as the tireless shoemaker. 'Intensely musical, a superb mime and a good actor' is how Powell recalls the great Russian performer (1992: 642).

Powell acknowledged that the ballet in *The Red Shoes* was a significant attempt on his part to 'lift storytelling onto a different level and leave naturalism behind' (1992: 652), and the theatrical gestural codes of the ballet draw on melodramatic practices to infuse the young woman's struggle with a poignant dimension of pathos as, in the finale, she gestures to the preacher to remove the shoes and dies exhausted in his arms.

Drawing on exaggerated, mimetic acting codes and music, the subjective realm of dance and inner desire in *The Red Shoes* articulates the dancer's aspirations beyond language into a life/death struggle. As Gledhill notes, melodramatic characters do not function in the interests of psychological interiority but as anthropomorphised, emblematic signs of social forces, personifying good, evil, virtue, vice, through exaggerated performance codes (Gledhill 1992: 139). And the young dancer in The Red Shoes ballet could emblematise Gledhill's 'victim of persecuted innocence' (Gledhill 1987: 32) through the sacred/secular struggle of the demonic shoemaker, the lover, and the preacher outside the church.

In the main narrative we see Vicky Page lured to career heights by the nineteenth-century Svengali-like figure of Lermontov, but prevented by patriarchal domesticity and the love of her husband. We can also identify a virtuous/fallen woman ideology in the mise-en-scène and camera angles as Vicky's ambition and success are cinematically inscribed in terms of a melodramatic rise and fall. At one point, she climbs the steps to a villa: 'a simple flight of steps up the mountain, but it has one hundred, two hundred, what do I know, maybe three hundred steps going heavenward, with no villa in sight' (Powell 1992: 638). And on reaching the fairy-tale heights of her career, she is told she will be the principal dancer. But this success becomes spatially demonised through her histrionic fall in the film's closure as her unadulterated artistic pleasure is morally punished.

Once Vicky has chosen dancing over marriage, and the red shoes impel her to her doom, the frame privileges a cast-iron spiral staircase. In extreme close-up the red shoes are followed running down the stairs, delineating the melodramatic fallen woman. Technically, this was a difficult sequence to shoot. In order to keep ahead of her shoes, the film-makers first tried putting the camera on an elevator, but so as to see more of her feet they used a spiral staircase on a turntable which rotated slowly as Moira Shearer ran down. By adjusting its speed to hers they kept her continually in view. They cut two takes of the same shot and edited them together to extend it to five seconds and thus draw out the suspense (Powell 1992: 652). The fall is further exaggerated as she throws herself over the edge of a balcony, her arms histrionically gesturing towards unspeakable desires which can find no place in her social framework. This image in itself thus becomes suggestive of the price the woman must pay for her deviance from patriarchal norms.

Vicky's death, as in the dramatic plunging to death of the heroine in both *Black Narcissus* and *Gone to Earth* (1950), shows that the dizzying heights that women aspire to in Powell and Pressburger's films also provide the locus for their fall. Hence, the Archers' post-war films have been read by some as belonging to a trend of films that aim to bring strong women down to size (Aspinall 1983: 284–285). But the energy and daring of their heroines create an excess of pleasure for female audiences that runs the risk of diminishing the punishing endings, and scholars such as Sue Harper have warned against an overarching feminist analysis: 'For Powell and Pressburger, females were not passive bearers of tradition but key speakers of it. Nor were they sacrificial victims of it' (Harper 1996: 110). In this sense, *The Red Shoes* conforms more to the spirit of Gainsborough melodramas, such as *Madonna of the Seven Moons* (Crabtree, 1943) and *The Wicked Lady* (Arliss, 1945), which 'were popular with war-time female audiences, not because good triumphs over evil, but because the case for pleasure is made so convincingly' (Aspinall 1983: 276). Hence, while the all-important tension between Vicky's career and home life is melodramatically realised through the extremity of the punishing closure that confirms the status quo and the prevailing ideology of femininity as homemaker, the melodramatic conventions of excess offer a more open reading of female resistance which allow us to sympathise with the pleasure of Vicky's artistic aspirations and the unfairness of her social position indicating a tension very pertinent to post-war British women.

Note

1 J. B. Mayer, *British Cinemas and Their Audiences: Sociological Studies*, London, Dennis Dobson, 1948, p. 107.

Further Reading

Sue Aspinall, 'Women, Realism and Reality in British Films, 1943–53' in James Curran and Vincent Porter (eds) *British Cinema History*, London, Weidenfeld & Nicholson, 1983, pp. 272–293.

Gail Braybon and Penny Summerfield, *Out of the Cage: Women's Experiences in Two World Wars*, London, Pandora Press, 1987.

Christine Gledhill (ed.) *Home is Where the Heart Is: Studies in Melodrama and the Woman's Film*, London, BFI, 1987.

Christine Gledhill, 'Between Melodrama and Realism: Anthony Asquith's *Underground* and King Vidor's *The Crowd*' in Jane Gaines (ed.) *Classical Hollywood Narrative: The Paradigm Wars*, Durham/London, Duke University Press, 1992, pp. 129–167.

Claudia Gorbman, *Unheard Melodies: Narrative Film Music*, London, BFI, 1987.

Sue Harper, 'Madonna of the Seven Moons', *History Today,* August 1995.

——, 'From Holiday Camp to High Camp' in Andrew Higson (ed.) *Dissolving Views: Key Writings on British Cinema*, London, Cassell, 1996, pp. 94–116.

Robert Murphy, 'Under the Shadow of Hollywood' in Charles Barr (ed.) *All Our Yesterdays: 90 Years of British Cinema*, London, BFI, 1986.

Michael Powell, 'Your Questions Answered', in R. K. Nielson Baxter, Roger Manvell and H. H. Wollenberg (eds), *The Penguin Film Review,* London, Penguin, 1946.

——, *A Life in Movies: An Autobiography*, London: Mandarin Paperbacks, 1992.

TRISH SHEIL

PASSPORT TO PIMLICO (1948)

[Production Company: Ealing Studios. Director: Henry Cornelius. Screenwriter: T. E. B. Clarke. Cinematographer: Lionel Banes. Music: Georges Auric. Editor: Michael Truman. Cast: Stanley Holloway (Arthur Pemberton), Betty Warren (Connie Pemberton), Barbara Murray (Shirley Pemberton), John Slater (Frank Huggins), Jane Hylton (Molly Reed), Raymond Huntley (Mr W.P.J Wix), Paul Dupuis (Duke of Burgundy), Margaret Rutherford (Professor Hatton-Jones).]

In keeping with Aristotle's definition of comedy, *Passport to Pimlico* deals with ordinary characters in everyday situations in an amusing way. And following a specific strand of the genre the ordinary and everyday is transformed into the brief liberation of a carnivalesque escape. But *Passport to Pimlico* can also be viewed as a satirical comedy, designed to expose the follies and vices of individuals and/or society (civil servants, bureaucrats and politicians, but also perhaps the self-centred middle class of Pimlico).

Passport to Pimlico does not employ the biting sarcasm used to attack corruption in Juvenalian satire but instead the relatively gentle laughter at people's vanity and hypocrisy found in Horatian satire.

69

This is comedy that lampoons over-inflated, self-important individuals, and exaggerates perceived weaknesses in society in order to highlight them. There is criticism of social institutions, but these are seen not as corrupt so much as in need of a little reform. Arrogance and insensitivity are defeated by simple good sense and compassion.

Ealing comedies in general involve this gentle social criticism. However, although the criticism is expressed most directly by a kindly character, Arthur Pemberton (played by the well-loved performer, Stanley Holloway), who tells the bureaucrats 'We're sick and tired of your voice in this country', this actually amounts to a pretty strong attack coming as it does from such a character. Furthermore, there is no disguising the rebellious glee with which the residents of Pimlico symbolically throw off the bureaucratic shackles by tearing up their ration books.

To understand the comedy we need to be alert to the ways in which this film expresses the nature of the historical moment. Ordinary people expected change after the sacrifices of the Second World War. They wanted new freedoms and a new society, and to some extent this was what they got following Labour's landslide victory of July 1945 with plans for a welfare state, free health service and widespread nationalisation. The rigid pre-war class system had disappeared: returning servicemen (and women) were not prepared to revert to being subservient to their 'betters' nor to accept 1930s-style economic hardships.

It was said that the war had 'eroded practically every traditional social barrier in Britain'.[1] However, from the end of the war through to the time *Passport to Pimlico* was released three years later, the public was also being urged to show restraint and being forced to accept increased austerity.

> We have come through difficult years and we are going to face difficult years and to get through them we will require no less effort, no less unselfishness and no less work than was needed to bring us through the war.
>
> (Clement Attlee, July 1945 in Johnson 1994: 300)

Rationing actually increased after the war, even bread and potatoes being included on the list of restricted foods. Clothing and furniture were rationed until 1949, food until 1954 and coal until 1958. Demobilisation was felt to be proceeding too slowly contributing to the dissatisfaction: numbers in the armed forces dropped from 2 million in 1946 to 800,000 by 1948, but this was still 300,000 up on pre-war levels. In the winter before *Passport to Pimlico* was released there was also a fuel crisis with electricity cuts, a shortened working week and factory closures that made rationing and post-war austerity seem all the more oppressive.

It is this frustration that *Passport to Pimlico* expresses. The question is whether in doing this the film ultimately aims to bring about change or convince people of the necessity of continuing to conform. Although the film focuses upon acts of rebellion, in the end it praises restraint and affirms the importance of law and order.

The new consumer society was not yet in place; but a supposed shift from wartime community spirit to selfish individualism (highlighted 11 years later in *I'm All Right Jack* (Boulting, 1959)) seems already to have been detected by the makers of *Passport to Pimlico*. Reflecting on their selfish materialism, Arthur asks council members: 'Don't you think of anything other than pounds, shillings and pence?' Burgundian Pimlico is always a fragile alliance of disparate types with their own agendas; as with Britain during the war perhaps, the main thing holding them together it seems is the threat from outside.

The war produced a need for cohesive images of British national identity based upon unity and togetherness, but once the threat was removed film-makers were able to take part in redefining the image of Britain and 'Britishness' for the post-war era. Should they re-assert traditional (pre-war) values or champion a new radicalism? Perhaps they had little choice in this but had their views shaped by the mood of the country. More fundamentally (and unfortunately more difficult to ascertain), when a film does portray a particular view of national identity what is the relationship of that constructed image to the reality on the streets?

In *Passport to Pimlico* there is nostalgia for the war years. Evidence of the war can still be seen but is beginning to disappear: 'Pamela' is supposed to be the last unexploded bomb in London (although another 'last' bomb is found later), and Arthur is said to miss 'that old white hat', his air-raid warden's helmet. Wartime films are recalled in the community singing that takes place after the ration books have been torn up, reflecting a longing for the (supposed?) sense of community found during that period. When it opened the film offered audiences the opportunity to re-live wartime experiences of solidarity and celebrate that key supposed aspect of 'Britishness', bulldog determination:

> If the Nazis couldn't drive me out of my home with all their bombs and rockets and doodlebugs, you don't catch me packing

up now. . . . We always have been English and we always will be
English, and it's just because we are English that we're sticking up
for our right to be Burgundian.

(Connie Pemberton's words also, of course, raise the issue of the
relationship between notions of Britishness and Englishness. 'Englishness' excludes three further parts of the United Kingdom. And
you might consider that locating the film so firmly in London potentially
operates to further exclude parts of England.)

Passport to Pimlico reflects a longing for continued national unity. As
the 'Siege of Burgundy' goes ahead spoof newsreel footage shows
politicians of all parties uniting:

> For the first time since World War Two Britain's party politics
> have been forgotten. The nation's leaders have come together to
> seek a solution to this unprecedented crisis.

Spivs and characters with an eye to the main chance although offered
as characters to laugh at also threaten chaos and disorder in *Passport to
Pimlico*.

Ultimately, *Passport to Pimlico* aims to reinforce what it sees as
positive images within the back catalogue of shared concepts of
Britishness. The difficulty is that it wants all the time to hark back to
the past which, while it may be of momentary comfort within the
darkness of the auditorium, immediately disappears as the audience
emerges from the cinema's fantasy safety zone. The film attempts to
reinforce aspects of the imagined national community existing within
the individual (and collective?) imagination. It attempts to shore up that
shared stock of images, ideas, norms and values, stories and traditions
the film-makers see as being the essence of Britishness.

National identity affects the way we see ourselves and the way we
perceive others who are classified as existing outside of the chosen
'in-group'. But, the nature of that identity is a site of struggle, so that
the identity itself is constantly undergoing a process of either re-
affirmation or re-definition. Put simply, national identity does not
exist in some singular, uncontested form. *Passport to Pimlico* works
within this arena, expressing disapproval of certain aspects of the
perceived state of the nation and positive approval of other potential
facets of a contested, shifting national identity.

With the end of the war and (to some extent) the end of the old
pre-war hierarchies of class, the nature of social order in Britain is
being particularly strongly fought over (or renegotiated). This film

reflects the accompanying turmoil and uncertainty as hegemony is being contested. The old certainties that attached to a well-formed sense of class and rank have been severely undermined. Deference to authority is a thing of the past. Younger women like Shirley are showing disturbing tendencies towards redefining social expectations of women. The old order is changing and the concept of British national identity is in a state of flux, ripe for redefinition. (Race may be a significant absence from *Passport to Pimlico* but this state of affairs won't last much longer.)

Henri Bergson, in his essay 'Laughter' (1900), suggested the usual object of humour was human rigidity, or inflexibility, whether of outlook or belief. The resulting laughter, he pointed out, produced two groups, 'those who laugh' and 'those who are laughed at'. The whole process, he said, operated as social criticism but with the aim of promoting social conformity. It could produce permanent alienation for the 'laughed at' group but could also bring about their re-incorporation into a renewed social order. The gentle approach to comedy offered by *Passport to Pimlico* it could be suggested would encourage 'laughed at' groups to more willingly accept implied criticisms.

In his essay 'The Argument of Comedy' (1948), Northrop Frye suggested that in ancient Greece there were two periods of comedy, 'old comedy' and a later 'new comedy'. The first, he said, accepted that society was unchangeable and that vice and folly could only be ridiculed in such a way as to enable a brief 'carnivalesque' holiday before a return to conformity. The second suggested an alienating social order could be reshaped; it often involved an escape to nature before a return to a regenerated society. How would *Passport to Pimlico* be seen in relation to this theory?

Ealing studio head, Michael Balcon, suggested that

> In the immediate post-war years there was as yet no mood of cynicism; the bloodless revolution of 1945 had taken place, but I think our first desire was to get rid of as many wartime restrictions as possible and get going. The country was tired of regulations and regimentation, and there was a mild anarchy in the air. In a sense our comedies were a reflection of this mood ... a safety valve for our more anti-social impulses.
>
> (Balcon 1971: 159)

The idea of getting rid of 'as many wartime restrictions as possible' and the country being 'tired of regulations and regimentation' is clearly relevant. And certainly the final comment here, suggesting

Ealing comedies could be seen as 'a safety valve for more anti-social impulses', offers a further interesting perspective upon the role of comedy within society. Far from instigating, or even attempting to instigate, social change, this would suggest comedy may actively work to prevent radical change.

Note

1 Anthony Howard, 'We Are the Masters Now' in Philip French and Michael Sissons (eds), *Age of Austerity*, Oxford, Oxford University Press, 1986, p. 18.

Further Reading

Michael Balcon, *Michael Balcon Presents: A Lifetime of Films*, London, Weidenfeld and Nicolson, 1971.
Charles Barr, *Ealing Studios*, Moffat, Cameron and Hollis, 1998.
James Curran and Vincent Porter (eds) *British Cinema History*, London, Weidenfeld and Nicolson, 1983.
Christine Geraghty, *British Cinema in the 1950s: Gender, Genre and the 'New Look'*, London, Routledge, 2000.
Philip Gillett, *The British Working Class in Post-war Film*, Manchester, Manchester University Press, 2003.
Sue Harper and Vincent Porter, *British Cinema of the 1950s: the Decline of Deference*, Oxford, Oxford University Press, 2003.
Andrew Higson, *Waving the Flag: Constructing a National Cinema in Britain*, Oxford, Clarendon Press, 1997.
Paul Johnson (ed.) *Twentieth Century Britain: Economic, Social and Cultural Change*, Harlow, Longman, 1994.
Ian Mackillop and Neil Sinyard (eds), *British Cinema in the 1950s: A Celebration*, Manchester, Manchester University Press, 2003.

JOHN WHITE

THE THIRD MAN (1949)

[Production Company: London Film Production. Director: Carol Reed. Screenwriter: Graham Greene. Cinematographer: Robert Krasker. Editor: Oswald Hafenrichter. Music: Anton Karas. Cast: Joseph Cotton (Holly Martins), Orson Welles (Harry Lime), Alida Valli (Anna Schmidt), Trevor Howard (Major Calloway).]

The Third Man has become an indisputable classic of British cinema, a mystery thriller with a wonderful twist, drawing on noir techniques, themes, characters, and moods. Based on a story by

Graham Greene, it charts the post-Second World War moral and material decay of Western Europe via the adventures of a naive American writer, Holly Martins, who goes to Vienna in search of his old friend Harry Lime (Orson Welles on magnificent form). At first told that he is dead, Martins is then disturbed to discover that Lime is alive and stands accused of being involved in black market drug-dealing, indirectly causing the death and suffering of hundreds of people, and hiding out in the Russian sector of the rubble-strewn city. Eventually Martins finds him but the story does not end easily for any of the characters involved. Such a simple tale and yet somehow *The Third Man* has succeeded in becoming one of the greatest British films of all time, with one of the most famous and memorable scenes in all cinema.

Before unravelling this film's apparent 'greatness', it is worth pondering its status as a 'British' film. Well before critics and academics began debating the complexities of 'transnational' cinema, along came a feature that posed a challenge to most of the traditional ways of deciding the national identity of a film. But surely *The Third Man's* credentials as a British film cannot be called into question? The film's iconic pre-titles image of Big Ben and accompanying text clearly establish its production 'home' as London, its celebrated director and writer were both British, and it was one of the first films to benefit from a new grants scheme set up to boost national cinema production.[1] And yet, before either Carol Reed or Graham Greene's names appear on screen, the spectator is informed that the film is 'presented by' Alexander Korda and David O. Selznick. Korda was the Hungarian-born founder of London Film Production, whose Austrian-held account was called upon while filming in Vienna, while Selznick was already widely considered as one of the most influential Hollywood producers of all time.[2] Furthermore, *The Third Man* tells the story of one American character (Harry Lime) from the point of view of another (Holly Martins), while the British actors Trevor Howard and Bernard Lee play only supporting roles. As Rob White points out, it would be 'misleading to call it simply a British film, given the central involvement of Selznick, Cotton and Welles' (2003: 9). Notwithstanding, while its national identity remains ambiguous, its status in British film culture is indisputable: in 2000, it came top of a poll of industry representatives designed to identify the best British films of the twentieth century, fighting off at least eight others made during the immediate post-war period when British cinema suddenly flourished.[3] Moreover, it led to its director being considered one of the greatest British film-makers of all time.

Perhaps its anomalous national status is part of what makes *The Third Man* so distinctive, especially since ambiguity is at the core of the film's thematic preoccupations. But of course the reasons for its longevity must extend far beyond its complicated production context which is already long forgotten. We need also to look at the way in which it draws so deftly on a range of cinematic influences, and crafts a story and characters of such interest as to create a work of overwhelming magnetism. Techniques of German expressionism, conventions of film noir and tricks of the thriller genre are all used to set up an engaging and unique portrayal of a post-war context that was steeped not in the more conservative ideals of conformity and unity, but in complex questions about the value of human life. Moral ambiguity is inscribed in its main characters, and the whiff of corruption, deception and betrayal pervades a city depicted as ravaged by conflict and ripped into four occupied zones along nationalist lines (British, American, French and Russian). In fact, the film foregrounds a constant blurring of physical, social, political and moral boundaries. Vienna is portrayed as a place of deep mistrust and a ubiquitous spy culture. Having suffered extensive damage from bomb attacks, its citizens are forced to survive despite relentless food and power shortages by relying on a thriving black market. The film's shifting mood, from bleak cynicism to dark humour, is deftly achieved as national stereotypes are set up and then torn apart, preventing us from ever being really sure when to take things seriously. Much of what is regarded as important by the authorities – passports, border patrols – is ridiculed by the lack of respect paid to such conventions by most of the film's main characters.

It is important also to emphasise the distinctive formal components of this magnificently composed film, since it is only through a thorough understanding of them that we can begin to comprehend the complexities of the chaotic situation it seeks to express. As Phillips has observed, '*The Third Man* is an accomplished example of the ways that *mise-en-scène*, cinematography, editing and sound can help reveal and support a film's settings, subjects, moods, and meanings' (2002: 179). While its cyclical narrative structure, starting and ending with the funerals (one a part of the deception, the other all too real) of one of its main characters is quite simple, what gives this film its classic status is its inventive cinematography and uncertain atmosphere. Robert Murphy describes it as a philosophical thriller, with just the right blend of: 'realistic locations + slanting shadow throws + deeply diagonal night-streets [...] + strong, insolent, secretive faces + charged acting + zithery-slithery vibrations tangling and unwinding our nerves, teasing and haunting us like a ghostly gurdy-hurdy' (2001: 144). Robert Krasker's Oscar-winning monochrome camera work accentuates the baroque contours of this once magnificent city, reminding the viewer of its high-culture status (statues and spires reaching up above the rubble) that has been largely deposed by a seedy underworld of criminality and deception.

The film's opening moments are particularly remarkable for the neat and concise way in which so much information is quickly conveyed. The image over which the titles appear is almost abstract with its extreme close-up of the moving strings and sound-hole of a zither, the music from which establishes the film's uncertain tone, jaunty and sinister at the same time as if concealing a sense of unease amidst its irritatingly upbeat chords. As Amy Sargeant points out, 'the Anton Karas score pervades the film, endorsing both its location [...] and its mood: the famous Harry Lime theme is woven into an almost continuous warp' (2005: 167). The director himself then anonymously provides a brisk and ironic voice-over commentary as a swift montage of images gives further warning of the tone and concerns of the piece: street racketeers shiftily reveal cheap, fake watches hidden in suitcases, a dead body floats along the Danube, soldiers march up and down under instruction to defend artificial borders that mark the beginning of Cold War frontlines; classical buildings lie in ruins or cluttered by rubble.[4]

Amidst this rubble, Reed's emotionally complex characters struggle with questions of loyalty and morality. Which is worse − betrayal of love, or deception and crimes against humanity? The answer should be clear but the beauty of *The Third Man* is that nothing is ever clear. Harry Lime may be morally repugnant, but he is charming and charismatic nevertheless. He doesn't even appear until just over halfway through the film and yet − thanks to that zither − his presence is felt throughout. Even after his death, his influence is such that his girlfriend will not acknowledge the 'friend' who finally betrayed him, despite his offer of help. Meanwhile, this friend, Holly Martins, who should be the hero of the piece, is constantly found wanting. He has only come to Vienna because Harry has promised him a job, and then tries to steal his girlfriend's affections. This girlfriend, Anna, is herself the embodiment of masquerade: as a comedy stage actress, she is used to performing for the sake of others and her grief at losing Harry is revealed only in her most private moments.[5] As the object of the male gaze and passive until the final moments of the film (to Holly's great disappointment), she operates in a kind of limbo throughout in terms of her own moral authority. Found guilty of identity fraud, she refuses to strike a deal with the authorities, but in taking that decision she becomes complicit in Harry's crimes and thus the whole notion of loyalty is called into question. And so it is left to Major Calloway, supported by his sidekick Sergeant Paine, to provide the moral backbone of the film, somehow bringing order to the chaos around him, sweeping up the mess and offering the voice of common sense. Perhaps this is what really confirms the film's national allegiance: its apparent alliance of the qualities of decency and valour with Britishness, and those of treachery, malevolence and violence with the Americans, the Czechs, the Hungarians and the Russians. Anyone but the British.

The ending of *The Third Man* was the subject of a major dispute between Reed and Greene, the latter unconvinced that audiences would tolerate anything other than a happy conclusion with Anna and Holly leaving together. The choice of closing image is even more striking for its bold use of a long-held deep-focus shot that allows Anna to walk towards and then past the camera, as the Harry Lime theme plays out. It worried Selznick also for expecting audiences to wait until the end (he shortened it), but its mixture of suspense and defiance works a treat. As Murphy suggests, 'like the strings pulling up the sails in a bottle it jerks everything into place' (2000: 198). In the end, questions have been answered and order is restored as Calloway drives off to resume service.

Notes

1 This scheme was administered by the newly established Film Finance Corporation, and Korda was successful in winning a grant of £1.2 million to support the making of *The Third Man*.

2 Selznick provided substantial funding although this came at a price. As Rob White explains, the formidable producer ordered controversial cuts in the American version (removing non-subtitled German speech and shortening the ending), and it was 50 years before the British version of the film was properly released in the US (2003: 9).

3 The US version was included in a poll of 100 Greatest American Films. The UK version fought off such classics as *Brief Encounter*, *The Red Shoes* and *A Matter of Life and Death* to come top of the British poll in 2000.

4 In all, 28 shots are shown in just 66 seconds of film during the montage sequence that opens the film.

5 Alida Valli (Anna) was already reasonably well known in Britain for her roles in Italian neo-realist films.

Further Reading

Robert Murphy, *British Cinema and the Second World War*, London and New York, Continuum, 2000.

——, *The British Cinema Book*, 2nd edition, London, BFI, 2001.
W. H. Phillips, 'Expressive Film Techniques in *The Third Man*', in *Film: An Introduction*, London, Palgrave, 2002, pp. 35–43.
Amy Sargeant, *British Cinema: A Critical History*, London, BFI, 2005.
Rob White, *The Third Man*, London, BFI, 2003.

SARAH BARROW

THE CRUEL SEA (1953)

[Production Company: Ealing Studios. Director: Charles Frend. Screenwriter: Eric Ambler. Cinematographer: Gordon Dines. Music: Alan Rawsthorne. Editor: Peter Tanner. Cast: Jack Hawkins (Captain Ericson), Donald Sinden (Lockhart), John Stratton (Ferraby), Denholm Elliott (Morrell), Stanley Baker (Bennett), Virginia McKenna (Julie Hallam), Moira Lister (Elaine Morrell), Liam Redmond (Jim Watts), Bruce Seton (Bob Tallow), Megs Jenkins (Tallow's sister).]

British war films made after 1945 are sometimes seen as distinctively different from those produced during the conflict, containing a nostalgic yearning for the unity of purpose achieved by the country in the war years; but there is actually a strong sense of thematic continuity in this genre throughout the 1940s and 1950s.[1] What does change is the context in which these films are viewed: while the conflict is taking place an idea such as the need for different classes to work together and the suggestion that there exists a quiet, determined, particularly British form of heroism are (at least debatably) acceptable to a majority of viewers, but with the post-war break-up of British overseas power and the increasing willingness of the working class to question their class subordination, such concepts appear to be an increasingly desperate attempt to stem the tide of a changing world order at home and abroad. In other words, the propaganda inherent in the genre comes to seem false, forced and increasingly out of tune with public opinion.

It is useful to compare *The Cruel Sea* both in terms of style and content with on the one hand, say, *In Which We Serve* (1942) and *The Way to the Stars* (1945) and on the other perhaps *The Dam Busters* (1954) and *The Colditz Story* (1955), but we should beware of making too easy assumptions and generalisations about films from the two different periods. It is worth considering to what extent and in what ways each film concerns itself with the horror and brutality of war; and relating these representations to the contexts of the different periods. How are issues of patriotism and the nature of 'Britishness' addressed? Are those taking part in the struggle shown as heroic; does the expression of heroism alter in any way, and if so, in what ways and for what reasons? How are the different classes represented and what role do women play in the films?

In line with other films from the period *The Cruel Sea* shows war, despite its brutality, bringing out the best in people; but it also clearly displays the horrific waste of decent ordinary people's lives (Watts and Seaton floating away from the life-rafts after the sinking of Compass Rose, for example), debates the value of war and points towards the madness of it all ('Number One, this is quite a moment. We've never seen the enemy before.'/'They don't look very different from us do they.').

This film is certainly one of a number made in post-war Britain that looked back at the war years as a heroic period in the history of a country that had opposed Hitler's Germany with Churchillian defiance. Each of these films contributes towards promoting a certain version of the war that is in line with the dominant middle-class outlook on the world and carefully avoids too much of the harsh reality.[2] But this film does attempt to push forward more uncomfortable questions about the war.[3] In terms of both plot and character development the film revolves around the moment Ericson makes the brutal war-driven decision to plough his ship through British seamen in the water in order to attempt a 'kill' on a German U-boat; but on the other hand the reality of conditions onboard for those below decks is never explored[4] and the gulf between the officer class and ordinary seamen is never seen from a below-decks perspective. In fact, men at every level or rank are shown to be not only content with their place within the order of things but also intensely aware of their role and place within an efficiently functioning hierarchical unit.

Attitudes towards war displayed in the film have been shaped by the dominant norms and values of 1950s British society. This is a highly selective view of things presented for the consumption of cinema audiences with a clear eye to shaping the way in which the war will be seen by the public. It is the product of a particular society at a particular historical moment made by middle-class film-makers from a middle-class perspective. And yet, in addition to the stereotypical officer class heroism of Ericson there is also an awareness of the quietly stoical heroism of very ordinary people.

One thing that has shifted considerably since the war years is the attitude towards Germans expressed in the film. As demonstrated by the quotation above they are seen as the enemy but also as ordinary human beings caught up in the events. In the context of the Cold

War there is an increasing need in the post-war period to see Germany as a potential ally rather than enemy. What appears to be a decision by the film-makers to identify the enemy as the 'cruel sea' and war itself as much as 'the Germans' could also be seen to address an ideological need. As with the comedy genre of *Passport to Pimlico* made a few years earlier what we see is the importance of considering genre not purely as a functional approach to film form but as operating within a specific socio-historical context. This is a war film reflecting a certain version of the experience of war and the nature of war. It is made at a specific point in British history, not during the war but eight years later.

At its heart *The Cruel Sea* is a love story between Ericson and Lockhart. When they first meet Ferraby is also present but the exchange that ensues is essentially between these two and subsequently they share a series of intensely intimate one-to-one scenes throughout the rest of the film ('You alright, sir?'/'No, I don't mind telling *you*, I'm not.'). He discusses this relationship with his female love-interest, Second Lieutenant Hallam:

> *Hallam*: You must be very fond of Ericson.
> *Lockhart*: I feel I want to finish the war with him and with no-one else: David and Jonathan. Does it sound silly?
> *Hallam*: No, but women don't often have that relationship and if they do it's not usually about something important like running a ship or fighting a war.

It is also a careful exploration of the psychological changes that come over the central character as he struggles to maintain both his sanity and his humanity in the face of the brutality. See, for example, the opening scene alone on the bridge of the new ship, Saltash Castle, in which the sight of the communication tubes creates a flashback to the remembered sounds of the screams from below decks on Compass Rose.

Both Ericson and Lockhart are clearly denoted as members of the well-to-do middle class, and class divisions are made apparent throughout the film. Filmic codes such as dress and language use mark out officers from other ranks. The middle-class officers, for example, use words and phrases such as 'I say', 'grand', 'terrific' and 'old chap'. In this connection, Bennett is immediately marked out as different, in a variety of ways, but certainly through his language use ('Snorkers, good oh.'). And he is different – he is from the wrong class:

Morrell: He sounds a very 'experienced' officer, the First Lieutenant.
Lockhart: Very, until four months ago he was a second-hand car salesman.
Morrell: Ah, I see.

When we first see Ericson he is wearing overalls and workingmen's gloves; the top of the overalls is open to reveal his officer's jacket and tie and he is wearing his captain's hat. He moves around the ship with purpose, constantly looking about him. He is the captain clearly but he is also able to join with and move amongst the ordinary seamen. Almost immediately we are given a contrast between not only the cut of his gloves compared with those worn by the First Lieutenant, Bennett, but also the way in which he wears them. See how Bennett is positioned above Ferraby and Lockhart when the three first meet and how the glove is used as an emblem of his character.

A range of women are shown in the film (helping perhaps to open the genre to a wider audience). Women have often been portrayed as either caring and selfless or uncaring and selfish; is this pattern followed in this film? Painted beauty, in the case of Morrell's wife, is clearly seen as deceptive and false; while plain beauty, in the case of Hallam, is not only real and true but also part of that which is able to nurture and support a man. The presence of women also allows some exploration of war on the Home Front and this is very much connected to a class division. Morrell's wife seems to be part of a stratum of society that continued to do well and live the high life during the war while others experience the hardship. Glad, by contrast, is a representative of the terraced house working class who took the brunt of the Blitz. She is common decent humanity that suffers and dies in war. Her death is dealt with in a low key way that demonstrates the understated best of this film.

Overall, what view of Britain does this film present? It was made eight years after the end of the war and in order to answer this question we would need to consider more carefully what Britain was like at this time, and why it chose to look back to World War Two in films from the period. This is a prejudiced middle-class film with, for example, the second-hand car salesman being unable to deal with the demands of being an officer and with little real understanding of the day-to-day hardship of working and living below decks on the Atlantic crossing. But it is also a film that in contrast to many from the period is prepared to explore harder questions about both the nature of war in general and the nature of the British experience of a specific war. Ultimately it offers no real analysis of the situation but does at least raise the issue of the madness of it all.

Ericson: It's the war, the whole bloody war. We've just got to do these things and say our prayers at the end.

Notes

1 Aldgate and Richards argue the key change occurs after 1950, when there is a shift from Ealing films showing 'the people as hero' to those portraying officers and gentlemen as heroes (Aldgate and Richards 2002: 136).
2 Member of the British Board of Film Censors at the time, John Trevelyan, suggested it was the public that did not want to know too much of the reality (Trevelyan 1973: 156). The most popular film of 1953 was Rank's pageantry-filled coverage of the Coronation, *A Queen Is Crowned*.
3 According to some *The Cruel Sea* is the closest war films from the 1950s came to making an anti-war statement (Medhurst 1984: 36).
4 It is true that the cinematography below decks does give a sense of the claustrophobia of these spaces and their potential for entrapment, something which culminates in Compass Rose entombing many of these seamen at the bottom of the Atlantic.

Further Reading

Anthony Aldgate and Jeffrey Richards, *Best of British: Cinema and Society from 1930 to the Present*, London, I.B. Tauris, 2002.

Charles Barr, *Ealing Studios*, Moffat, Cameron and Hollis, 1998.

Marcia Landy, *British Genres: Cinema and Society, 1930–1960*, Princeton, NJ, Princeton University, 1991.

Andy Medhurst, '1950s War Films' in Geoff Hurd (ed.) *National Fictions: World War Two in British Films and Television*, London, BFI, 1984.

Robert Murphy, *British Cinema and the Second World War*, London, Continuum, 2000.

John Trevelyan, *What the Censor Saw*, London, Michael Joseph, 1973.

JOHN WHITE

THE LADYKILLERS (1955)

[Production Company: Ealing Studios. Director: Alexander Mackendrick. Screenwriter: William Rose. Cinematographer: Otto Heller. Music: Tristram Cary. Editor: Jack Harris. Cast: Katie Johnson (Mrs Wilberforce), Alec Guinness (Professor Marcus), Cecil Parker (Major Courtney), Herbert Lom (Louis), Peter Sellers (Harry), Danny Green (One-Round).]

The Ladykillers is widely recognised as the last of the major Ealing comedies and thereby acts as coda for this sequence of films. *Hue and Cry* (1947) is usually taken as the starting point and the other substantial landmarks include *Passport to Pimlico* (1949), *Whiskey Galore* (1949), *Kind Hearts and Coronets* (1949), *The Lavender Hill Mob* (1951) and *The Man in the White Suit* (1951). Along with several minor films, they form a body of work which has retained its popular appeal and become synonymous with a particular vein in British film comedy. In *The Encyclopedia of British Film*, Charles Barr describes them as 'gentle, cosy, whimsical' (McFarlane 2003: 193). They typically celebrate the British love of eccentricity and side with the uncommon individual against larger corporate or state institutions. In doing so, there is often a fascination with the minutiae of British life, from schoolboy comics to those endless cups of tea. Individuals or whole communities frequently find themselves having to rebel or even turn to crime to protect themselves against bureaucracy or big business. Despite the potential seriousness of this as a topic, the handling is consistently light and warmly sympathetic.

Much of the responsibility for the company's ethos can be attributed to its head of production, Michael Balcon. Although Balcon often takes the producer credit on Ealing's films (including *The Ladykillers*), the job of producing individual films was usually in the hands of an associate producer (in this case, Seth Holt). Nonetheless, Balcon's influence was writ large throughout the company. Ealing adopted the slogan 'The Studio with the Team Spirit' and its symbol 'became the Round Table at which, every week, producers, writers and directors consulted freely together' (Barr 1977: 6). Balcon seems to have viewed the studio as a family unit, with himself cast in the role of the firm, but kindly father (Balcon 1969: 138). A communal spirit was both part of the company's production ethic and also reflected in the films they made. By the late 1940s Ealing had established a reputation for both populist comedies (with a strong appeal to working-class audiences) and for documentary-realism (as seen in the propagandist films they produced during World War Two). Elements of both approaches are apparent in the Ealing comedies. Realism is evident in the use of location shooting, the strong sense of place and the focus on ordinary citizens, although this realism is often overlaid by fantasy and visual stylisation, as is the case with *The Ladykillers*.

Balcon was also concerned that Ealing's films should reflect the intrinsic nature of Britain and then project this image out to a wider world. When the studio was sold in 1955 he provided the wording for a commemorative plaque: 'Here during a quarter of a century

were made many films projecting Britain and the British character.'
As a result, Ealing's films often reflect in a direct way on the contemporary condition of Britain. The political landscape of the
immediate post-war period was radically shaped by the election of
Clement Atlee's Labour government in 1945. Atlee's administration
set about realising the socialist dream of a welfare state which would
offer its citizens care and opportunity 'from the cradle to the grave',
whatever their individual social background.[1] This was a social
experiment which Balcon broadly supported, although not without a
sense of ambivalence:

> Though we were radical in our points of view, we did not want
> to tear down institutions ... We were people of the immediate
> post-war generation and we voted Labour for the first time after
> the war: this was our mild revolution.
>
> (Ellis 1975: 119)

However, by 1951 the Conservatives were back in office, where they
were to remain for the next 13 years. The forces of reaction had
seemingly prevailed over Labour's short-lived 'mild revolution'. It is
against this context that *The Ladykillers* needs to be read.

Another factor in assessing the film is the position within Ealing of
its director and its writer, Alexander Mackendrick and William Rose.
Rose was an American, whilst Mackendrick was born in Boston and
brought up in Scotland. Although it's easy to over-interpret the
importance of their backgrounds, at Ealing, the most English of studios,
they seem to have shared a sense of distance from the prevailing ethos
which Balcon fostered. Roy Armes suggests that Mackendrick's work
'transcends the self-imposed limitations of the Ealing style' (Armes
1978: 190). Similarly, in his study of Mackendrick, Philip Kemp
suggests that 'by disdaining the bland, conciliatory endings that Ealing
favoured, he constantly questions the studio's assumptions even while
ostensibly operating within them' (Kemp 1991: 135). Mackendrick
was frequently at odds with Balcon and *The Ladykillers* has the air of a
final declaration of intent before his departure for America.

At first sight, the film has many characteristics which position it
firmly within the canon of Ealing comedies. It sympathetically
portrays a criminal gang and its action is rooted in a strong sense of
place, with the central robbery taking place at Kings Cross Station
and several sequences shot in nearby streets. The minutiae of English
life are recreated with Ealing's typical attention to mundane detail,
from the rank of shops near Mrs Wilberforce's home to the cluttered

interior of her house. The love of eccentricity is embodied in all the characterisations and encapsulated by the attitude of the local police superintendent (Jack Warner) towards Mrs Wilberforce; we are first introduced to her when she makes one of her regular visits to the police station to explain that her friend Amelia's sighting of a spaceship was actually just a dream. The police treat her with characteristic kindness and indulgence. The film even offers a little gentle knockabout humour in the sequence following the robbery when Mrs Wilberforce manages to inadvertently cause a street brawl between a barrow boy and a cab driver, played by the two popular comics Frankie Howerd and Kenneth Connor.

However, the film is more remarkable for the ways in which it deviates from the Ealing norm. From its opening, when the sinister, grotesque Professor Marcus (Alec Guinness) arrives to rent the spare room in Mrs Wilberforce's house, the film abandons Ealing's usual reliance on surface realism and adopts a stylisation which borders on the Gothic. This stylisation is apparent in the depiction of the interior of Mrs Wilberforce's house, with its mountains of bric-a-brac, caged birds and heavy drapery. The house itself is 'lopsided' from subsidence caused by wartime bombing and the plumbing can only be persuaded to work if the pipes are pounded with a wooden mallet. The cramped interior creates a feeling of claustrophobia, rather than the cosy comfort one might expect in an Ealing comedy, and Otto Heller's colour cinematography, with its palette of garish greens and yellows, gives the film an ambience of decay. The underlying menace comes to the surface in the second half of the film as the humour gradually drains out of Rose's script and we are faced with a modern morality play, as the criminal gang destroy themselves, leaving the scene scattered with bodies in the manner of a Jacobean revenge tragedy.

At the core of the film's approach is the ambiguous presentation of Mrs Wilberforce herself. In more conventional Ealing fare she would simply be a loveable old lady, but she proves to be rather more formidable and destructive than might be expected. After all, she sees off a hardened gang of train robbers and ends up with the loot herself. At the film's conclusion, the increasingly deranged Professor Marcus is forced to conclude that she is too strong for them; even with a hundred men they wouldn't have been able to beat her. Her chosen weapons are the endless cups of tea with which she attacks the gang, but they prove more potent than Louis's (Herbert Lom) gun. For Philip Kemp, Mrs Wilberforce is a representation of traditional England: 'what she patently symbolises, besides innocence, is the past in which

England is mired' (Kemp 1991: 120). The film presents Mrs Wilberforce, and her house, as a metaphor for post-war Britain, a place crippled by inertia, clinging to the past and blindly ignoring the fact that the whole construction is falling to bits. Mrs Wilberforce, and all her friends, dress in Edwardian clothes and have names like Constance and Lettice; they seem to have been preserved from an era before World War One. This world certainly has its appeal; it is genteel, polite and ordered, but it also doesn't work properly (the plumbing) and has no room at all for the modern. Mrs Wilberforce's victory over the gang is a clear indication of the real power of 'old England' to maintain the status quo.

Aldgate and Richards suggest that the film provides an oblique commentary on the nature of 1950s Britain, or 'cul-de-sac England' as their essay is called. They interpret the gang as representatives of the social forces (youth, the working class, intellectuals) which would soon come to the fore and radically alter British society during the 1960s. Their defeat by the forces of repression and reaction (Mrs Wilberforce) encapsulates a key historical moment, as '1955 is almost the last year in which these dissident elements can be contained, for they are about to burst forth in all directions' (Aldgate and Richards 1999: 163). This is most perfectly captured in the scene when the gang are forced to join the tea party which Mrs Wilberforce throws for her friends. Charles Barr, slightly playfully, pushes this reading even further by suggesting that the gang actually represents Atlee's post-war Labour government. (Barr 1977: 171–172) They take over 'the house' (parliament), with plans to redistribute wealth (the robbery), but find themselves unable to surmount the forces of conservatism which eventually defeat them (the Tories' election victory of 1951). Barr offers this reading in a tongue-in-cheek manner, but nonetheless argues that the film illustrates 'the absorption of the dynamic by the static, of change by tradition, of the new by the old, which is the essential pattern of post-war British history' (Barr 1977: 172).

A further fascinating level of metaphor, which is picked up by Aldgate and Richards, is that the film's allegory is a critique of both post-war Britain and Ealing itself (Aldgate and Richards 1999: 159). Mrs Wilberforce stands for Balcon, the eternal nanny, benevolently overseeing her slightly wayward young men and trying to keep them on the right path. It's hardly surprising that Mackendrick left for America after making the film. The remarkable achievement of *The Ladykillers* lies in its ability to move beyond the familiar comforts provided by the secure world of the Ealing comedy and provide instead a mischievous portrait of a country caught on the brink of change. With a foot in both camps, it offers us a picture of traditional English values in the form of Mrs Wilberforce, a figure as likely to induce alarm as affection.

Note

1 See 'That Topic All-Absorbing: Class' and 'The Welfare State' in Arthur Marwick, *British Society Since 1945*, London, Penguin, 1986.

Further Reading

Anthony Aldgate and Jeffrey Richards, *Best of British: Cinema and Society from 1930 to the Present*, London, I.B. Tauris, 1999.

Roy Armes, *A Critical History of British Cinema*, London, Secker and Warburg, 1978.

Michael Balcon, *A Lifetime of Films*, London, Hutchinson, 1969.

Charles Barr, *Ealing Studios*, New York, The Overlook Press, 1977.

John Ellis, 'Made in Ealing', *Screen*, 16, Spring 1975.

Philip Kemp, *Lethal Innocence: The Cinema of Alexander Mackendrick*, London, Methuen, 1991.

Brian McFarlane, *The Encyclopedia of British Film*, London, Methuen, 2003.

Robert Murphy, *Realism and Tinsel: Cinema and Society in Britain, 1939–1949*, London, Routledge, 1989.

Tim Pulleine, 'A Song and Dance at the Local: Thoughts on Ealing' in Robert Murphy (ed.) *The British Cinema Book*, London, BFI, 2001.

ROBERT SHAIL

SAPPHIRE (1959)

[Production Company: Artna Films. Director: Basil Dearden. Screenwriter: Janet Green (additional dialogue: Lukas Heller). Cinematographer: Harry Waxman. Music: Philip Green. Editor: John Guthridge. Cast: Nigel Patrick (Superintendent Bob Hazzard), Michael Craig (Inspector Phil Learoyd), Earl Cameron (Dr Robbins), Yvonne Mitchell (Mildred), Paul Massie (David Harris), Bernard Miles (Ted Harris), Olga Lindo (Mrs Harris), Gordon Heath (Paul Slade), Harry Baird (Johnnie Fiddle), Robert Adams (Horace 'Big Cigar').]

In *Sapphire* (Dearden, 1959) African-Caribbean faces fill the screen in scene after scene; and for mainstream cinema audiences of the time, used only to the essentially voiceless presence of black natives as the threatening hordes of Empire in their films, this would have made *Sapphire* challenging viewing. The central characters are two white police officers but the enigma at the heart of the film is a murdered black woman, a 'lilywhite' who has attempted to pass as white. In plot terms the police officers are investigating the death of this woman, Sapphire, but thematically their journey represents an effort to come to terms with the presence of a growing black community within traditionally white British society. Superintendent Bob Hazzard and Inspector Phil Learoyd are effectively investigating the collective psychological make-up of British society in relation to this black presence.

Apart from Earl Cameron as Dr Robbins, the brother of the murdered Sapphire, none of the black characters has a leading role but their multifaceted presence as an ethnic community is emphasised; and this is in a film that was made and released immediately after the Notting Hill riots of 1958 when gangs of young whites had taken to the streets 'nigger hunting' during the late August Bank Holiday and into early September.

The audience is placed in the position of watching one black character, Johnny Fiddler, being chased by a white gang. After several groups have refused to offer him shelter, including (interestingly) a black couple who don't want to get involved and whites in a pub who call him 'nigger' and 'dirty black', a white woman persuades her husband to let Johnny into their shop to save him from the mob. A similar incident actually happened to one Seymour Manning from Derby who arrived in Notting Hill during the Bank Holiday to visit relatives. He was saved by a white woman who let him into her greengrocer's shop. The aftermath was covered by Pathé News and released as a newsreel that the same audiences who watched *Sapphire* might well have seen.

The attacks and riots in Notting Hill (which were preceded by similar events in Nottingham) were covered extensively in the newspapers, but this open violence was only the most visible expression of deep-seated prejudice amongst sections of the British public. In *Sapphire* the officers investigating Sapphire's murder go to the International Club where they see a black pianist, and this results in direct social comment from Hazzard, who concludes, 'He's lucky, *he'll* be accepted for what he is: a good pianist'.

Sporadic violence continued in the Notting Hill area after the main riots and culminated in the death of Kelso Cochrane in May 1959, the year of *Sapphire*'s release. In the film, Hazzard refers directly to the idea of riots against minority groups: 'Given the right atmosphere you can organise riots against anyone: Jews, Catholics, Negroes, Irishmen'. In the context of the war, which had ended just 14 years before, the mention of 'Jews' is especially powerful (a similar comparison is made in a BBC TV play from 1956, *A Man From the Sun*); and the use of 'Catholics' and 'Irishmen' highlights the situation for the other main group facing discrimination in Britain in the late 1950s.[1]

During this period Britain continued to maintain a false impression of itself as an imperial power. In 1951 the Festival of Britain celebrated British achievements, in 1952 Churchill revealed Britain now had the atomic bomb, and in 1953 the coronation of Elizabeth II took place amid incredible pageantry with the Queen then setting out on a six-month tour of the Commonwealth. Victory in the war, and the nostalgic and heroic representation of this success through the media, especially film, helped shape the outlook of ordinary Britons. Britain may no longer have enjoyed a monopoly of world trade and the Empire may have been disintegrating through a series of, often bloody, struggles for independence, but the attitude of Britons of all classes towards the former colonies remained one of racial superiority.

When migrants from the West Indies began to arrive in Tilbury in 1948 they found plenty of work – their labour was useful to the economy, but they were confronted by open discrimination. Immigrants were ghettoised into areas of poor housing (as seen in *Sapphire*) and the resulting communities naturally attracted new arrivals. Organisations like London Transport and several regional hospital boards (see the black nurse in *Sapphire*, Miss Dawson) went to the West Indies on recruitment drives. By late 1958 London Transport employed almost 4,000 black workers, with about a quarter recruited directly from the Caribbean. In the 10 years from 1951 to 1961

- the estimated number of West Africans in Britain rose from 6,000 to 20,000;
- the number of Pakistanis from 5,000 to 25,000;
- the number of immigrants from the Far East from 12,000 to 30,000;
- the number of Indians from 30,000 to 80,000;
- and the number of West Indians from 15,000 to 170,000.

What would have been called in 1961 the 'coloured' population was therefore four times what it was 10 years earlier, and within this the West Indian population had increased tenfold. Even so, West Indians still represented only just over a quarter of one per cent of the country's population.

Commonwealth citizens were absent from most post-war British films. Occasionally they were a token presence as in *A Matter of Life and Death* (Powell and Pressburger, 1947) where there is some recognition that more then 2.5 million Indians, for example, had been in the armed forces during the war with 36,000 killed in action; often they were a source of jokes as in the 'Doctor in the House' film series; and only rarely were they seen within a serious dramatic context as in *Simba* (1955), dealing with Mau Mau attacks in Kenya in which Cameron played the humanitarian, Dr Karanja. Social problem films were a feature of the 1950s, but *Sapphire* (voted Best British Film for 1959 by the British Film Academy) is rare in dealing with the race issue in such a direct fashion. *Pool of London* (with Cameron controversially shown in a relationship with a white girl) had been made in 1950 and *Flame in the Streets* (with the same star attempting to overcome discrimination) was to be made two years later in 1961.

Pool of London, directed by Dearden, tells the story of Johnnie, a Jamaican merchant seaman who through his friendship with a white sailor becomes implicated in a diamond theft. As with *Sapphire* it displays open prejudice (with the central black character again being called 'dirty', for instance) but also has a clear social message:

> *Johnnie*: You wonder why one man is born white and another black.
> *Pat*: It doesn't matter.
> *Johnnie*: It does you know: one day maybe it won't.

It does not contain the sheer number of black characters and racism is not as central to the narrative as in *Sapphire*, but this film could be considered the more effective anti-racist text: Cameron's character has a more central role, is the embodiment of honesty, integrity and gentleness, and is loved for these human qualities by two further key characters (both white, one male and one female). Which is not to say there are not stereotypical representations within this film (as there are within *Sapphire*): see Cameron in several scenes for instance as the simple, happy, black 'servant'.

The way West Indians are represented in these texts and the relationship of these representations to socio-historical context is certainly questionable in some respects. Sapphire, the character, is an absence from the film that bears her name: we, like the detectives, have to construct her from snippets of information gleaned from a series of sources each with their own perspective on the issue. It seems she has found she can pass for being white and as a result has left her black friendship groups and passed over into the white world. It could be suggested this is her ultimate crime: she has attempted to transcend the boundaries of race. Threateningly for racists she is not only the alien 'other' but also the 'other' that cannot be recognised as such. Whilst purporting to deal with a social issue in an enlightened liberal way, this film could be seen as an expression of white fear of the black 'other' that could soon through the 'horror' of miscegenation become the unrecognisable presence within our midst (or even within each of us individually).

When two (or more) ethnic communities come into contact there are three generalised possible outcomes:

- separatism – the two communities continue to exist each as it were in a vacuum;
- integration – the two communities mix or intermingle (rather than clash) on the basis of equality and mutual respect for each other's culture;
- assimilation – one ethnic group is prepared to renounce its cultural identity in order to achieve membership status within the other community.

Would the implied messages and values to be found in *Sapphire* seem to advocate any one of these outcomes?

The diversity of perspectives open to the spectator will always make it impossible to allocate any categorical positioning of audience in relation to text: readers are able to make of texts what they will. However, it remains the case that for a sizeable proportion of the mainstream film-going public at the end of the 1950s this film would be unusual in bringing into question the security of the taken-for-granted Anglo-centrality[2] of their world.

The film industry does deal with the retreat from Empire in various ways in the early 1960s. In *Guns at Batasi* (John Guillermin, 1964) the quintessential regimental sergeant major, bridging the officer class-ordinary ranks gulf, is given lines such as 'Our good is as good as their good, and their bad is as bad as our bad'. In *Zulu* (Cy Endfield, 1964) the main Zulu victory occurring at Isandlwana is ignored in order to concentrate on what was merely a sideshow skirmish to the main battle. In general, ethnic groups are denied a voice in films from the period and issues of race are thoroughly ignored. In this context the work of Dearden, screenwriter Janet Green and producer Michael Relph (a further common factor between this film and *Pool of London*) does seem at the very least laudable.

Ethnic minority communities might be said to experience a range of racist attitudes:

- everyday white prejudice and discrimination, hinging on a determined social and cultural exclusion of the threatening 'other';
- institutional racism, involving for instance entrenched attitudes within the police force;
- extremist white racism, ultimately involving unprovoked physical violence.

Sapphire, particularly in the script, determinedly confronts each of these areas, even attempting to force liberals to question their own perhaps too cosy, self-congratulatory value system at certain points, as well as exposing the imposed poverty and deprivation accompanying such race-based exclusion. This text succeeds in raising issues about the ways in which migrating people experience identity, ethnicity and diasporic-belonging; and, even more importantly, confronts the way individuals within the audience who are members of the white majority experience 'otherness' within what they would tend to see as 'their' society.

Notes

1 Lukas Heller, who provided additional dialogue for the script, was a German Jewish refugee who came to England before the Second World War.
2 If Eurocentrism is a perspective from which Europe is seen as the unique source of meaning, 'Anglo-centralism' represents a similar British outlook on the world. Stam (2000: 269) defines Eurocentrism as:

> a form of vestigial thinking which permeates and structures contemporary practices and representations even after the formal end of colonialism.

Further Reading

Alan Burton, Tim O'Sullivan and Paul Wells (eds) *Liberal Directions: Basil Dearden and Postwar British Film Culture*, Trowbridge, Flick Books, 1997.
Raymond Durgnat, *A Mirror for England*, London, Faber, 1970.
John Hill, *Sex, Class and Realism: British Cinema 1956–1963*, London, BFI, 1986.
Robert Stam, *Film Theory: An Introduction*, Oxford, Blackwell, 2000.

JOHN WHITE

WE ARE THE LAMBETH BOYS (1959)

[Production Company: Graphic Films. Director: Karel Reisz. Cinematographer: Walter Lassally. Music: Johnny Dankworth. Editor: John Fletcher. Commentary: John Rollason.]

During the 1950s many of Britain's younger artists, writers, filmmakers and cultural critics took as their subject matter 'ordinary' people and 'ordinary' life. This may have reflected in part the increasing post-war importance of democracy – ordinary people had done their bit to defeat fascism, they had voted for the benefits of the Welfare State and now they were being represented in all kinds of cultural practices. It may also have owed something to the now familiar desire of younger generations to sweep away the favoured images and ideas of their predecessors which in 1950s Britain were often unadventurous, middle-aged and middle class or nostalgically historical.

From the mid-1950s, new playwrights like John Osborne and Harold Pinter were characterised somewhat loosely as 'angry young men' and a group of young artists including John Bratby and Jack Smith were known as the 'Kitchen Sink Painters'. Two key publications celebrated the culture of ordinary people and pointed the way to the development of British Cultural Studies: one was *Culture and Society* by Raymond Williams, the second *The Uses of Literacy* by Richard Hoggart.

In 1959 Hoggart contributed an article to *Sight and Sound* on a new British documentary film, *We Are the Lambeth Boys*, suggesting

> the questions which the film is bound to raise for anyone interested in the way 'ordinary life' is treated in popular art and entertainments nowadays.

He identified and generally praised the 'subjective approach' of the director Karel Reisz, contrasting it with more cautious documentary work which in seeking 'comprehensive, objectivity and balance' sacrifices 'meaning (and) . . . the sense of life itself'. By contrast, Hoggart suggested *We Are the Lambeth Boys* demonstrated 'characteristics of art' in setting out 'to show, not the whole truth, but some aspects of the truth wholly'.

The film offers an account of young people in a London youth club on the southern side of the Thames. It was shown for the first time just along the road from its location, at the National Film Theatre in March 1959, having been shot over six weeks during the previous summer. It had been sponsored by the Ford Motor Company as part of a cinema series called 'Look at Britain'. At its premiere it was one of four documentaries shown together under the title 'Free Cinema 6'. Christophe Dupin (2006) says Free Cinema was

> Essentially ... the general title given to a series of six programmes of (mainly) short documentaries shown at the National Film Theatre (NFT) in London between February 1956 and March 1959.
>
> (Dupin 2006: 1)

In February 1956 a group of participating young directors had issued a 'manifesto' claiming a common approach in their films. They defined this as including an 'implicit ... belief in freedom' alongside the 'importance of people and ... the significance of the everyday'. This attitude was very similar to that found in much of the art, drama and critical writing of the time.

We Are the Lambeth Boys was one of the films in the last programme of these short documentaries, after which Reisz and his fellow directors Lindsay Anderson and Tony Richardson moved into feature films as the leading figures of the short-lived but successful British 'New Wave' which again took as its subjects ordinary people in contemporary Britain.

So in part, the significance of *We Are the Lambeth Boys* is as one of a set of films that allowed this group of young directors to develop their skills before moving into fictional feature films. But if this experience were merely an apprenticeship these short films would not warrant inclusion in any list of significant British films. The Free Cinema movement reflected the growing desire for greater democracy in class-conscious Britain but was also tied to the growing recognition of film as a significant artistic, intellectual and cultural practice. The films, produced in the late 1950s, were linked to new publications, specialist screenings, manifestos and the growing study of film in universities and colleges. For example Anderson and Reisz both wrote for the new film journal *Sight and Sound*.

While the films of the Free Cinema had a serious intent they were produced by relatively young directors and a number offered representations of emerging youth cultures. The first programme of the Free Cinema included a film directed by Reisz and Richardson and funded by the British Film Institute. Its subject was a jazz club in Wood Green, north London and it had the title of a jazz song, *Momma Don't Allow*, performed in the film by the Chris Barber Jazz

Band – one of Britain's most popular jazz bands. The shooting budget of £250 was approved at the end of 1954 and the completion budget of £175 in mid-1955, so this film offers a view of British youth culture just months before Elvis Presley's first British hit and the cinema 'riots' that accompanied the first screenings of *Rock Around the Clock*. At the time jazz and its English off-shoot skiffle were at the hipper end of the popular music spectrum and jazz clubs or coffee bars were the location for the emergence of youth culture.

By the time *We Are the Lambeth Boys* was shot three years later, skiffle was virtually over and jazz had given way to USA pop in the affections of most young people. The soundtrack was provided by Johnny Dankworth who with his vocalist wife Cleo Laine was another key figure of the British jazz scene: but while Barber provided a 'retro' jazz soundtrack for *Momma Don't Allow*, Dankworth was, albeit tentatively, exploring the modern style.

We Are the Lambeth Boys then offers a record of young English people in the summer of 1958 just prior to the emergence of the first Mods but with the Teddy Boys on the wane and popular culture taking an increasingly ubiquitous hold. The Lambeth teenagers are neither in a jazz club nor in the less structured surroundings of a coffee bar but in the organised, secular surroundings of a local council youth club. Through the 1950s and 1960s these clubs provided social spaces for young people to interact in a relatively 'safe' environment (all but two of the Lambeth boys and girls have left school and are in employment but we do not see them in pubs, drinking alcohol or mixing with adults). By contrast, just one year later, Reisz's *Saturday Night and Sunday Morning* shows a young rebellious factory worker sharing social spaces with adults, drinking copious quantities of alcohol and pursuing an affair with an older woman. In these respects the Lambeth youngsters anticipate more accurately the social groupings of young people separating themselves by choice from their elders, which would have such an impact in the 1960s and beyond.

The most obvious adult presence in *We Are the Lambeth Boys* is the disembodied commentator (John Rollason) and his role is not straightforward. His authoritative commentary is perhaps too didactic, determined to guide our interpretation of what we see rather than allowing the spectator to interpret more actively what is on offer. The directors of the Free Cinema admired the 1940s documentary films of Humphrey Jennings, yet his major film *Listen to Britain* offers a more open example of documentation, resisting the didactic tradition of John Grierson and other British documentary-makers. In France in the 1950s, Jean Rouch was exploring a more open approach to documentary and his work was paralleled in the USA by the American innovators Robert Drew, Richard Leacock, DA Pennebaker and the Maysles brothers. Rollason's commentary seems dated today but it is worth noting that Hoggart too criticised its addition to the images and live speech on offer, not least because it contributed to an over-idealistic depiction of young people.

But while Free Cinema pursued new attitudes and *We Are the Lambeth Boys* records a new youth-oriented world, we can see half-a-century later that much of that world has changed significantly. The film opens with some of the young people walking towards the youth club on a bright summer's evening. Others join them and we soon see the boys bowling and batting in a cricket net while the 'Lambeth Girls' stand around chatting. These young working people in their late teens smoke copiously but don't drink and there is no hint of the spread of drug-taking which is now a significant part of teenage life. Almost without exception they dress smartly to relax, while Lambeth 1958 appears to be almost wholly white and working class. Halfway through the film we see two girls walking towards the club past three younger boys in short trousers, one of whom is black, but it is a fleeting moment. They appear to be playing happily together but in that same late summer there were extensive disturbances in the streets of north London, characterised as 'race riots'. Similar problems occurred in Nottingham and the protagonists were mainly young white working-class hooligans, intent on trouble.

Two passages do hint at the possibility of gang violence which the popular press would cover over the following decades in their pursuit of what Stanley Cohen described as 'folk devils' and 'moral panics' (Cohen 1972). In the opening minutes we see 'Harry and his gang' dressed more like Teddy Boys and preferring to smoke and 'hang about'. Later, during a work-place sequence we overhear a discussion about 'Smithy's mob' who may be threatening trouble locally. We hear that Smithy 'don't look hard ... he looks a queer' but he may 'fuckin' have about fifty ... ' – the only bad language in the film.

Subsequently, cultural commentators like Dick Hebdige (1979) noted the creative influence of black taste and style on the young working-class subcultural groups. The early stages of this can be discerned in the film's Saturday night dance sequence where we see the youngsters jiving to a typical twelve-bar rhythm & blues instrumental. Percy, one of the key figures in the film, seems older perhaps because of his pencil moustache or his preference for white ties and dark shirts more reminiscent of the gangster look of *Brighton Rock* (Boulting, 1947). But on this Saturday night, his Brylcreemed quiff has been brushed forward and he sports a silk pocket handkerchief, hinting at the embryonic mod style which would soon invade the south London estates.

The boys have already declared their interest in clothes in a discussion in the club where one asserts that he would spend 15 guineas on a suit (£15.75) – probably a week's wages for a working man. They also discuss the morality of shop-lifting and the case for and against capital punishment which was then still legal.

The Lambeth boys and girls have apprenticeships or work as unskilled labour in a variety of places including a butcher's, a post office, a dress-maker's, a factory and an office reception. This is a period of full employment and while it is not mentioned, most of these young men will be among the first generation not called up for National Service, enabling them to experience freedoms previously unavailable. Nonetheless we are reminded of the powerful class divide in Britain at the time on the boys' annual trip to Mill Hill public school for an afternoon of cricket, swimming and socialising. While these educational divisions still exist, young people today share a more common popular culture which in 1958 was hardly widespread and appears not to have touched the public school at all.

On the evening of the cricket match back in Lambeth there is more dancing with chips to follow while the commentary reassures us that 'a good evening for young people is much as it always has been'. Would a contemporary version of the film be able to make the same claim?

Further Reading

Stanley Cohen, *Folk Devils and Moral Panics: the Creation of the Mods and Rockers*, London, MacGibbon and Kee, 1972.

Christophe Dupin, '*Free Cinema*' DVD booklet notes, London, BFI, 2006.

Dick Hebdige, *Subculture: the Meaning of Style*, London, Routledge, 1979.

Richard Hoggart, *The Uses of Literacy*, London, Penguin, 1957.

——, 'We are the Lambeth Boys', *Sight and Sound*, Vol. 28, Nos. 3 and 4, 1959, pp. 164–165.

Raymond Williams, *Culture and Society 1780–1950*, Harmondsworth, Penguin, 1958.

DAVE ALLEN

SATURDAY NIGHT AND SUNDAY MORNING (1960)

[Production Company: Woodfall Film Productions. Director: Karel Reisz. Screenwriter: Alan Sillitoe. Cinematographer: Freddie Francis.

Editor: Seth Hilton. Cast: Albert Finney (Arthur Seaton), Shirley Anne Field (Doreen), Rachel Roberts (Brenda), Hylda Baker (Aunt Ada), Norman Rossington (Bert).]

Released in 1960, *Saturday Night and Sunday Morning* is rooted in the new cinematic and literary movements of its day. Its screenplay, written by so-called 'angry young man' Alan Sillitoe, was based on his novel of the same name, and its director Karel Reisz was involved in the Free Cinema movement of the late 1950s. This, Reisz's first fiction feature, was at the forefront of the short-lived 'British New Wave' (1959–1963). With its working-class protagonists, focus on controversial yet ordinary issues, and a commitment to represent working-class life, this ground-breaking movement included films that took a resolutely humanistic, poetic and non-commercial approach to cinema. They were also collectively known as 'kitchen sink' films.[1]

The 1960s saw the rise of the independent film company as a significant force in British cinema and Woodfall was a prestigious example. Formed by another of the 'angries', John Osborne, in partnership with Tony Richardson, it was financed by the proceeds of Osborne's stage success, *Look Back in Anger*. Woodfall's aim, according to Richardson, was 'to get into British film the same sort of impact and sense of life that the Angry Young Man cult has had in the theatre and literary worlds' (Hill 1986: 40).

Independent production gave directors the freedom to represent their society in original ways and tackle issues previously considered taboo. They were helped in this by the new 'X' certificate, introduced by the BBFC in 1951 and granted to all the 'new wave' films apart from *Billy Liar* (John Schlesinger, 1963). This allowed them to be more daring in content, albeit within reason: for example, Arthur (Albert Finney) was allowed the contentious use of the word 'bloody', but 'bugger' was too much and had to be changed to 'beggar'; likewise, a reference to the gin and hot bath abortion had to be cut.[2] Nevertheless, the frank presentation of Arthur's sexual attitudes, Brenda's (Rachel Roberts) adultery, and the unwanted pregnancy seemed adult and contemporary next to Hollywood films still labouring under a draconian Production Code.

It is unsurprising therefore that *Saturday Night and Sunday Morning*, like *Room at the Top* (Jack Clayton, 1959) before it, hit a nerve with the cinema audience. Despite a small publicity budget, it was the third most successful film at the box office in 1961, won the BAFTA for Best Film and was the first film to take £100,000 in the three weeks of its London run alone. This film reflected the political and social changes shaping British society at this time. It was released in the middle of the prosperous consumer boom of the 1950s, but before the 'swinging sixties'. Considered daring on its release for its representation of sexuality and working-class youth, its moral values look old-fashioned even compared to *Georgy Girl* (Silvio Narizzano, 1966) and *Alfie* (Lewis Gilbert, 1966), let alone *Blow Up* (Michelangelo Anonioni, 1966) and *Performance* (Donald Cammell and Nicolas Roeg, 1970). By 1963, gritty realism and working-class angst were no longer box-office draws.

Nevertheless, the fact that radical representations of working-class life were at the heart of these new literary and cinematic movements is explained by contemporary changes in society. The economic boom of the 1950s had brought unprecedented prosperity to a class used to defining itself in terms of the battle for a living wage. This led to new tensions around class identity and working-class masculinity in particular, defined as it was in its opposition to oppression in the workplace. After the 'hungry thirties' and the austerity of the war years, the 1950s were the 'never had it so good' Macmillan years. Wages doubled between 1951 and 1959, inflation and bank rates were low. Between 1957 and 1959, television ownership went up by 32%; between 1952 and 1959 ownership of cars doubled. Advertising investment increased fourfold between 1947 and 1960. In 1959 alone 200,000 motorbike licences were issued (Sandbrook 2006: 97).

Jack's (Bryan Pringle) motorbike and sidecar and his promise to buy Brenda a television; Robbo's (Robert Cawdron) outrage at Arthur's pay packet of over £14; Doreen's (Shirley Anne Field) comments about Arthur's suits – 'Are all these clothes your'n? They must have cost you a pretty penny' – are all precise contemporary details. A class that had previously defined itself as producers now had to redefine itself as consumers. Increased wealth plus access to university education offered greater class mobility than ever before, but also challenged established ideas of what it meant to be working class. From the perspective of 1960, it seemed conceivable that the working class as it had been was an endangered species, and *Saturday Night and Sunday Morning* reflects these feelings of uncertainty, confusion and social paranoia.

The seminal text setting the agenda for intellectual debate about working-class identity was Hoggart's *Uses of Literacy* (1957). Hoggart contrasts the 'good' authentic working-class culture of the past with the 'shiny barbarism' of the modern consumer culture he sees as destroying it. Most of the 'new wave' films produce representations of working-class life premised on this binary opposition. Sillitoe read

Hoggart after writing *Saturday Night and Sunday Morning*, but agreed that his novel 'pointed out more or less the same thing' (Hill 1986: 203). The opening shot frames Arthur as traditionally working class, shirt sleeves rolled up and working at his lathe, voicing his combative attitude to authority and his determination not to be ground down. Doreen's new council house, with its modern furnishings, is seen as an unfriendly and repressive place set against the homely welcome of Arthur's traditional terraced home, reflecting the distrust of middle-class aspirations. Arthur's scathing comment that television produces people who are 'dead from the neck down' is a recurring motif found in most of the 'new wave' films.

Saturday Night and Sunday Morning pushes beyond this fixed ideological model to present a more ambivalent view. Jack, staid on his motorbike, seems more old-fashioned than Arthur on his pushbike; in the club, the younger generation listens to their pop music and the older generation enjoy their sing-song: neither group is held up as more desirable than the other. This is different from the clear privileging of the rich brass band concert over the television quiz show in *A Kind of Loving* (John Schlesinger, 1962). Even the final sequence, where Arthur throws a stone at the modern housing development and expresses his preference for an older house, finishes with a resigned acceptance that he and Doreen may live there. Moreover, several times in the film, Arthur himself expresses disdain for 'the good old days'. While this is framed within an awareness of how hard those times were, there is no nostalgic admiration for the people who lived through them.

Most of the 'new wave' films sidestep uncomfortable exploration of class identity by projecting all the problems onto the female characters, who become embodiments of the threats posed to traditional working-class culture. A stereotype of the new wave is the woman obsessed with consumer goods and middle-class aspirations. This neat containment of the debate lets the men off the hook; demonising the women prevents further uncomfortable debate over class identity. *Saturday Night and Sunday Morning* shares this misogynistic tendency, but whereas in other new wave films, the male view is privileged, this one is more ambivalent in its audience positioning. Effective examples include the sequence where Arthur deliberately tips a pint of beer over the woman in the club, the sequence where he puts a dead rat on the bench of a female worker and the sequence where he shoots Mrs Bull (Edna Morris). In the first two incidents there is a lack of clear motivation, while in the third we are encouraged to assume it is a payback for Mrs Bull helping to bring about the arrest of the man who threw the brick through the shop window. Reaction shots of Arthur laughing after each incident suggest this is part of Arthur's rebellious streak, or his addiction to 'having a good time', but in neither sequence are Arthur's values prioritised as superior. The messages regarding class and gender remain quite ambivalent.

The extremity of Bert and Arthur's hatred for Mrs Bull is disturbing. They call her 'a bitch and a whore', 'rat face', 'old bag', and suggest she 'wants pole-axing'. Because this hatred cannot be masked by the more acceptable guise of class resentment, it can be seen as straightforward antagonism towards women. It is tempting therefore to read the film as emphatically sexist. The sexually attractive 'good girl' gets her man, while the transgressive woman is punished for her deviance.

Doreen seems to fit this first stereotype, described by some as 'a smashing bit of stuff', but 'first kiss and she'll expect a ring'. When Arthur does agree to marry Doreen, despite the film's analogies between marriage and fishing, the film is ambivalent about their relationship. Has Arthur's rebellious masculinity been tamed like Jack's before him (as suggested by the shot of the brick-throwing man being restrained by a group of threatening women), or does his relationship signal a more adult recognition of who he is? In the final sequence his comment that it will not be the last stone he throws, and the mildness of Doreen's rebuke, further resist misogynistic readings about the female emasculation of the male.

Similarly, while Brenda's agency in the narrative (adulterous wife who is punished for her transgression) seems unambiguous, the representation of her is more complex. For example, in the 'Sunday morning' sequence we see her in three conflicting stereotypical roles: in bed with Arthur confirming her pleasure with their sexual relationship; serving him breakfast in a way which recalls the servile role of Mrs Seaton; and, finally, hugging her child. Her ease and confidence in all these roles of lover, wife and mother constructs a representation at odds with the more misogynistic elements of the film. Her courage in deciding to go ahead with the pregnancy and 'face whatever comes of it', her speech about what it means to be a mother, and the final shot we see of her in the film, trapped in the spotlight with a crowd of hostile spectators around her just after she has been publicly slapped by Jack, invite the audience to sympathise with her. Meanwhile, in the penultimate sequence of the film where Arthur consummates his relationship with Doreen after their engagement, the camera privileges Doreen's unease. This, combined with the sequences involving Brenda, gives a complex and empathetic look at the female experience of sexuality and marriage in the late 1950s, before the contraceptive pill and the abortion law started to have a real effect on women's lives.

Saturday Night and Sunday Morning is unusual in its implicit criticism of the ways in which challenges to working-class male identity manifest themselves. Like the 'angry young men' of the time, Arthur's anger is real but its focus remains unclear. The film gives a real sense of Arthur's unhappiness with his situation but is less clear about why he feels like this or what the solution may be. Arthur articulates this crisis of identity in juxtaposition with searching shots of his face in the mirror: 'I'm me and nobody else. Whatever people say I am that's what I'm not. . . . God knows what I am'. To this extent the film is a more provocative and searching exploration of its time than some of the other 'kitchen sink' films which present a more apparently coherent picture of what 'working class' might mean.

Notes

1 Susan Hayward, 'Free Cinema', in *Cinema Studies: The Key Concepts*, London & New York, Routledge, 1996, pp. 132–135.
2 Tom Dewe Mathews, *Censored*, London, Chatto and Windus,1994, pp. 151–152.

Further Reading

John Hill, *Sex, Class and Realism*, London, BFI, 1986.
Richard Hoggart, *The Uses of Literacy: Aspects of Working Class Life*, London, Chatto & Windus, 1957.
Dominic Sandbrook, *Never Had it So Good: A History of Britain from Suez to the Beatles*, Oxford, Abacus, 2006.

JEAN WELSH

PEEPING TOM (1960)

[Production Company: Michael Powell (Theatre). Director: Michael Powell. Screenwriter: Leo Marks. Cinematographer: Otto Heller. Editor: Noreen Ackland. Music: Brian Easdale. Cast: Carl Boehm (Mark Lewis), Anna Massey (Helen Stephens), Moira Shearer (Vivian).]

It is always creepy and fascinating when the cinema screen looks back at you, turning that fundamental element of film – the gaze – back onto the viewer. This is what Michael Powell's *Peeping Tom* does to us from the outset. It opens with an extreme close-up of a pair of blue eyes, closed at first then wide open and alert, as though suddenly engaged in the activity of looking. We are so close that we cannot judge their expression. Are they peeping at something, captured by the sight of a spectacle they should not be seeing? Or is that fear twitching at the corner of the eye, are they watching some unaccountable horror? The cleverness of this opening, whose ambiguity remains even once the film is over, is that the captivated yet terrified gaze of the horror movie spectator is laid bare. In other words this shot mirrors from the start our own gaze as we watch the film, letting us know in no uncertain terms that the film will, in a sense, be watching us watching. *We* are the peeping Toms of the title and the film 'knows' it too. *Peeping Tom* is almost as famous for the bad press it received on its release as for its subsequent rehabilitation in the 1970s by British film critics such as Ian Christie, and US film-makers like Martin Scorsese. In 1960 it was vilified as exploitative, perverse and downright nasty, in spite of the fact that there is very little explicit violence or sex. What could be more disturbing, however, than a film that probes the very mechanisms of cinema itself, revealing our own perversity as obsessive watchers and highlighting our sadistic sense of mastery over the image? As Mark Lewis, the psychopathic protagonist of the film, knows, nothing is more shocking than seeing one's mirror image looking into the abyss of human terror. The critics' initial outcry captures this uncomfortable feeling of being caught in the act.

Peeping Tom might arguably be situated in relation to the slasher genre, which developed in the wake of Alfred Hitchcock's *Psycho* (1960 US), during the 1970s and 1980s. Carol Clover describes as follows the essential elements from the Hitchcock film, referenced by numerous later productions:

> ... the killer is the psychotic product of a sick family, but still recognizably human; the victim is a beautiful, sexually active woman; the location is not-home, at a Terrible Place; the weapon is something other than a gun; the attack is registered from the victim's point of view and comes with shocking suddenness.
>
> (1992: 23–24)

Peeping Tom was financed, as part of a series of low-budget films, by Anglo-Amalgamated, hoping to emulate the success of British horror production company Hammer in the late 1950s. It is strikingly similar to the slasher model Clover outlines, most notably in the figure of the killer, whose childhood relations with a cold-hearted scientist father and sexually attractive stepmother are shown to have led directly to his psychopathic affliction: the urge to film the death agonies of women whose sexuality is a crucial part of their identity. What is more, *Peeping Tom* goes further than *Psycho* towards anticipating the genre by introducing both the series of female victims and the 'Final Girl', in the figure of the bright and sympathetic Helen Stephens, who both discovers Mark's secret and manages to survive the experience. It is true that *Peeping Tom* may have influenced later practitioners of slasher films, in particular Brian de Palma who was one of the 1970s 'movie brats' who rediscovered the films of Powell and former partner Emeric Pressburger (Christie 1994: 95). However, it is clearly *Psycho* that is most explicitly referenced by subsequent films. What is interesting then about *Peeping Tom*'s resonance with the slasher genre is the way it appears both to anticipate and deconstruct this particular mode of horror from within.

The complex patterns of identification and perspective offered to the viewer are the primary means of this deconstruction. As will become commonplace in slasher films, our gaze is initially aligned with the killer's, switching towards the end to the perspective of the Final Girl, who takes on the 'active investigative gaze' (Clover 1992: 60). However the interplay of narrative and perspective in *Peeping Tom* complicates this pattern. The 'killer's' point of view is explicitly designated as that of a camera, whether in the process of filming, signalled by the grid of a viewfinder across the screen, or at the moment of replay, in the black and white 16 mm films Mark projects in his darkroom after the murders. Not only this but the murder weapon, the sharpened end of the tripod of Mark's Bell and Howell camera, is itself part of the apparatus, while Viv's murder is staged by Mark on a studio set under the auspices of a horror movie audition piece. This all conspires to bind the sadistic murders inextricably to the process of making and watching movies, implicating the spectator in Mark's 'scoptophilia', as the caricature psychiatrist calls his 'morbid urge to gaze'.[1] The Final Girl's attack sequence also complicates perspective, for it reveals the terrifying device of the mirror showing victims their own fear of death, but not before we have witnessed Helen watching the film of Viv's murder. Here, rather than registering her point of view, the camera remains fixed on her offering to the spectator precisely the spectacle of terror Mark himself seeks to record. Perhaps even more disturbingly, Mark's condition supposedly stems from his appalling childhood as guinea-pig for his father's experimental exploration and filming of the mechanisms of fear, suggesting that the excuses we make for obsessive watching – such as being a scientist or, say, a film critic – are just covers for a morbid and unhealthy subjugation of the desired image to our devouring eye. That there might be something inherently 'morbid' about watching films, something that goes beyond curiosity and into the realm of horror, is not only indicated by the success of the horror genre per se. It also connects with the workings of film itself, which as an inherently photographic medium has a particular relation to death. As Roland Barthes has argued, the photographic image, by preserving the image of life in the face of death, creates, as its subjects pass away, a disturbing 'future anterior' tense: between the shot being taken and the image being viewed by us in the present, the subject 'will have' died: 'whether or not the subject is already dead, every photograph is this catastrophe' (1980: 96). Although Barthes felt that the narrative flow of cinema denied it this uncanny power, *Peeping Tom* constantly reminds us of the photographic referent at the heart of cinema. Still photography plays an important part in the narrative of the film, in the ironic contrast between Mark's after-hours job taking erotic snaps and Helen's plans for a children's book about a magic camera. More significantly, both still photography and the moving image are referred to as 'photography' by characters in the film, highlighting their common element, the capturing and fixing onto film of images. Mark's collection of female victims, each stabbed through the throat like a pinned butterfly, thereby parallels both his father's scientific 'collection' of his childhood emotions and the elderly gentleman's collection of pornographic images purchased from the newsagent. The stillness or movement of the image is not at issue, rather the mechanical containment of the image allowing it to be mastered by the viewer. Even the film's real cinematographer Otto Heller is credited with the words 'Photographed in Eastman Colour by ... '. This blurring of the distinction between photography and cinema foregrounds the secret morbidity of film. Combined with the self-reflexive focus on the voyeurism of cinematic viewing, it means that the spectator of *Peeping Tom* is not free simply to shift unthinkingly between identificatory positions, but is instead constantly reminded of his or her own position as viewer, steeped in a complicity that goes well beyond mere 'sympathy' for the murderer.

One of the results of this is that the diegetic space of the film is precisely *not* as contained as we expect it to be, destabilising the mastery over the filmed image that we, like Mark, conventionally require from cinema. This is set in motion by the eye-opening first image and continued as the credits roll over the play-back of the murder scene we have just witnessed through a viewfinder. The boundaries between events within the film and outside it are blurred. The *mise-en-abyme* created by the production for which Mark works as focus-puller contributes to this effect, particularly in the scene where, cameras rolling, the female star opens the trunk to find Viv's dead body. Presumably a horror flick itself given its title, 'The Walls are Closing in', this represents the moment where real horror intrudes upon the artificial world of the film set. Another, more critical moment of confusion occurs when Helen, having discovered and watched the film of Viv's murder in Mark's darkroom, cries in desperation to Mark, 'that film is just a film, isn't it?' The film's persistent disturbance of the parameters of fiction adds to the feeling of disquiet it creates in the spectator. Yet ultimately we never question that this *is* just a film we are watching. For equally persistent are the comic and ironic touches undermining the film's realism. When glamour model Milly says that Mark 'might be more fun' if it wasn't safe to be alone with him, or the policeman quips 'we're going to be stars' when he catches Mark filming him; when the film director fumes, 'the silly bitch, she fainted in the wrong scene!' as his fluffy female star discovers a real dead body, the dramatic irony and humour of such remarks serves to distance us from the events even as the stability of cinema screen as boundary is being disturbed. Likewise, the tight, carefully constructed narrative structure provides a framework to guide us through the complex thematic layering.[2]

In the end this perhaps accounts for the strangeness – and brilliance – of the film. It makes us as spectators feel both at home and not at home in the perverse cinematic universe it evokes. Like the Terrible Place described by Clover as the slasher film's prime location, the film is uncanny because it is a 'not-home', both familiar and frightening. This is to follow Freud's exploration of the uncanny through an analysis of the way the German word *unheimlich* (uncanny, unhomely) meets *heimlich* (homely) since the latter word also signals that which is private and therefore concealed, hidden. The uncanny is therefore 'something which ought to have remained hidden but has come to light' (1990: 364). Within *Peeping Tom's* diegesis, the Terrible Place is Mark's darkroom, the secret heart of the family home containing the archives of all his father's cruel experiments on him as a child as well as his own murderous 'experiments'. It is a site that excites curiosity, not only in Helen but also in her blind, alcoholic mother, who tells Mark she visits it each night through the sounds of his footsteps and the whirring of his projector. For the auditory is not forgotten in the film's self-reflexive stripping bare of the fascination of cinema: the revelation at the end that every room in the house is wired for sound furnishes the darkroom with aural secrets to match its visual horrors. Helen and her mother are like cinema spectators drawn irresistibly to the hidden spectacle of cruelty. Like them, we are confronted by an uncanny filmic space that uncovers repressed desire, both revealing and undermining our mastery of that which it contains.

Notes

1 This is now more usually termed 'scopophilia'.
2 See William Johnson's thorough analysis of the narrative in '*Peeping Tom*: A Second Look', *Film Quarterly*, Vol. 33, No. 3 (Spring, 1980), pp. 2–10.

Further Reading

Roland Barthes, *Camera Lucida*, trans. Richard Howard, London, Vintage, 1980.
Ian Christie, *Arrows of Desire: The Films of Michael Powell and Emeric Pressburger*, London, Faber and Faber, 1994.
Carol Clover, *Men, Women and Chainsaws*, London, BFI, 1992.
Sigmund Freud, 'The Uncanny', in *Art and Literature*, The Penguin Freud Library, Vol. 14, London, Penguin, 1990, pp. 339–376.

ISABELLE MCNEILL

THE INNOCENTS (1961)

[Production Company: Achilles/20th Century Fox. Director: Jack Clayton. Screenwriter: Truman Capote. Cinematographer: Freddie Francis. Editor: Jim Clark. Music: George Auric. Cast: Deborah Kerr (Miss Giddens), Martin Stephens (Miles), Pamela Franklin (Flora), Megs Jenkins (Mrs Grose), Michael Redgrave (Uncle), Peter Wyngarde (Peter Quint), Clytie Jessop (Miss Jessel), Isla Cameron (Anna).]

For the successful debutant director, the second film is always a tricky prospect. Should it follow in the footsteps of its predecessor, repeating a tried and trusted formula, or should it be completely different, the director taking advantage of a power and freedom in the industry he or she may never again experience? After the international critical and commercial triumph of his first feature, *Room at the Top* (1959), which is often credited with launching the British New Wave, Jack Clayton was offered several projects in a similar vein of gritty realism: *Sons and Lovers, Saturday Night and Sunday Morning,*

The L-Shaped Room and *Term of Trial*. The films were all subsequently made – but not by Clayton. Instead he unexpectedly turned to a famous late-Victorian ghost story by the American master Henry James, *The Turn of the Screw* (1898), which Clayton had read and been enthralled by as a boy. The rights were owned by Twentieth Century Fox after a successful stage adaptation of it by William Archibald; after initial preparatory work with Archibald in adapting his play for the screen, Clayton reverted back to the novella for his inspiration, bringing in Truman Capote to write the screenplay.[1]

Even at that stage of his career, the ghost story was not unfamiliar territory for him. He had been an associate producer on Thorold Dickinson's stylish adaptation of Pushkin's *Queen of Spades* (1949), where a Russian soldier is haunted to the point of madness by the ghost of a wealthy Countess whose death he has caused; and his Oscar-winning short film, *The Bespoke Overcoat* (1955), was based on a supernatural tale by Gogol. Yet, as close friend and director Karel Reisz was later to reveal, Clayton might also have felt a personal connection with the James story. Not knowing who his father was, and brought up by a succession of nannies in a household full of secrets, Clayton empathises with the situation of the children in the story as they struggle to survive in an adult world that they already perceive to be fearful and duplicitous.

At that time the British horror film was a subject of considerable controversy. Michael Powell's *Peeping Tom* (1960) had outraged many with its tortured portrayal of a psychologically wounded, voyeuristic psychopath, and the blood-soaked horror rhapsodies of Hammer had yet to find critical acceptance. *The Innocents*, however, sidestepped that kind of indignation by skilfully situating itself in two critically respected traditions. Like the Ealing compendium classic, *Dead of Night* (Robert Hamer et al., 1945), its horror was implied rather than overt: here, a shot of a teardrop on a child's school slate could elicit the requisite shiver of dread. In that sense, it was being absolutely true to the narrative strategy James himself had outlined in his Preface to the tale, where he felt the horror should be suggestive rather than specific: 'Make the reader think the evil, make him think it for himself,' he wrote, 'and you are released from weak specification' (1907: 176). *The Innocents* could also be seen as one of British cinema's most distinguished adaptations of a literary classic, being true to the spirit of the story but highly imaginative in its cinematic realisation.

James's 'little pot-boiler' of a story (as he put it) has become one of the great literary conundrums. Two ghosts – the former valet, Peter Quint and the former governess, Miss Jessel – haunt the grounds of

Bly House, where a new governess and the housekeeper, Mrs Grose, are in charge of two children, Miles and Flora. Are the ghosts demonic presences, trying to possess the souls of the children and, through them, re-kindle their illicit affair? Or are they figments of the new governess's imagination, symptoms of a sexual repression perhaps breached by her infatuation with the children's uncle, whom she met (and was carried away by) when interviewed for the post? The tale is a masterclass in literary ambiguity: could the film replicate its richness?

From the outset, Clayton recognised that the tale presented formidable filmic challenges. Because the story has a limited number of ingredients – basically, two adults, two children, two ghosts, and a house – he realised it was essential that the tension must never be allowed to sag: each scene must have some point of intensity or disquiet, underlined by a visual detail, say, or an unusual camera angle, or a look. As examples, one might cite the way the governess's first approach to the house is filmed as if she is being followed; or the look exchanged between Miles and Flora when he enquires whether the governess's previous home was 'big enough to have secrets'. The film's opening is more atmospheric than the story's, because Clayton felt it essential to establish the mood of apprehension right from the start, and he frames the whole thing as a subjective flashback. Even a tiny verbal slip by Mrs Grose, which is the first allusion to Quint ('He had the devil's own eye') is more pointed in the film than in the story. Unconventionally, the ghosts appear in daylight and had to be presented in a way that communicated their threat to the children but also distinguished between them. We never get a close look at Miss Jessel, though we do pick up the aura of sadness around her, whereas Quint is thrust before us as a figure, in James's phrase, 'reeking of evil', never more so than in a superb sequence of hide-and-seek, when the governess, playfully hiding from the children, becomes suddenly aware of a spectral, malevolent presence behind her staring in at the window.

Contractually obliged by Twentieth Century Fox to shoot the film in wide-screen Cinemascope format, Clayton and his cameraman Freddie Francis devised a strategy of putting objects at the corner of the frames slightly out of focus, to give the sense of something unnervingly glimpsed on the fringes of perception. Challenged by the prospect of respecting the story's ambiguity but needing to give the ghosts a palpable presence, Clayton and his editor Jim Clark hit upon the ingenious solution of reversing cause and effect by invariably showing the governess's reaction to what she sees before revealing the thing itself, thus suggesting that it is the response that might be producing the visions rather than the other way round.

A sequence early in the film exemplifies a number of its themes and strategies. Miles has unexpectedly returned home, expelled from school for reasons as yet unclear. On the night of his return, the governess has paused outside his room and then been surprised when a voice from within invites her to enter: how has he known she was there? Is this evidence of Miles's supernatural powers or is it simply, as he explains, that this is a very old house and he has heard her foot-steps? There is a similar moment at the end of the scene when the candle suddenly goes out at the point when the governess is begin-ning to press Miles about his school experience: is it the flash of his eyes that causes this, as if warning her not to get too close, or is it, as he suggests, a gust of wind? Clayton makes such incidents eerily ambiguous, offering explanations that are more or less equally plau-sible. While tantalising us with these ghostly elements, he also has his eye on the human drama. How well he and Deborah Kerr catch the governess's nervousness here, as she tries to raise the subject of the boy's expulsion without upsetting him, and also her defensiveness when Miles moves the subject on to the uncle's indifference. How well he and young Stephens convey Miles's ostensible man-of-the-house precocity as he calmly describes his uncle's lack of concern, only to disclose his sensitivity when the governess, professing her own devotion, is surprised to find Miles silently crying.[2]

Dissolve to a huge rose in the garden as the governess clips it: a subliminal romantic reminder to her of the uncle perhaps (he has already been associated with roses in the film) and also an image that reminds us of a tendency in her to magnify things. It is a beautiful sunny morning; Flora is singing quietly in the background; every-thing seems right with the world. The governess spies an opening in the garden but is disconcerted by the sight of a broken Cupid statue that first echoes then fractures her reverie, all the more so when a black beetle drops from its mouth like a tongue. Suddenly the atmosphere of contented drowsiness changes: the sound dips, an electric hum fills the soundtrack as if something unearthly is stirring, and the governess looks up into the sun to see the hazy figure of a man standing at the top of the tower and looking down at her. The shot is held momentarily; a pigeon flutters past in seeming slow motion; and then the governess drops her scissors in the fountain, the sound resumes as normal, the spell is broken. But what has hap-pened? Finding Miles at the top of the tower tending to some pigeons, she asks if he has seen the person, but Miles denies it.

'Maybe you imagined it,' he says. Has it been a hallucination, or is there a suggestion at this early stage of a diabolical complicity between Miles and Quint? This tightrope of possibilities will be grippingly maintained as governess and ghosts do battle. The finale is terrifying, because the governess has herself become a figure of fear, her behaviour veering into self-vindication as much as self-sacrifice. After all, if the children were actually as innocent as they claim, what does that make her?

There is a perfect match between Deborah Kerr's performance and her persona. Appearing in every scene, she develops a characterisation seen so deeply from the inside that she seems to change physically under the pressure of events. As her performances in films such as *Black Narcissus* (Powell and Pressburger, 1947), *Tea and Sympathy* (Minnelli, 1956) and *Heaven Knows, Mr Allison* (Huston, 1957) demonstrate, she was at her best when suggesting repressed passion beneath a surface of prim respectability. One could even see her performance here as a nuanced neurotic counterpart to her governess in *The King and I* (Lang, 1956). In that film, whenever she feels afraid, she whistles a happy tune. In *The Innocents*, whenever she feels afraid, she takes it out on the children.

Although highly praised at the time, the film was not a box-office success, perhaps being too artily obscure and downbeat for mass appeal. With subsequent films such as *The Pumpkin Eater* (1964) and *The Lonely Passion of Judith Hearne* (1987), Clayton was again to show his facility and compassion in exploring feminine feeling, something first signaled in Simone Signoret's revelatory performance in *Room at the Top*. However, as Pauline Kael once remarked of Charles Laughton's thriller, *The Night of the Hunter* (1955), truly frightening films become classics of a kind even if unappreciated at the time, and over the years, the reputation of *The Innocents* has grown (1968: 397). One particular accolade stands out. Dining in a restaurant in France in the early 1980s, Clayton was handed a message by a waiter from one of the diners sitting opposite. It read simply: '*The Innocents* – the best English film since Hitchcock left for America'. The signatory was François Truffaut – never the most complimentary commentator on British cinema, but, in this instance, absolutely right.

Notes

1 William Archibald and John Mortimer were also involved in work on the screenplay at various stages.
2 Stephens was already an experienced child actor who had recently given a sinister performance in *Village of the Damned* (Wolf Rilla, 1960).

Further Reading

Gordon Gow, 'The Way Things Are: An Interview with Jack Clayton', *Films and Filming*, April 1974, pp. 10–14.

Henry James, *The Art of the Novel: Critical Prefaces*, New York, Charles Scribner's Sons, 1907.

Pauline Kael, *Kiss Kiss Bang Bang*, Boston, MA, Little Brown, 1968.

Brian McFarlane, *An Autobiography of British Cinema*, London, Methuen, 1997.

Neil Sinyard, *Jack Clayton*, Manchester, Manchester University Press, 2000.

NEIL SINYARD

A TASTE OF HONEY (1961)

[Production Company: Woodfall Film Productions. Director and producer: Tony Richardson. Screenwriters: Shelagh Delaney and Tony Richardson. Cinematographer: Walter Lassally. Music: John Addison. Editor: Anthony Gibbs. Cast: Dora Bryan (Helen), Rita Tushingham (Jo), Robert Stephens (Peter), Murray Melvin (Geoffrey), Paul Danquah (Jimmy).]

A Taste of Honey is a central film of the British New Wave. The origins of the New Wave lie, at least partly, outside of the realm of cinema, in developments which occurred in literature and the theatre during the late 1950s. The sources for these films are almost always to be found among the group of young writers (John Osborne, Alan Sillitoe, Shelagh Delaney, Stan Barstow) whose work changed the face of British fiction and drama in this period and which was dubbed by the popular press as the 'kitchen sink' or 'angry young man' style. Their adoption of social realism as a form and their depiction of working-class frustration broke radically with dominant literary trends, particularly in the theatre where the 1956 production of Osborne's *Look Back in Anger* was a landmark. For Stephen Lacey, its significance lay in the way it challenged the common perception of 1950s theatre as being 'dominated by pre-war personnel and reactionary social and aesthetic values' (Lacey 1995: 22). The first production of Osborne's play by the English Stage Company at the Royal Court Theatre was directed by Tony Richardson, who would go on to helm a number of the New Wave films, including *A Taste of Honey*.

Another source which the New Wave drew upon was the realist tradition within both British and European cinema. Richardson described the experience of seeing the films of the Italian Neo-Realists as 'like emerging from a house whose windows and rooms have long been boarded over and air and places and people being revealed outside' (Richardson 1993: 67). The work of the British documentary movement, especially the films of Humphrey Jennings, provided another reference point for the New Wave directors and in part led to the use of the documentary form by all of them at some stage in their careers. Several of these documentaries were shown as part of a series of six programmes at the National Film Theatre (1956–1959) under the banner 'Free Cinema'. These were organised by Lindsay Anderson and Karel Reisz who, along with Richardson, formed the nucleus of the New Wave group.

All three film-makers shared a common view of contemporary British cinema, and the wider national culture, which reacted angrily to its middle-class timidity and conformism. As chief polemicist, Anderson proclaimed that British films were 'snobbish, anti-intelligent, emotionally inhibited, wilfully blind to the conditions and problems of the present, dedicated to an out-of-date, exhausted national idea' (Anderson 2004: 234). Their aim was to revitalise British film-making by making it relevant to contemporary audiences. In practice, this meant adopting the techniques of documentary-realism to give their films a sense of authenticity and immediacy. At the same time, they were dedicated to a cinema of personal vision which should strive towards art and reflect the sensibility of the individual film-maker. This combination of naturalism and auteurism drew heavily on the examples set by Humphrey Jennings and the directors of the Italian Neo-Realist movement such as Roberto Rossellini. The aim was not sociology, but social commitment. This is also reflected in what might otherwise seem to be a wilfully eclectic critical standpoint, whereby Anderson was an acknowledged admirer of both documentarists like Jennings and Hollywood auteurs like John Ford.

To further his cinematic ambitions, Richardson founded the production company Woodfall in collaboration with Osborne and the producer Harry Saltzman. Their initial intention was to film versions of Osborne's plays, but both *Look Back in Anger* (1959) and *The Entertainer* (1960) were hampered by their theatrical origins, remaining defiantly uncinematic and retaining interest principally as a record of the plays. A more successful model was provided by Jack Clayton's film of John Braine's novel *Room at the Top* (1958). The film's depiction of a working-class hero on the rise, along with its frank attitude towards sex, chimed with the mood of the time and the film was a box-office success. Woodfall's commercial breakthrough was to come with *Saturday Night and Sunday Morning* (1960), produced by Richardson,

directed by Reisz and adapted from Alan Sillitoe's novel. Its affectionate, dynamic portrayal of a discontented lathe operator, played
with charismatic gusto by Albert Finney, had enormous appeal, particularly to young working-class audiences who identified with the
central character. The increasing confidence of Woodfall, along with
their desire to move away from the staginess of their first films,
provided the context for the making of *A Taste of Honey*.

The New Wave films have provoked considerable academic debate
as to their merits and deficiencies. Roy Armes was among the first to
offer a critique, focusing on what he saw as a lack of emotional
engagement on the part of the film-makers with the subjects they
were filming (Armes 1978: 263–279). Armes attributes this to their
middle-class backgrounds which, he suggests, prevents them from
feeling any personal identification with the characters depicted. A
more systematic approach is taken by John Hill who takes issue with
many aspects of these films. Expanding on Armes's position, he
argues that the film-makers' distance from their subject matter is
reflected in their depiction of northern industrial landscapes as little
more than a form of visual tourism (Hill 1986: 132–133). He also
suggests that the working-class male is presented as a figure motivated
by 'an ideology of individualism', where personal gain is foregrounded over any sense of community or class loyalty and no political solution is offered (Hill 1983: 110–111). For Hill, this is
indicative of the middle-class, conformist ideology of the New Wave
films. Hill then raises issues relating to gender politics, suggesting
'there was more than a streak of misogyny running through the films
and a failure to acknowledge the changing social and economic role
of women in British society' (Hill 1986: 174). Female characters,
therefore, are inevitably associated negatively with the social pressure
applied to the male hero to conform via marriage and fatherhood.
Considering that these films were supposed to represent a break from
the dominant attitudes of the 1950s, Hill concludes that 'the "new"
British cinema, in this respect, was neither as novel nor, certainly, as
radical as has sometimes been claimed' (Hill 1986: 179).

A more sympathetic account of the films is offered by Robert
Murphy, who accuses Hill of adhering to a rigid form of Marxist
analysis: 'His Marxist Puritanism leads him into dangerously wide
generalisations' (Murphy 1992: 31). As an example of this, he points
to the fact that the selfish actions of the male heroes in these films,
particularly in relation to the female characters, are always shown to have
their consequences. The nature of their relationship with the women in
their lives is always both central and complex within the narrative; the

dilemmas they face reflect the contingencies of the time. He also argues forcefully for the significance of the roles allowed to women within these allegedly misogynistic texts: 'These incandescently intense women have a seriousness, an emotional weight, altogether lacking in the pathetically trivial roles women had to play in most 1950s British films' (Murphy 1992: 33).

It is useful to analyse *A Taste of Honey* in light of these debates. The film certainly doesn't conform to Hill's argument regarding the misogynistic nature of the New Wave. The central character, Jo (Rita Tushingham), is female and the audience is openly invited to share her viewpoint. Although her mother, Helen (Dora Bryan), might fall into the category of the female stereotype which Hill describes (she is certainly materialistic and views marriage principally as a means to financial security), her ambiguous relationship with Jo complicates matters considerably. Even the sense that she is stifling Jo's chances of happiness is undercut by the obvious affection between the two; a sequence near the film's conclusion shows them fighting, but when Geoffrey (Murray Melvin) tries to intervene Helen shoos him off, saying: 'Don't be so silly, we enjoy it'. Although Jo's lover, Jimmy (Paul Danquah), abandons her, there is no sense of gender antagonism, only of regret. Geoffrey, who is Jo's closest friend, is a long way from the swaggering braggadocio of the typical New Wave hero, being sensitive, gentle and gay. Although the script deals with his homosexuality in a mainly indirect manner, the character is drawn with considerable sympathy.

Hill suggests that the New Wave directors betray their sense of distance from their subjects through an overly pictorial visual style, typified by what Andrew Higson has called 'That Long Shot Of Our Town From That Hill' (Higson 1996: 134). Of course, it might be argued that the industrial townscapes of Northern England are as beautiful in their way as more traditional landscapes and that the views of Higson and Hill betray a certain snobbery. There are certainly many examples in *A Taste of Honey* which conform to this critique. Richardson and his cameraman Walter Lassally frequently linger on shots of the grey Salford backstreets and its misty canals in a dreamy, lyrical manner. However, reading Richardson's account of the location shooting indicates the degree to which these scenes represented a form of liberation for the director (Richardson 1993: 120–122). Finally away from the studio and the controlling interference of executives, Richardson uses camera movement, cinematography and music to convey a feeling of spontaneity and freedom, even in these grim settings. The visual lyricism might be read as an indication of the spirit of the characters, rather than a sense of distance in the film-maker. Higson suggests this is a long way from documentary realism and Richardson certainly appears to be striving to move beyond the limitations of surface naturalism towards a more overtly personal style.

Another key criticism of the New Wave films relates to their endorsement of personal self-interest over communal values. Again, a close examination of *A Taste of Honey* tends to contradict this. It is hard to see Jo as a self-interested character; she tends to be portrayed as confused and vulnerable. Her decision to go ahead with her pregnancy suggests altruism, rather than selfishness, and her relationships with Jimmy, Geoffrey and even her mother are marked by empathy and mutual support. The household she creates with Geoffrey is a form of improvised family unit, with the roles of father and mother open to constant renegotiation. The final image of Jo, clutching a sparkler, seems cautiously optimistic. An earlier sequence of Jo and Geoffrey out walking is full of youthful vigour and energy ('We're bloody fantastic'), prefiguring the youth explosion of swinging London. Jo and Geoffrey are contrasted sharply with an older generation who are blatantly materialistic in outlook. In retrospect, the film's sympathetic depiction of a black man, a young woman and a gay man, mark it as an indicator of changing attitudes and the liberalisation of British culture.

Further Reading

Lindsay Anderson, 'Get Out and Push!' in Paul Ryan, *Never Apologise – The Collected Writings: Lindsay Anderson*, London, Plexus, 2004. Originally published in Tom Maschler, *Declaration*, 1957.

Roy Armes, *A Critical History of British Cinema*, London, Secker and Warburg, 1978.

Andrew Higson, 'Space, Place, Spectacle: Landscape and Townscape in the "Kitchen Sink" Film' in Andrew Higson (ed.) *Dissolving Views: Key Writings on British Cinema*, London and New York, Cassell, 1996. Originally published in *Screen*, Vol. 25, Nos. 4 & 5, July & October 1984.

John Hill, 'Working Class Realism and Sexual Reaction: Some Theses on the British "New Wave"' in James Curran and Vincent Porter (eds) *British Cinema History*, London, Weidenfeld and Nicolson, 1983.

——, *Sex, Class and Realism: British Cinema 1956–1963*, London, BFI, 1986.

Stephen Lacey, *British Realist Theatre: The New Wave in its Context 1956–1965*, London, Routledge, 1995.

Robert Murphy, *Sixties British Cinema*, London, BFI, 1992.

Tony Richardson, *Long Distance Runner: A Memoir*, London, Faber, 1993.

Alexander Walker, *Hollywood England: The British Film Industry in the Sixties*, London, Harrap, 1986.

ROBERT SHAIL

LAWRENCE OF ARABIA (1962)

[Production Company: Horizon Pictures. Director: David Lean. Screenwriters: Robert Bolt and Michael Wilson. Cinematographer: Freddie Young. Music: Maurice Jarre. Editor: Anne V. Coates. Cast: Peter O'Toole (T. E. Lawrence), Alec Guinness (Prince Feisal), Anthony Quinn (Auda abu Tayi), Jack Hawkins (General Lord Allenby), Omar Sharif (Sherif Ali).]

Academy Award winning *Lawrence of Arabia* is a film of its time, resplendent in the grandeur of the British Empire and in offering a challenge to orthodoxy to be echoed across the 1960s. An epic, shot in Super Panavision 70 mm on location in the deserts of Jordan and Morocco, and in Spain, it is British film-making at its best, and in terms of its cinematography and score it offers an evocative, emotional, and profound experience.

Beginning with T. E. Lawrence's accidental death in the leafy country lanes of the Home Counties, the film adopts a traditional conceit of having newspaper reporters researching background to the story of this remarkable man. Flashing back to a series of World War I exploits, *Lawrence of Arabia* enables director David Lean to explore issues of 'Britishness', duty, personal identity, violence, and sexuality.

Casting Peter O'Toole as Lawrence, Lean presented him with an opportunity to show his range on a grand scale. O'Toole exploited this to the full, creating a tour de force and what is often cited as his greatest performance. However, O'Toole was not to play the recalcitrant, elusive figure that history suggests was the real Lawrence, but instead a man of contradictions and masochistic tendencies, who was an egotist, and, most contentiously, homosexual. Across the original 221 minutes running time, the screenwriters played out this characterisation against a cinematic backdrop that allowed audiences to see what widescreen could be used to achieve.

Cinematographer Freddie Young chose to emphasise the vastness of landscape and de-emphasise individuals within it. This was in line with Lean's vision of the disconnected Lawrence who seemed to grow more in tune with the nature and rhythms of desert life and more alienated by the regimentation and restriction of 'civilised' army life. Indeed this duality and the conflict it caused are central to Lean's story, and Young reflects this through his composition, camera movement, and lighting. There are many bold aspects of cinematography such as the oasis introduction of Sherif Ali (Omar Sharif). The script demanded that Sherif Ali emerge out of a desert mirage, something notoriously difficult to capture on film due to its inherent 'distant' nature, but Young solved this through the use of an extremely long lens allowing effectively the production of a 'close up' of Sherif Ali through the mirage. The resulting image is of a 'dot' on screen slowly being revealed as an Arab riding a camel, and duly coming to prominence over the juxtaposed image of Lawrence and another native at the oasis; a truly cinematic sequence through its outstanding cinematography, the rhythm and tension of its editing, the build of the soundtrack, and an overall boldness in presenting the lengthy arrival in virtually real time. (Of course, the sequence completely fails to have the same effect on television where Sherif Ali remains less than a pixel for much of his journey.)

In the shooting of Lawrence's companion, Lean presents the audience with a divergence of cultures, between the restraint and 'fair play' of the young British officer, and the perceived 'barbarism' of the Arab (there is irony here in the fact that the gun the Arab companion was running for was given to him by Lawrence – a commentary on the cause of problems in the region that is built upon through the film). Lean however does not simply dismiss Sherif Ali's actions as barbaric, but allows Lawrence to become influenced by such approaches; and it could be suggested that in not overtly criticising such actions Lean has some sympathy for this clarity and purity of decision and action. He certainly allows his Lawrence to lose his British values and adopt those of the tribesmen, and increasingly depicts Lawrence's superiors as inept, suffocated and repressed individuals who would prefer to lose than adopt any tactic that seemed somehow un-British.

Lawrence's relationship with his superior General Allenby (Jack Hawkins) is re-visioned for the film and bears little resemblance to historical truth. Of course, a difficult relationship between subordinate and superior is the stuff of conflict, and as such is almost an inevitable path for a screenwriter if given the option, but the choice of such a depiction is more likely to have been fostered in order to structure an anti-war message, whilst retaining the protagonist's war-focused actions. Co-writer Michael Wilson was blacklisted in the McCarthy Congressional hearings into anti-American behaviour, and his left-leaning sympathies, coupled with an understandably strong anti-authoritarian stance, led to his creating a fictional world where the 'civilised' nations were in moral crisis, and where he celebrated the 'natural' societal ordering of the tribesmen.

The anti-war message can be read as deriding the 'dishonour' of modern warfare in favour of the courage and purity in battle presented by the Arab tribesmen. Certainly, in looking at Lawrence leading a band of 50 tribesmen into battle against superior forces with superior weaponry, their 'honour' and valour re-contextualises any perceived pacifist views. This honour is placed to the fore in a scene where, to resolve a blood feud that looks set to wreck his plans of uniting the Arab tribes, Lawrence has to execute a killer who is revealed to be Gasim (I. S. Johar), a tribesman he saved from death previously. Lawrence conducts the execution regardless of this fact (and shows little concern in carrying it out) and honour is restored, but he is already now moving away from his British proscribed values and embracing the more emotionally attuned values of the tribesmen.

This theme could reflect world events of the time, with the Korean War having ended in a stalemate under a decade earlier and Vietnam entering a wider public consciousness with American involvement moving towards outright war. Both Korea and Vietnam would have held particular parallels with the Middle East at the time of Lawrence, with great empires playing out their political moves over a battlefield that in itself held little value yet offered significant strategic value to a post-war victor.

The issue of identity is co-joined inexorably with that of duty and is most clearly explored in O'Toole's anguished portrayal of Lawrence, torn between his British identity and his emerging Arab identity (with his 'purer' loyalty to those fighting beside him). This again is reflected in the use of setting within the film, with Lawrence seemingly most comfortable when isolated and surrounded only by the arid widescreen desert, and at his most uncomfortable when in his pressed uniform and crowded by the military machine and the cityscape. There is a duplicity in the British officers that is not portrayed in the Arab tribesmen who live by strict tribal codes and customs. When with 'his own people' Lawrence develops suspicions as to the post-conflict political aspirations of the colonial powers and becomes conscious of the complex web underpinning the relative simplicity of his war.

This understanding of political motives marks a turning point in the film and in the character of Lawrence with both film and character becoming darker and more troubled. Lawrence takes to adopting guerrilla warfare tactics and using the natural advantages presented by native knowledge and the landscape to secure victories over an 'alien' occupier. This would again resonate with an audience familiar with the Korean War and with the experiences of the French in Vietnam. Lawrence's approach slowly becomes more aggressive, and to some eyes more barbaric. His shooting of one of his injured men rather than leave him to the Turks is another milestone on his transformation and forces the spectator to confront their own cultural views in deciding whether this was a civilised act or an act of barbarism indicating a decline in values.

A further turning point is when Lawrence is rounded up with a number of Arabs whilst scouting the enemy city of Dara. Taken to the Turkish Bey (played with camp decadence by Jose Ferrer) Lawrence is tortured for the Bey's pleasure, and there is a clear implication that he is raped before being returned to the streets of Dara. Male rape was certainly not a subject for feature films at the time, and was one that the censors would have dealt with quickly and assiduously, and yet Lean evidently believed this was an important sequence for the exploration of Lawrence's sexuality. O'Toole's rather effeminate Lawrence is unquestionably traumatised by the event, and suffers a crisis of identity, returning to the safety (and repression) of his British culture.

Back in Jerusalem (British Army Headquarters) Lawrence is seen to have undergone a significant transformation through the direct challenge to his sexuality, leading to a change in temperament and morality. The impact of one empire (the Turkish Bey) on another (Lawrence) is to propel one towards ever increasing barbarism, and this is reflected in Lawrence ordering the execution of any potential prisoners in the battle at Tafas, leading to a massacre of fleeing Turkish troops – a massacre that would for the audience at the time have been reminiscent of stories of Nazi or Japanese atrocities during World War II. Lawrence has adopted the culture of the tribesmen, and in doing so has succumbed to the allure of violence.

Unsurprisingly for a war film, *Lawrence of Arabia* structures much of its narrative progression around violent acts. The violence of the film is particularly visceral (for its time) and is foregrounded within the natural landscape dwarfing the actions of humankind. The truly shocking context of the violence however is that it is largely presented as a matter of fact, often with little or no emotional impact on the characters, and often as casual or even ritualistic. There is a lonely feel to much of the violence, as if it segregates those involved from a wider community, whilst this wider community expects the violence to be carried out as a cultural duty. This loneliness is again reflected in the landscape of the film and emphasised by the widescreen compositions.

Lean's brutal tribesmen are unable to work together constructively to administer Damascus when they drive out the Turks and achieve their victory, and consequently allow the British to take control (symbolically allowing them post-war control of the region). Lawrence, who culturally is now more Arab than British, is also unable to bring the tribesmen together and clearly Lean is celebrating a set of British 'qualities' that Lawrence has lost by assuming Arab identity. In 'going native' Lawrence is seen to have lost the very thing that allowed him to bring the disparate tribes together in the first place, and so finds himself of use to neither culture. Left in the lonely landscape once more, Lawrence is sent home and fights the loneliness of a different, restrictive landscape by thrill-seeking and riding his motorbike too fast down slow-paced English country lanes.

Lean's story ends where it begins, offering a circular narrative, a symbolically rich device that indicates an inevitability that mirrors some of the philosophy of the Arab world in which fate plays a significant hand (Lawrence indicates the hand of Destiny at several places in the film). Within this circular narrative there is an emptiness that is amplified by the vast scale of the images, which whilst at times heavily populated, still have an uncompromising loneliness at their centre, perhaps suggesting this was at the centre of Lean's Lawrence as he fought to discover who he was rather than what he was expected to be, or perhaps suggesting that this loneliness, this lack of self-initiated identity, is central to the region's continuing problems.

Further Reading

Steven Caton, 'Lawrence of Arabia': A Film's Anthropology, Berkeley, University of California, 1999.

L. Robert Morris and Lawrence Raskin, 'Lawrence of Arabia': the 30th Anniversary Pictorial History, New York, Doubleday, 1992.

ScreenOnline's Lawrence of Arabia (http://www.screenonline.org.uk/film/id/477570/index.html).

Britmovie's Lawrence of Arabia (http://www.britmovie.co.uk/directors/d_lean/filmography/004.html).

Adrian Turner, The Making of David Lean's 'Lawrence of Arabia', Limpsfield, Dragon's World, 1994.

FREDDIE GAFFNEY

A HARD DAY'S NIGHT (1964)

[Production Company: Proscenium Films/United Artists. Director: Richard Lester. Screenwriter: Alun Owen. Cinematographer: Gilbert Taylor. Editor: John Jympson. Music: John Lennon, Paul McCartney. Cast: The Beatles, Wilfrid Brambell (Paul's grandfather), Norman Rossington (Norm), John Junkin (Shake), Anna Quayle (Milie), Lionel Blair (TV Choreographer).]

Although originally intended as little more than an 'exploitation' film, made hurriedly to cash in on the latest pop sensation whose fame was not expected to last, *A Hard Day's Night* has instead proved to be a remarkably durable piece of film-making – just as the fame of its stars, The Beatles, has long outlasted their 1960s heyday. The film was backed by the Hollywood studio United Artists who had already had a number of international commercial hits with films made in Britain such as the first of the James Bond franchise *Dr No* (Terence Young, 1962) and the bawdy literary adaptation *Tom Jones* (Tony Richardson, 1963), and were keen to develop the British-based arm of their operation. Like many other British films of the 1960s, *A Hard Day's Night* should be regarded as an Anglo-American film rather than strictly British, for as Alexander Walker points out, 'to talk of "British" cinema in these years is to ignore the reality of what underpinned the industry – namely, American finance' (2005: 16). In Richard Lester, the film even had an American director, albeit one who had made his home in Britain. A child prodigy who had attended university as a teenager, Lester had already worked in television and advertising in America and Britain, and had also directed several films, including the pop film *It's Trad, Dad!* (1962), when he took on *A Hard Day's Night*. However, what most impressed the Beatles was his association with the anarchic comedy troupe, the Goons (Spike Milligan, Peter Sellers, Harry Secombe and Michael Bentine), having directed and composed the score for their home-movie-turned-art-house-hit *The Running, Jumping and Standing Still Film* (1959) as well as overseeing their forays into television.

Lester's background in the surreal, establishment-mocking comedy of the Goons was one of the things that helped give *A Hard Day's Night* a tone that was distinctly different from previous British pop films, like the well-behaved star vehicles for Cliff Richard and Tommy Steele. Along with visuals influenced by the French New Wave and contemporary documentary, characterised by choppy handheld camerawork and staccato editing (and the decision to film in black and white), Lester invented 'a style which helped carry the group forward to another stage of development rather than pushing them into the arms of traditional show-business' (Murphy 1992: 136). Considerable credit for the breakthrough should also go to Alun Owen, the film's script-writer, whose previous experience writing gritty television drama, often set in Liverpool (most famously his 1959 ITV play, *No Trams to Lime Street*) enabled him to bring a version of the Beatles to the screen that was sharply colloquial rather than soppily anodyne. However, Owen's freedom to write that way was only achieved thanks to the efforts of producer Walter Shenson, who had learnt from the American success of his Ealing-esque comedy *The Mouse That Roared* (Jack Arnold, 1959) that a very British movie could still be a transatlantic hit; it was Shenson who insisted on the Liverpudlian idiom being used in *A Hard Day's Night*. As Alexander Walker points out, 'a less resolute producer, whose confidence in local accents hadn't been boosted by a fortune at the international box-office, might have yielded to pressure to give the film an American slant' (2005: 229–230).

Shenson was also behind the decision to give each of the band members their own scene to overturn the idea of them as four indistinguishable mop-tops. He outlined his aims in an article for the *Evening Standard* in June 1964: 'Get each boy on his own for a stretch of film and show him as an individual. Get away from any notion of the Beatles as a four-headed monster.'[1] Both George's and John's solo moments revolve around mistaken identity (George is mixed up with an advertising stooge when he accidentally goes into the wrong room, John is recognised by a woman at the TV studio who then changes her mind and tells him that he doesn't look very much like himself at all), while Ringo's interlude, the longest and arguably most successful in the film, has him temporarily escaping from his duties to do normal things like go for a walk and have a drink in a pub. Wandering by the river, he chats to a truanting schoolboy whom he recognises as a fellow 'deserter'. The sequence blends slapstick humour (Ringo's attempts to play various games in the pub, from bar billiards to darts, all end in disaster) with an undertow of melancholy about the losses inherent in the proscribed lifestyle of a Beatle. Throughout the film, Ringo is depicted as the least self-assured, most vulnerable member of the band, and as George Melly noted, his 'loveably plain' persona provided 'a bridge, reassuring proof that the Beatles bear some relation to ordinary people' (1972: 69). Paul is the only Beatle missing a solo scene – his planned scene, an encounter with an actress rehearsing her lines, was cut because it didn't fit into the overall flow of the final film and held up the action too much.

A Hard Day's Night opens with a sequence focused on rapid physical movement – George, John and Ringo running towards the camera, away from a hoard of screaming fans, to the accompaniment of the film's title song – and a sense of perpetual motion dominates the film, right through to its final moments, in which the band leap onto a helicopter waiting to whisk them away to yet another engagement. The film's loose episodic narrative is kept from meandering too much by what Lester calls its 'time clock' element (Gelmis 1971: 260), the countdown to the big event, their televised concert. But this is jeopardised by the sudden disappearance of Ringo, who goes AWOL after sly encouragement from Paul's mischievous grandfather, 'Mixing' John McCartney (Wilfred Brambell), accompanying them on their tour.

The inclusion of McCartney Senior was a smart move: he acts as an important dramatic catalyst by continually getting into scrapes and causing arguments. Brambell, an experienced stage and television performer, also brought a backbone of reliable professionalism to a film whose four main performers were all novices to acting.[2] Brambell's character also utters what is perhaps the key line of dialogue in the film, complaining, 'I thought I was getting a change of scenery and so far I've been in a train and a room and a car and a room and a room and a room'. This deliberately echoes something Lennon said to Lester about their tour dates in Sweden; to him, Stockholm had been nothing more than 'a plane and a room and a car and a cheese sandwich'.[3] This is the obverse of the band's continual movement from place to place: their state of near captivity in a succession of enclosed spaces (the car, the train carriage, the hotel room) because of their fame but also their tight promotional schedule. The film even shows them being bullied into spending their free evenings answering fan letters by their manager Norm (Norman Rossington) – the most obvious case of the film's bowdlerisation of the Beatles' real-life existence at the time, much more likely to involve groupies and drinking than letter-writing.

The one unambiguous moment of freedom in the film comes when all four of the band clatter down the TV studio fire escape and go to a nearby playing field, to do some running and jumping (but hardly any standing still) while *Can't Buy Me Love* accompanies their antics. Slow motion and speeded-up footage are employed, along with aerial photography (about the only time in the film we get to see any outdoor space) and the film's familiar techniques of handheld camera and rapid editing, to create what Neil Sinyard calls 'a definitive short ballet of youthful high spirits' (1985: 25). But even this is curtailed when a groundskeeper turns up to tell them they're trespassing on private property – a moment that Stephen Glynn compares to the arrival of the policeman at the end of Gene Kelly's rain-dance in *Singin' in the Rain* (2005: 72); another authority figure interrupting a display of joyous physical exuberance.

This moment of mutual misunderstanding could be read as an example of the widening generation gap which reached its zenith in the 1960s. The most notable example of this in *A Hard Day's Night* is the confrontation at the beginning of the film between the band and a pompous commuter on the train. He asserts his right to have the window closed because he travels regularly on the train (even though all the other occupants of the carriage want it kept open) and reminds the boys 'I fought the war for your sort', to which Ringo pithily replies 'I bet you're sorry you won'. Perhaps more sinister is the attempt of the older generation to appropriate and capitalise upon youth culture, as illustrated by George's brief encounter with the advertising executive who hands him a couple of shirts and informs him 'you'll like these, you'll really dig them, they're fab and all the other pimply hyperboles', although George tells him that they're 'grotty' (a word Alun Owen made up for the occasion) and refuses to be taken in by the older man's hard sell. But compared to a later 1960s film such as *If . . .* (Lindsay Anderson, 1968), the existence of a generation gap is gently hinted at rather than central to the drama, and the most anti-authoritarian, rebellious figure in the film is Paul's granddad.

The film reaches its climax with the successful televised concert, echoing their actual career-making appearances on British TV; as Glynn recounts, '15 million watch[ed] them top the bill on *Sunday Night at the London Palladium* (13 October 1963) while 26 million saw their appearance on the *Royal Variety Performance* (4 November 1963)' (2005: 65). The final concert also provides an important showcase for several of the soundtrack album's songs, as well as replaying older favourites like *She Loves You*. During that track, the camera swish-pans across the screaming audience and picks out individual cameos, including one blonde-haired girl to whom it returns several times as her state of frantic excitement tips over into tearful melancholy, suggesting a darker side of the young women's orgiastic adoration of the Beatles.

A Hard Day's Night is the definitive visual document of Beatlemania at its height, showing both the passionate pursuit of the fans but also the difficulty for the band of being, to use Lester's apposite phrase, 'revolutionaries in a goldfish bowl' (Gelmis 1971: 316). The film continues to exert an influence on contemporary film-making (most obviously perhaps in *Spiceworld: The Movie* (Bob Spiers 1997), which closely follows its 'day-in-the-life of a band' template) and Lester's influence on the nascent form of the music video was openly acknowledged by MTV who sent the director a scroll declaring him to be the father of the channel. But the film's ultimate achievement is to encapsulate what the Beatles brought to British (and later international) popular culture in the 1960s, 'the emergence of a new spirit: post-war, clever, nonconformist, and above all cool' (Melly 1972: 75).

Notes

1 Article taken from BFI microfiche on *A Hard Day's Night*.
2 Brambell was best known for his role as the weasly patriarch in the BBC comedy series *Steptoe and Son* (1962–1974), alluded to throughout this film by constant protestations from the cast that the TV show's 'dirty old man' Steptoe is actually 'very clean'.
3 Quoted in Sinyard, 1985, p. 24.

Further Reading

Joseph Gelmis, *The Film Director as Superstar*, London, Secker and Warburg, 1971.
Stephen Glynn, *A Hard Day's Night*, London, I.B. Tauris, 2005.
George Melly, *Revolt into Style: The Pop Arts in Britain*, Harmondsworth, Penguin, 1972.
Robert Murphy, *Sixties British Cinema*, London, BFI, 1992.
Neil Sinyard, *The Films of Richard Lester*, London, Croom Helm, 1985.
Alexander Walker, *Hollywood England*, London, Orion, 2005.

MELANIE WILLIAMS

GOLDFINGER (1964)

[Production Company: Danjaq and Eon Productions. Director: Guy Hamilton. Screenwriter: Richard Maibaum, Paul Dehn. Cinematographer: Ted Moore. Editor: Peter Hunt. Music: John Barry. Cast: Sean Connery (James Bond), Honor Blackman (Pussy Galore), Gert Frobe (Auric Goldfinger), Shirley Eaton (Jill Masterson), Harold Sakata (Oddjob), Bernard Lee (M).]

The erosion of modern commercial cinema – where spectacle takes precedence over narrative logic – began with a stuffed seagull. What may seem like an insolent statement describes an insolent moment in the history of British cinema. After the established trademark Bond-shooting-through-the-gun-barrel motif, *Goldfinger* opens with a crane shot, pulling away from an industrial refinery to the waterfront beside it, on which the aforementioned seabird is paddling. Only it is not a seagull: it's a disguise – a disguise on the head of 007. Enter James Bond and what follows in the pre-credits sequence is what can only be described as a 'mini-adventure', narratively having no relation to the rest of the film (apart from serving to send Bond to Miami where he will first encounter Goldfinger). So while the pre-credits sequence may have no narrative reason to be there, and does not feature in Ian Fleming's original novel, it is important for thematic and commercial reasons.

James Bond had burst onto British cinema screens in 1962 with *Dr. No* (Terence Young), presenting a colourful and exotic change from the black and white kitchen-sink dramas of the British New Wave. The following year, James Bond returned in *From Russia with Love* (Young), which introduced the series' tradition of a pre-credits sequence. However, unlike *Goldfinger*, this sequence was important narratively: despite the shock of apparently killing off Bond, it introduced the machinations of SPECTRE and the threat posed by Red Grant (Robert Shaw). While Bond was becoming an established part of the cinematic landscape, the formula of the films was being refined. *Dr. No* introduced the essential elements: Bond himself, the 'Bond girl', the villain and his lair, shooting abroad, humour, and technology verging on science-fiction; whereas *From Russia with Love* remains the closest in the series to a straight spy-thriller, even with the arrival of *Casino Royale* (Martin Campbell, 2006). But it is *Goldfinger* which perfects the formula, so much so that many commentators have described it as 'the archetypal Bond film in terms of its narrative structure and balance of thriller, science-fiction and comedy elements' (Chapman 1999: 111).

It's the comedy elements that come to the fore in the opening of *Goldfinger*. Back to the stuffed seagull – the notion that Britain's top secret agent would utilise such a gimmick is ridiculous. For the first time in the series, the audience is invited to laugh at James Bond rather than with him; previously, Bond's humour had taken the form of cruel or sardonic witticisms in one-liners, often after a villain has been violently dispatched (since appropriated by the Hollywood blockbuster). However, the ridiculous nature of the image is mitigated by the persona of Bond, established and embodied by Sean Connery, and is cast aside as soon as Bond discards the disguise. Yet, it sends out a clear signal to the audience: don't take anything too seriously over the next 109 minutes. As Penelope Houston observed, *Goldfinger* 'assumes a mood of good-humoured complicity with the audience' (1964–1965: 16). Few British films, outside of comedy, had done this before; it went against the perceived national tradition of quality and realism.

Back to the stuffed seagull: it isn't real, it's a decoy. A recurring theme in *Goldfinger* is that appearances are deceptive: nothing is quite what it seems. This is nothing new to the spy thriller of course, but taken to extremes here and, once more, insolently going against the British notion of 'realism'. Apart from the seagull, the pre-credits sequence features silos hiding heroin factories, bananas hiding heroin, the duplicitous belly dancer, Bonita, and Bond's wetsuit stripped off to reveal an immaculate white tuxedo beneath. The latter is another example of Houston's 'good-humoured complicity', but it goes a bit further. There's a game going on between the film-makers and the audience. It's a playful way of inviting the audience to work out what's really going on: take in the spectacle and see the truth beneath. The world of spies and espionage is a dangerous game, but in the sphere of Bond it's a world where cars contain ejector seats and a playroom can be turned into a base of operations at the flick of a few switches. Through it all, the audience's compass is Bond; the majority of the point-of-view shots belong to 007, and his reactions reflect those of the spectator: 'An ejector seat? You've got to be joking!' is his reaction to Q's demonstration of the gadgets contained within the Austin Martin DB5.

Game playing is also central to the narrative of the film itself, as it is to the Bond 'formula'. Analysing the narrative structure of Fleming's original novels, Umberto Eco used a chess analogy. James Chapman explains that:

> Eco [...] argues that the narrative construction of all the Bond novels is the same and can best be understood as a series of 'moves' in which characters play out familiar situations: Bond is given a mission by M (Head of the British Secret Service); Bond gives first check to the villain, or the villain gives first check to Bond; Bond meets the heroine and seduces her; or begins the process of doing so; Bond and the heroine are captured by the villain; the villain tortures Bond; Bond conquers the villain and possesses the heroine; and so on.
>
> (1999: 32–33)

With some variations, *Goldfinger* acknowledges this structure and foregrounds the game playing through the situations and dialogue. There's the 'customary by-play' between Bond and Moneypenny to quote M. 'What's your game, Mr. Bond?' asks Goldfinger during their first face-to-face encounter on the golf course. We already know, thanks to Jill Masterson (Shirley Eaton), that 'Goldfinger likes to win'. Like all Bond villains, he is a bad loser and what ensues, as in all Bond's encounters with authority figures, is a game of one-upmanship. The same also applies to his encounters with Oddjob (Harold Sakata) and Pussy Galore (Honor Blackman). 'Now let's both play!' says Bond to Pussy during their judo bout prior to the inevitable seduction.

It's here, in the field of sexual politics, that *Goldfinger*'s theme of game playing comes somewhat unstuck. Reflecting the hedonistic ethos of *Playboy* magazine, which frequently published pieces by Fleming, women are there to reinforce Bond's potency and sexual allure. Those who resist are punished: Bonita is knocked out, Tilly Masterson is killed off. Those who indulge his whims survive: Moneypenny's teasing domesticity and Dink the masseuse (whose treatment is probably the most sexist moment in a Bond film until the arrival of Roger Moore in the lead role). This reading becomes problematic when applied to Jill Masterson: she succumbs to Bond but dies. Her role is reduced to that of a trophy to be fought over between Bond and Goldfinger. Her death by gold paint results in one of the most fetishised spectacles in British cinema (and a major selling point for the film), a moment of erotic, even necrophiliac, contemplation. This does give Bond the motivation for revenge, but the narrative strand becomes lost with the introduction of Tilly.

Finally, there's Pussy Galore. Her seduction could have been the most reactionary moment in any Bond film. A lesbian in the original novel (as, indeed, was Tilly), censorship restrictions left only the merest hint of this in *Goldfinger*. She's certainly butch, wears trousers throughout and tells Bond to 'Skip the charm, I'm immune'. But that's the sum of it. The character owes more to the already established persona of Honor Blackman as Cathy Gale in the television series *The Avengers* (1961–1963); indeed the judo scenes were added once she was cast. Blackman was the first Bond girl to have an established acting background, and the first to be given her own voice (previous leading ladies had been dubbed). By the rules of the Bond formula, such a strong female character had to succumb to Bond to bring her ideologically into line, accepting his values: indeed this is the only act he does during the second half of the film which helps bring about the resolution. As Tony Bennett observes, the seduction has the effect of putting her back in the 'correct' place:

> In thus replacing the girl in a subordinate position in relation to men, Bond simultaneously repositions her within the sphere of ideology in general, detaching her from the service of the villain and recruiting her in support of his own mission.
>
> (Bennett and Woollacott 1987: 13)

This reactionary depiction of Bond's potency does stretch the good-humoured complicity of some members of the audience; something the film-makers tried to redress in the following film, *Thunderball*. After a night spent with Bond, the SPECTRE assassin Fiona Volpe (Luciana Paluzzi) taunts him with the words: 'James Bond, who only has to make love to a woman and she starts to hear heavenly choirs singing. She repents and then immediately returns to the side of right and virtue. But not this one!' Inevitably, she is killed off soon after.

While some women remained resistant to Bond's charms, in the real world there was an important market proving equally resistant. Although *Dr. No* and *From Russia With Love* had done well across the world, they had only lukewarm box-office success in America.[1] Part of the problem was that financiers United Artists were unsure how to pitch the product, particularly the British element. With *Goldfinger*, the producers decided to aim squarely at the US market; something British cinema had tried in the past with only a modicum of success. Hence, most of *Goldfinger* is set in Kentucky and Miami and the finale is set in the bastion of American wealth, Fort Knox. Whilst retaining their quintessential British values, Bond films had already appropriated Hollywood production values, particularly through the playful and spectacular set designs of Ken Adam. His interior of Fort Knox bears absolutely no relation to the real thing, yet for a British film it's on an unprecedented scale.

But back to the stuffed seagull: the pre-credits mini-adventure serves to introduce a new audience to the character of Bond, encapsulating his persona in a sequence. It worked. *Goldfinger* received a simultaneous opening in America and Canada of 150 cinemas (small by today's standards, but big in 1964), where box-office quickly passed the $10 million mark, living up to the promise on the film's trailer that it was a 'Bond-Buster!' Following in its wake was the phenomenon of 'Bondmania', a merchandising bonanza ranging from magazine articles, model kits to games and lunch boxes. American cinema responded with their own variations of Bond: *Our Man Flint* (Daniel Mann, 1965) and the *Matt Helm* series starring Dean Martin (four films, 1966–1968), not to mention the television series *The Man from U.N.C.L.E.* (1964–1968). For once, British cinema was showing Hollywood how to make large-scale contemporary action movies.

Yet the stuffed seagull also ushers in the age of cinematic excess. A sequence, filled with spectacle, which had no narrative reason to exist, led the way. From this point, the Bond series would feature action spectacles with bigger and better stunts, often with little narrative logic. And where Bond was successful, others would follow, resulting in the hyperbolic action excess of Hollywood cinema from the 1980s onwards; one particular action hero, Arnold Schwarzenegger, even strips off his wetsuit to reveal a tuxedo underneath in James Cameron's *True Lies* (1994). As Bond himself exclaims: 'Shocking! Positively shocking!'

Note

1 *From Russia with Love* took $9.9 m rentals in North America compared to $19.5 m elsewhere.

Further Reading

Tony Bennett and Janet Woollacott, *Bond and Beyond: The Political Career of a Popular Hero*, London, Macmillan, 1987.
James Chapman, *Licence to Thrill: A Cultural History of the James Bond Films*, London & New York, I. B. Tauris, 1999.
Penelope Houston, '007', *Sight and Sound*, 34/1, Winter 1964–65.
Adrian Turner, *Goldfinger: Bloomsbury Movie Guide No. 2*, London, Bloomsbury, 1998.

NIGEL HERWIN

IF ... (1968)

[Production Company: Memorial Enterprises. Director: Lindsay Anderson. Screenwriters: David Sherwin and Anderson from script 'Crusaders' by Sherwin and John Howlett. Cinematographer: Miroslav Ondricek. Music: Marc Wilkinson. Editor: David Gladwell. Cast: Malcolm McDowell (Mick Travis), David Wood (Johnny Knightly), Richard Warwick (Wallace), Christine Noonan (The Girl), Rupert Webster (Bobby Phillips), Robert Swann (Rowntree), Hugh Thomas (Denson), Peter Jeffrey (Headmaster), Arthur Lowe (Mr Kemp), Mary MacLeod (Mrs Kemp).]

Being firmly located within the public school environment *If* ... announces itself clearly as a British film and yet the use of this quintessentially national institution as a metaphor for society means the film has much wider resonance. The school system has a clear hierarchy of power and authority maintained by ritual and physical discipline. New boys, like Jute, are indoctrinated into this quasi-society with frightening aggression by those just above them in the pecking order, who are themselves cowed into compliance by the threat of physical violence ('One word wrong and you fail the whole test.'/ 'And we get beaten.'). Non-conformists, like Travis, Knightly and Wallace, who question the values of the current social order, receive brutal, often sadistic, treatment.

The striking use of images of revolution helps to place this film within the context of a period of intense social upheaval. The common-room walls have pictures of Che Guevara and Geronimo in direct opposition to the paintings of traditionalists, past headmasters or benefactors, looking down on the boys from the dining hall wall. A magazine photograph of a black freedom fighter on Travis's wall is referred to as 'magnificent' and the images of lions asleep in a tree references Percy Shelley's 'The Mask of Anarchy'[1]:

Rise like lions after slumber
In unvanquishable number–
Shake your chains to earth like dew
Which in sleep have fallen on you–
Ye are many – they are few.

The year the film was released saw the ongoing student rebellion and impetus towards social change[2] which were such features of the early 1960s culminate in riots in Paris that threatened the de Gaulle government. This is a film that has at its heart contemporary student concerns from the period such as nuclear holocaust ('The whole world will end very soon – black brittle bones peeling into ash.'[3]) and Third World poverty and inequality in the distribution of wealth ('In Calcutta somebody dies of starvation every eight minutes.').

Anderson was a key figure in the Free Cinema documentary movement and is often associated with the early 1960s British New Wave but this film actually sits a little uneasily in relation to these developments in cinema. Free Cinema did focus upon ordinary people and everyday life, and as a result did point towards New Wave social realism, but it also emphasised the importance of personal film statements and artistic freedom. This was Anderson's focus, highlighting the director as artist or auteur, bringing their own distinctive vision to the screen. At the heart of Free Cinema for Anderson was a belief in film-making as an art that centred on personal expression and rejected commercial values.

If ... is clearly of its time and yet also distinctively different from other British films of the period. Both its form and its content, expressed in the radical attitudes and actions of the central characters, made it challenging to the conservative mainstream. These characteristics link it to an earlier film, *The Loneliness of the Long Distance Runner* (Richardson, 1962); and these two films, one based firmly within an upper middle-class experience and the other within the working class, suggest the widespread nature of the challenge to the old order in the 1960s.[4] And yet, Anderson had his own view on the extent to which *If ...* could be said to advocate revolutionary change since he saw the right to challenge authority as central to the British tradition:

You could say the boys in *If . . .* were traditionalists . . . They are part of the tradition of independence, the rights of the individual, the right to question authority, and to behave freely. When traditions have become fossilized, and instances of reaction as well, then they have to be rebelled against. That act in itself is a tradition.

(Friedman and Stewart 1994: 167)

Anarchy is a social and political philosophy which puts the highest possible values on responsibility. The film is not about responsibility against irresponsibility. It is about rival notions of responsibility and consequently well within a strong Puritan tradition.

(Aldgate and Richards 2002: 209)

Coming from a theatre background, Anderson was interested in exploring the use of Brecht's 'alienation effect'[5] within film. This film offered him the opportunity of bringing to a wider commercial audience the sort of challenging material theatre audiences were becoming used to seeing in the 1960s. The film is divided into eight chapters, much as a novel might be, with chapter headings appearing on screen as inter-titles. On the stage Brecht used text in a similar way; in *Mother Courage and Her Children*, for example, a summary of what is about to happen is displayed before each scene. This is an anti-illusionistic technique designed to prevent the audience becoming passive watchers and encourage them to become actively engaged in thinking about what is being presented on stage or screen. The act of reading breaks the illusion of reality that film (and drama) has conventionally been so interested in attempting to achieve, forcing the reader to see the work as a construct that demands to be thought about in an active way. Theoretically, this enables what is shown to be considered in relation to the way in which the viewer can see society as operating outside of the cinema (or theatre). It was a technique employed in theatre in Britain in the period; for example in John Arden's *Serjeant Musgrave's Dance* directed by Anderson at the Royal Court when it was first staged in 1959.[6] This play which according to Arden does not 'advocate bloody revolution' contains a third act in which a group of army deserters train a Gatling gun on a group of townspeople and threaten to open fire.

Anderson also uses the device of changing from colour to black and white film stock to further prevent the audience becoming engaged with the film as a realist text. These changes occur between scenes but also within sequences, and indeed as has been noted seem to obey no particular logic.

> Anderson's use of colour and black and white seems to obey a not always comprehensible logic.

(Murphy 1992: 158)

In Brechtian terms this lack of clear patterning within the choice is part and parcel of the process of disrupting the audience's viewing of the film. The process of film construction is again foregrounded in such a way that the audience is unable to forget they are watching a film that has been put together or constructed. The aim is again to encourage them to think about what is being presented. Usually mainstream film (certainly prior to 1960) would do everything possible to suggest what was on offer was a realistic slice of life. Anderson works to bring this reality status into question, to make the nature of film and the audience experience of it problematic and open to reflection and intellectual consideration. The supposed and usually taken-for-granted 'truth' of film is brought into question and our position as readers who need to make sense of the text is emphasised. The status of the classic realist narrative (in this particular film but also in all other films claiming that status) is undermined and brought into question.

The third key method used by Anderson to disrupt the viewing process is the movement between fantasy and realism, and indeed making the viewer unsure as to whether what he or she is watching is fantasy or realism. In his book on the director John Ford, Anderson quotes the scriptwriter Dudley Nichols saying Hollywood had been half-destroyed by its efforts to achieve 'realism': 'making everything appear exactly as it does to the average man, or to a goat, instead of sifting it through the feelings of an artist' (Anderson 1981: 86).

Unlike Sillitoe, the author of the original short story and scriptwriter for *The Loneliness of the Long Distance Runner*, Anderson and those involved in writing the script for *If . . .* are from the Oxbridge middle classes and their connection with the working class can never be more than that of privileged outsiders. *Every Day Except Christmas* (1957), one of Anderson's key contributions to Free Cinema, was supposed to make ordinary people 'feel their dignity and their importance' (Armes 1978: 266) but in fact comes across as patronising. With the subject matter of *If . . .* Anderson is able to work from material comfortably within his own experience and create a film that can be seen to stand as a metaphor for society as a whole.

Notes

1 And perhaps points towards the final scenes although it is noticeable that the boys do not rise in 'unvanquishable' numbers, with most of them continuing to align themselves with the current order.

2 In Britain, through popular music and fashion, and in their lifestyle choices, young people were challenging tradition values. In America, in cities such as Los Angeles and Detroit, there were black uprisings and increasing identification with the revolutionary aims of the Black Panthers. In 1968 there were student demonstrations and occupations of university buildings across the United States and Europe. The most dramatic events occurred in France where on the 'Night of the Barricades' (May 10) the police were driven from the Left Bank in Paris by students and there followed two weeks of strikes and factory occupations as workers joined the protests.

3 In 1962 the Cuban Missile Crisis had brought the world to the edge of nuclear war.

4 At times *If ...* seems to directly parallel *The Loneliness of the Long Distance Runner*: in the final scenes of both, for example, representatives of the various elements of the upper/ruling classes gather to witness the final act of rebellion. But Anderson's film should also be seen alongside Jean Vigo's *Zero de Conduite* (1933) not only in terms of storyline and themes but also in relation to notions of the auteur and the challenge to mainstream society.

5 Brecht's idea was that the audience needed to be 'alienated' from what they were seeing, distanced from what they were watching in order to be able to maintain the position of thoughtful, detached observers. His effort was to break the illusion of reality and prevent that identification with characters he saw other dramatists as attempting to create.

6 Arden described this as 'a realistic play, but not a naturalistic play' and this is very much in line with Anderson's thoughts on *If. ...*

Further Reading

Anthony Aldgate and Jeffrey Richards, *Best of British: Cinema and Society from 1930 to the Present*, London and New York, I. B.Tauris, 2002.

Lindsay Anderson, *About John Ford*, London, Plexus, 1981.

Roy Armes, *A Critical History of British Cinema*, London, Secker and Warburg, 1978.

Ali Catterall and Simon Wells, *Your Face Here: British Cult Movies Since the Sixties*, London, Fourth Estate, 2002.

Lester Friedman and Scott Stewart 'The Tradition of Independence: An Interview with Lindsay Anderson' in Wheeler Winston Dixon (ed.), *Re-Viewing British Cinema, 1900–1992*, New York, State University of New York, 1994.

Jonathan Hacker and David Price, *Take 10: Contemporary British Film Directors*, New York, Oxford University Press, 1991.

Erik Hedling, *Lindsay Anderson: Maverick Film-Maker*, London and New York, Cassell, 1998.

Gavin Lambert, *Mainly About Lindsay Anderson*, London, Faber, 2000.

Robert Murphy, *Sixties British Cinema*, London, BFI, 1992.

JOHN WHITE

CARRY ON UP THE KHYBER (1968)

[Production Company: Rank Film Distributors. Director: Gerald Thomas. Screenwriter: Talbot Rothwell. Cinematographer: Ernest Steward. Music: Eric Rogers. Editor: Alfred Roome. Cast: Sidney James (Sir Sidney Ruff-Diamond), Joan Sims (Lady Ruff-Diamond), Kenneth Williams (Randi-Lal), Bernard Bresslaw (Bunghit-Din), Charles Hawtrey (Corporal Widdle), Terry Scott (Sgt-Maj. McNutt), Angela Douglas (Princess Jelhi), Roy Castle (Captain Keen), Peter Butterworth (Brother Belcher).]

> If one flag deserves to fly over the hot-pot of the sixties, no doubt that it should be the Union Jack. That England which the continentals imagine to be always corseted and controlled by Victorian principles ... [1]

The *Carry On* series occupies an almost unique position in British film. Reviled by academics such as Marion Jordan,[2] adored by the public, the 31 strong movie franchise negotiated and bridged the socio-sexual-political arena from 1958 to 1992, during a period whereby Britain moved from austerity, through radicalism to end in dislocation. The low-budget, ribald comedies expanded upon the British music hall tradition and saucy seaside postcard humour of Donald McGill. Mocking British institutions like the National Health Service in *Carry On Nurse* (1959) or trade unionism in *Carry On At Your Convenience* (1971), they also parodied populist genres or offered historical pastiches. Examples are *Carry On Spying* (1964), which successfully aped the James Bond saga, *Carry On Screaming* (1966), which surpassed Britain's ghoulish Hammer Film productions, or *Carry On Cleo* (1964) which deconstructed the story of Cleopatra, and the media farrago that surrounded the overblown histrionics of Burton and Taylor's *Cleopatra* (USA 1963: Joseph Mankiewicz).

Importantly, the films are an ensemble effort. The 'public face' of the team was fundamental to the franchise's success; well-known, popular radio, film and television stars, fleshed out archetypal, conservative characters adorning innuendo-laden scripts. Through familiarity and adherence to narrative, and genre conventions, the formulaic representations of characters and plots, whilst arguably reductive and negative, allowed audience engagement with the texts. If Richard Dyer's notion of the Hollywood star is as a particular 'type' (Dyer 2002: 47–59), the *Carry Ons* subvert this concept. For example, when Sid James appears, audience awareness is of his on-screen persona as a working-class, work-shy, hard-drinking, gambling, woman-chasing 'bloke'; yet here he represents the upper-class Briton abroad. With the conservative nature of stereotyping clear, these constructions are invaluable in relaying textual information to the audience with filmic economy. Andy Medhurst defends this idea of the economy stating that, 'Attacking a *Carry On* for using stereotypes is like criticising a musical because it's unrealistic for people to burst into song like that' (Medhurst 1992: 18). Therefore the attraction in using stereotypes; the *Carry Ons* stereotype everybody and criticism against this appears redundant. Frances Gray writes about stereotyping, suggesting that female characters became replaced by the actor's persona,[3] suggesting that the canon subverts dominant ideologies to present new ways of investigating and navigating difficult arenas such as sexuality and race.[4] But if stereotypes are constantly employed and often negative conclusions drawn from them, for example Jordan likens Williams's effeminacy as 'sickly, or even mentally deficient'[5] why should *Carry On Up the Khyber* be discussed as a key British film?

Through adopting a historical approach the value of *Khyber* as a document that creates an understanding of British attitudes towards social upheavals of the 1960s can be appreciated. Engaging with colonial epics like *Northwest Frontier* (Thompson, 1958) *Khyber* affectionately critiques that quintessential, naïve trait of British imperialism. As the film's subtitle states, the story is concerned with the 'British position in India', and Britain, in the form of Sir Sidney Ruff-Diamond and 'the mem', Lady Joan, must survive an onslaught by the Khasi of Khalibar, and his cohort led by Bunghit Din of Jacksey who are attempting 'to drive the British out of Khalibar!'.

Through a barrage of double-entendres and innuendo the film paradigmatically constructs two contextual arguments. *Khyber* parodies *Zulu* (Endfield, 1964). The representation of exoticism in both films suggests the use of a foreign location as a means of negotiating British attitudes to the nation-state, whereby placing the familiar British cast of both movies into 'other' locations suggests a feeling of contextual incongruity for both. For example, the Khyber Pass, which is a wooden gate with a small sign saying 'Please shut the gate' pinned to it is open to ridicule through the sheer chutzpah of it, whilst in *Zulu* the horror of the violence yet to come is signposted through a shot of a compound gate swinging open.

With locations vital to both film's battle sequences, there are two scenes from *Khyber* that warrant attention; the dining-room sequence discussed later in this chapter, and when the escaping British find the Pass's soldiers massacred in battle. In the latter, a slow panning-shot captures the horrors of war with soldiers lying dead at the Pass until it rests on the escapees – four men in drag (a very British tradition) and two women. The characters discuss the massacre:

> *Lady Ruff-Diamond*: Oh, how awful. What can have happened?
> *Captain Keen*: I don't like making guesses but I wouldn't be at all surprised if there hadn't been a spot of foul play here.
> *Brother Belcher*: Foul play? Look at 'em. Lying around like a load of unwanted cocktail snacks!

With Burpars attacking, Captain Keen flees the battleground. Widdle and McNutt defend the Pass. In an outrageous gag the British etiquette of war as 'fair play' is ridiculed, as is the expertise of the British forces led by Michael Caine (upper-class Lt Bromhead) and Stanley Baker (working-class Lt Chard) in *Zulu*. McNutt cranks the field-gun and rather than bullets spraying out of the end the only thing to emerge is the cacophony of an old 78rpm recording. Attempting to use the cannon, it blows up in their faces due to a barrel-blocking bung. If this is compared to the vivid battle sequences of *Zulu* the parody becomes obvious.

Working-class Brother Belcher offers a comparison with *Zulu*'s Reverend Otto Witt (Jack Hawkins). Belcher encapsulates Britain's tradition of the knowledgeable fool.[6] Dressed in stark black and white, carrying his umbrella, he assumes paramount importance, representing, like Wilt, a British 'outsider' within his own society. Although part of the establishment he attempts to resist it. For example, Wilt goes to the regiment to warn of impending attacks but is lambasted for his views; Belcher demystifies British imperialism when asked to keep a stiff-upper lip, saying 'Well, I'm not standing around here waiting for mine to stiffen!' This creates two ideas of class-critiquing: effective representation of the working classes through humour and that the upper classes are arrogant and out of touch with their incumbent situation. With the rise of the cinematic working-class hero most profoundly noticeable in the 1960s, Rothwell is arguably critiquing those outside working-class strictures.

With *Khyber* placed within its historical framework the importance of the film becomes evident. With the independence of India from Britain in 1947 and the Suez Crisis still fresh in the public's memory the film demolishes notions of imperialism. Whilst the Khasi is an inverted, Gandhi-like figure who says, 'As a further mark of my respect I shall then exhibit your distinguished, but neatly severed head from the walls of the palace', Rothwell places the film into both historical (1895) and contextual settings. When the Khasi attacks the Residency Rothwell offers a critique of the collapse of the British Empire, attacking Britain's social/class structure.

The final scenes of the film have become arguably the paramount sequence in the entire canon. Whilst the Khasi attacks the Residency, the Ruff-Diamonds remain eating their food. Blasé about the cataclysmic destruction around them, they display nonchalance about their eroding imperial power. During the breathtakingly edited attack the scene cuts between three stratified social representations; the Khasi fights outside, representing an upper-class ruler bound by the constraints of the British – as if he is trying to become independent yet live within British society; the Residency compound becomes a negotiation arena between cultures and classes – the Indian and British soldiers are both 'foreign', yet working class, whilst their rulers are upper class; the dining room becomes a bastion of upper-class stoicism (Lady Joan, says 'Oh dear, I seem to have got a little plastered' when hit by a piece of collapsing ceiling) alongside the working-class cowardice of Belcher, who like Wilt turns to alcohol to combat the attack.

As the film is an essay about Empire, so Arthur Marwick argues that in regards to Indian autonomy ' . . . the official line was one of self-congratulation that Britain once more was leading the way in granting independence to former colonial peoples'.[7] With the contextual drive for former colonies to simultaneously achieve independence and for native-colonial families to be integrated into British society, Rothwell critiques this 'official line' arguing that the white-British must stay inside the Residency (Empire) whilst the Khasi (colony), despite his Oxford-education, is considered as 'other' and as such must be contained by the British, but outside its social sphere. Khyber critiques a contextual British argument whereby local councils banned Sikh bus drivers from wearing turbans; Rothwell has Din saying: 'That'll teach them to ban turbans on the buses'. In the internal context of the film this is meaningless, but contextually it would have been resonant.

At the film's climax Ruff-Diamond tells his troops to face the enemy. On a given command they grab and raise their kilts, revealing ... ? The answer is never known. The scene ends with the Khasi and his subordinates fleeing at whatever they've seen. The final moments sees Ruff-Diamond and the remaining upper classes retiring to the Residency. Interestingly, Princess Jelhi is to marry Captain Keen, showing how contextually tolerant Rothwell's script is. The final words go to Brother Belcher who, upon seeing a Union flag with the contextual slogan 'I'm Backing Britain' emblazoned upon it, looks directly at the camera, and therefore us, saying 'Of course, they're all mad you know'. These final moments reveal the extent to which Rothwell has taken (pre)1960s' attitudes of class in Britain and subverted them. The upper classes remain stagnant; Belcher, representing 1960s-working-class man ends up with the final word on the subject. Therefore, *Khyber* becomes a celebration of the working-class hero, and Belcher's satirical 'edge' emphasises that the *Carry Ons* are more than simple comedies. They are traditional. They are subversive. They reflect the pre-occupations of the nation-state. They emphasise the culturally familiar but cipher through them important messages debunking Britain's rigid social strata. Above all else, they gave their audience the ability to laugh at themselves. As such, *Carry On Up The Khyber* is a key British film.

Notes

1 Michael Winnock, 'Chronique des années soixante' (1987) in Arthur Marwick, *The Sixties,* Oxford, Oxford University Press, 1998, p. 456.
2 Marion Jordan, 'Carry On – Follow That Stereotype' in James Curran and Vincent Porter, *British Cinema History,* London, Weidenfeld and Nicolson, 1983, pp. 312–327.
3 For example, Barbara Windsor as the 'cheeky Cockney'.
4 Frances Gray, 'Female Performance in the *Carry On* Films' in Stephen Wagg (ed.) *Because I Tell a Joke or Two: Comedy, Politics and Social Difference,* London, Routledge, 1998, p. 101.
5 Marion Jordan, p. 320.
6 Notably Dickens's Pecksniff in *Martin Chuzzlewit.*
7 Arthur Marwick, *British Society Since 1945,* London, Penguin, 1982, p. 107.

Further Reading

Richard Dyer, *Stars,* London, BFI, 2002.
Morris Bright and Robert Ross, *Mr Carry On,* London, BBC Worldwide, 2000.
Arthur Marwick, *The Sixties,* Oxford, Oxford University Press, 1998.

Andy Medhurst, 'Carry On Camp', *Sight and Sound*, Vol. 2, No. 4, August 1992, pp. 16–19.

Robert Ross, *The Carry On Companion*, London, B T Batsford, 1996.

Simon Sheridan and Johnny Vegas, *Keeping the British End Up: Four Decades of Saucy Cinema*, London, Reynolds and Hearn, 2005.

STEVEN GERRARD

KES (1969)

[Production Company: Kestrel Films/Woodhall Film Productions. Director: Kenneth Loach. Screenwriters: Barry Hines, Ken Loach, Tony Garnett. Cinematographer: Chris Menges. Editor: Roy Watts. Music: John Cameron. Cast: David Bradley (Billy Casper), Lynne Perrie (Mrs Casper), Freddie Fletcher (Jud Casper), Colin Welland (Mr Farthing), Brian Glover (Mr Sugden), Bob Bowes (Mr Gryce).]

Once *Kes* was completed, its US financiers United Artists found they had a problem on their hands: a new kind of film which didn't quite fit into the existing market. The subject, style and sentiment of the film were all problematic: the story was a few months in the life of an under-achieving 15-year-old boy in a Yorkshire mining town who finds hope in training a kestrel, only for his aspirations to be thwarted by a combination of the harshness and indifference of school and family life. Subject-wise, was it a Northern working-class drama to be viewed in the same way as British New Wave titles of the early 1960s? It was classified as a 'U', but would the naturalistic style mean too much reflection and not enough action for a kids' movie? Would a wider audience respond to the universality of human aspiration, or had United Artists inadvertently funded a propaganda piece for the art-house?

Interested at that time in the commercial return on investing in British films using British locations, United Artists had come on board as funders for *Kes* at the eleventh hour. Tony Richardson approached them on behalf of producer Tony Garnett and director Ken Loach, whose film was on the point of collapse after their original backers pulled out. Conveniently hands-off during production, United Artists continued to be hands-off getting the film into distribution and over the summer of 1969 it went nowhere. Alexander Mitchell suggested some of what *Kes* was up against when he reported United Artists' Sales Director as having explained that, 'cinemas had been booked with films like *The Carry Ons*, *Chitty Chitty Bang*

Bang, Funny Girl and *The Battle of Britain*. Kes might get a Northern circuit next March ... '.[1]

Kes was first seen by a public audience in the UK at the London Film Festival in November 1969. It received an enthusiastic response from festival audiences and critics alike for its naturalistic approach to social realism, its poetic qualities and damning critique of the school system. Critic Paul Barker wrote that: 'All education committees should see it, compulsorily'.[2] Finally, ABC Cinemas bought the distribution rights and, despite stiff competition, *Kes* went on to be so popular on its release in five cinemas in Yorkshire in spring 1970 that it opened in the south in May and went on to be a huge commercial success throughout the UK.

Why was *Kes* so popular? Its social comment, new approach to naturalism on screen and the universality of human aspiration can be seen in retrospect within the broader contexts of social realist cinema and the filmography of director Ken Loach. At the time, these three elements had not been seen together in British cinemas in this way, although similar approaches had been seen on TV. The starting point for *Kes* had been Tony Garnett, one of the producers on the BBC's *Wednesday Play*. BBC Drama producers were at that time encouraged to engage with current affairs. The play was programmed directly after the evening news, which not only held a captive audience, but also, in looking deeper into social and political issues, built on the audience's mindset for impartiality.

This approach to film-making and programming could have a huge impact: one of Garnett's previous TV films with Loach as director, *Cathy Come Home* (transmitted November 1966), prompted government action on homelessness and the setting up of the charity Shelter. It also opened up a new way of constructing reality which was perceived by some right-wing critics as very dangerous indeed: the BBC's film *The War Game* (Peter Watkins 1965) presented a view of Kent if hit by Soviet nuclear missiles. Transmission was cancelled for fear of traumatising audiences with its potentially confusing use of newsreel-style footage and handheld camera to create a look of documentary.

Garnett and Loach were ready to break away from the fears and bureaucracy of the BBC. They created their own company to produce issue-based films true to their socialist ideals, in which ordinary people would see themselves reflected on screen, in cinemas. The first, *Kes*, was based on a novel, *A Kestrel for a Knave* (1968). Author Barry Hines had contacted Garnett directly from his home in the area of Yorkshire where the story is set. Hines's father had been a miner and, before becoming a writer, Hines was a teacher in one of the Secondary Moderns that offers Billy so little joy. He wrote of what he knew, using local dialect and recognisable locations, and his message regarding the wasted lives of the youth that he saw around him was unmistakable.

The mining industry was a major part of the British economy, reliant on the labour generated by the tight-knit communities. Mines were dug in rural areas away from towns and cities, creating a land-scape in which the grime and mechanisation of the colliery was cheek by jowl with unspoilt natural surroundings. For most young people in these towns, school was pointless: although the 1944 Education Act had been established on the socialist ideal of creating parity between social classes via three kinds of secondary education, in prac-tice there were few Technical Colleges and Grammar Schools were selective, so Secondary Moderns took all the rest. *Kes* follows Billy, a working-class boy, let down by a system not designed to help him grow. The narrative of the film takes place over his last term where, as an 'Easter leaver', his education would end without any qualifications.

Loach explains his attraction to the novel as follows:

> I was struck by the simplicity of the story's metaphor. It was not too political. It was basically a story about one boy and his bird but with plenty to say about working class culture and aspirations of that time. We'd all seen the social realism films of the late 50s and early 60s and we both felt that there must be another way forward from there.
>
> (Ojumu 1999: 6–7)

Moreover, choice of subject matter and style were influenced by the respectful approach to the stories of ordinary people made with energy, humour and compassion by film-making movements beyond Britain: the Italian Neo-Realists, the French and the Czech New Waves in particular. Loach said of the work of Czech directors like Jiri Menzel and Milos Forman that, 'They weren't soft in any way, but had a very sharp, wry wit . . . They made us feel that they were the kinds of films we wanted to make' (Fuller 1998: 38).

The wit in *Kes* relies in part on creating stereotypical characters, including the bullying PE teacher Mr Sugden's (Brian Glover) delu-sions of football heroics on the sports field, the harshness of Billy's mum's (Lynne Perrie) indifference to her young son, his brother Jud's (Freddie Fletcher) aggression. But these are not overplayed or turned into caricature; it feels that this is just the way that people in these situations behave. To this end, casting was also affected by fresh approaches to representing reality: all actors, bar Colin Welland, were non-professionals cast locally in and around Barnsley.[3]

For the film-makers, the cast's local accents and colloquialisms played a key part in the authentic representation of place. Small, under-fed looking Bradley was the son of a miner and went to the Secondary Modern where Hines had taught; Brian Glover was a teacher friend of Hines; and Lynne Perrie was a local cabaret star. Kes was played by three birds named after a chain of shoe shops, *Freeman, Hardy and Willis* and trained by Hines's brother. Loach drew out naturalistic performances from his cast, his technique including an element of surprise, as recalled by Welland:

> In the school assembly scene Ken had organised a real member of staff to pick a particular boy who had been coughing and drag him out of the room. At the last minute, Loach told the actor playing the headmaster to pick a completely different teacher who obviously chose the wrong child. So in the finished film, the unlucky boy was really protesting his innocence as he's dragged out into the hallway. There was a tremendous freshness about that scene.
>
> (Ojumu 1999: 6–7)

They filmed for eight weeks during the school summer holidays in 1968, shooting on location in the school, the streets of thin-walled post-war housing, the colliery, pubs and surrounding woods and fields. Cinematographer Chris Menges had planned to shoot in black and white, the conventional format then for TV work and social realist films, but funders United Artists demanded audience-attracting colour. Concerned that the rural settings might look too rustic and cosy, the film-makers pre-exposed the 35 mm film stock to de-saturate it and take out some of the colour. In post-production, the sound-track of largely location sound added another layer to this new approach to expressing reality. John Cameron's score was barely 20 minutes long, and used only to reveal the childlike innocence and beauty in the secret relationship between Billy and Kes. Led by a simple, delicate flute, it refers to traditional folk music as much as it subtly underlines the different moods of the film.

Menges lit the space rather than the action and kept the camera controlled and at an observational distance, rather than using the camera handheld, as had been another convention of naturalism to that point. This allowed actors to move naturally without fear of stepping out of the camera frame. When there are close-ups, particularly on Billy, they are all the more moving for the distance from which most of his story is viewed. In scenes making use of the landscape, such as when Billy sits on the hill reading aloud from a comic, he is tiny in comparison to the huge, black, noisy colliery in the background. It is a moment of happiness for him but a moment of foreboding as well. Would Billy hold on to the sense of freedom which Kes had helped him to understand, or give up and join Jud down the pit? From the inherently critical point of view of the naturalist style which *Kes* deploys so effectively, we guess probably the latter. As Deborah Knight suggests, 'the central protagonists of naturalistic narratives are not "heroic". Heroes are capable of great actions. The protagonists or naturalist narratives are seldom able to break free from the constraints of their socio-cultural environments' (1997: 67).

In 1969, audiences recognised that *Kes* was an interventionist piece: a call for action to address the social problems young people like Billy were facing. It remains a key work in the filmography of Loach, whose films have covered a huge range of stories of the lives of ordinary people, all told with his now signature naturalist approach and sense of righteous protest. However, *Kes* stands alone, as a film which finds contemporary audiences anew via the combination of subject, style and sentiment so different when first released, and still unique to this day.

Notes

1 Alexander Mitchell, 'Top film hits snags', *The Sunday Times*, 16 November 1969, p. 11.
2 Paul Barker, 'Arts in Society: Boy in a Cage', *New Society*, 20 November 1969, p. 17.
3 Welland was well known at the time for his character in BBC TV police drama *Z Cars* (1962–1978).

Further Reading

Graham Fuller (ed), *Loach on Loach*, London, Faber & Faber, 1998.
Bert Hogenkamp, *Film, Television and the Left 1950–1970*, London, Laurence & Wishart, 2000
Deborah Knight, 'Naturalism, Narration and Critical Perspective: Ken Loach and the Experimental Method' in George McKnight (ed.) *Agent of Challenge and Defiance: The Films of Ken Loach*, Trowbridge, Flicks Books, 1997.
Akin Ojumu, 'A typical reaction was a snigger . . . I was making a film about the wrong sort of bird', *The Observer: Screen*, 29 August 1999, pp. 6–7.

CORINNA DOWNING

PERFORMANCE (1970)

[Production Company: Goodtimes Enterprises. Directors: Donald Cammell and Nicolas Roeg. Screenwriter: Donald Cammell. Cinematographer: Roeg. Editors: Antony Gibbs, Brian Smedley-Aston and Frank Mazzola (uncredited). Music: Jack Nitzsche. Cast: James Fox (Chas), Mick Jagger (Turner), Anita Pallenberg (Pherber), Michèle Breton (Lucy), Anthony Valentine (Joey Maddocks), Ann Sidney (Dana), John Bindon (Moody), Stanley Meadows (Rosebloom), Allan Cuthbertson (the lawyer), Johnny Shannon (Harry Flowers), Kenneth Colley (Tony Farrell).]

Performance is an important British film for three reasons. First, it broke new ground aesthetically, in terms of its visual style. Second, as a social document it gives cultural expression to a particular historical moment. And third, it demonstrates how innovation in cinema is always dependent upon a particular set of industrial as well as cultural circumstances.

Colin MacCabe dubs *Performance* 'the finest British gangster film ever made' (MacCabe 1998: 8). Yet Donald Cammell's rendition of 1960s London gangland is but a point of departure. The film documents the formal dissembling of that acutely rendered underworld by the transgressive spirit of the counter-culture's hallucinatory drug scene. This is embodied in the iconic rock star Turner (Mick Jagger) who 'takes over' the identity of gangland drop-out Chas (James Fox) in the gothic gloom of a Powis Square mansion. His provocative accomplices in this bohemian *ménage-à-trois* are Pherber (Anita Pallenberg) and Lucy (Michèle Breton). Depending on your view, it is a film about Romantic disillusion and dissolution; a Nietzschean fable of the twilight of the idols; a depiction of the hangover after the party that was Swinging London; a Marcusean exploration of the mythic potential of free love to overthrow class-bound capitalism; or, according to Cammell himself, a poetic treatise on violence.

The film owes its distinctive visual style to four key elements: the creative adaptation of key locations, the central performances, the photography of co-director Nicolas Roeg, and Frank Mazzola's post-hoc re-editing. The first part of the narrative offers a grimly realistic view of London. Donald Cammell's brother David was hired as production manager and his thorough location scout yielded a brazen view of the capital, by turns run down and tarted up, alighting at last upon the dilapidated former gambling club in Lowndes Square for Turner's Notting Hill retreat in which Chas takes refuge in the second part of the film. The décor of these interiors – a combination of faded grandeur, prosaic dereliction and bohemian chic – was designed by Christopher Gibbs who had decorated the flat in Courtfield Road which Pallenberg had shared with Rolling Stone, Brian Jones. Jones's drug-induced demise is believed to have provided Cammell with the model for Jagger's Turner. This combination of friends-and-family film-making with a darker concern for the border between reality and fiction, distinguishes the nature of the film's central performances.

Cammell, an artist by training and a dilettante writer by inclination, had never made a film, though he had sold a couple of screenplays. Perhaps his singular talent was social entry into the Chelsea set of the mid-1960s. This was a bizarre côterie in which Establishment figures rubbed shoulders with London's criminal fraternity at parties thrown by artists, fashion designers and pop stars on budgets provided by television executives, advertising agents, record moguls and pornographers. This was a select milieu but one which, at least temporarily, forgot class boundaries. New money was the great leveller, hedonism the common currency. But it was a vibrant, cocksure scene from which some, like Jones, ultimately dropped out. It provided Cammell with his creative inspiration, but also gave him the connections with those, including producer Sanford Lieberson and co-director Nicolas Roeg, who enabled him to realise his vision on film.

Of the central performers, only Fox and Pallenberg were trained actors. Fox was cast against type as the arrogant young villain Chas forced into hiding when, against orders, he over-reaches himself in an attack on Joey Maddocks (Anthony Valentine). Fox's 'method' training in the Elephant and Castle pubs frequented by 'chaps' from 'the firm', was overseen by boxing trainer, print-worker and friend of the mob, Johnny Shannon, who relishes his screen debut as gang boss Harry Flowers (MacCabe 1998: 24–27 and 38–43). In a late interview Donald Cammell credited Pallenberg with much of the inspiration for the second part of the film (Savage 1999: 110–116), in particular through her ability to totally be herself on screen (rather than playing a part called Pherber) and the effect this had on others (especially Fox). Fox told MacCabe she taunted him for being too 'straight', a conflict which comes across on screen. Her experience of working in the experimental tradition of Artaud's *Theatre of Cruelty* brought an emotional intensity to her performance (MacCabe 1998: 53–54). Fox suffered from the experience of the film, withdrawing from acting during the 1970s in pursuit of personal spirituality (Walker 1986: 423).

Fox's 'professional' willingness to succumb to the experiment of *Performance* was, ironically, quite at odds with Jagger's 'amateur' reluctance to play the part of Turner, based as it so clearly was on the demise of Brian Jones. Jagger's equivocation, between being himself and playing the part, between the personal charisma and iconic signification he brings to the performance, and the vulnerability and ordinariness visible through his untrained technique, is a tension at the heart of this film. Of course, it accounts perfectly for the nihilistic demise of the reclusive Turner which satisfies the narrative motivation, but it does more than this. It opens up the traditionally hermeneutic nature of screen stardom to a much more fluid, less deterministic, emotional register. The result is a powerful, charismatic quality which engages the viewer on a new kind of emotional level. It is because of the rawness of its improvised performance style that the characters communicate so directly, so accessibly to the viewer.

This directness is exacerbated by Roeg's intimate photography, just as it is deflected by the disorientation of the complex editing style. Indeed, the viewing experience is an emotional fort/da game which mirrors Chas's own subjective ordeal. The handheld camerawork of the Powis Square interiors, much of it shot on 16 mm and naturally lit, lends a claustrophobic domesticity and an awkward, voyeuristic prurience to the unfolding pantomime of mixed sex, mixed drugs and re-mixed rock 'n' roll.

Despite pushing the boundaries, the finished film ran into more problems with its paymasters (Warner Brothers) than with the censor. The deal, which Sandy Lieberson had struck with his friend and head of production Ken Hyman (whose father's Seven Arts media corporation had taken over the studio following the retirement of Jack Warner), represented a modest studio investment of £400,000 for a film they believed would cash-in on the high profile of Jagger. However, as originally shot, the film not only delayed Jagger's entry into proceedings for more than 30 minutes, but offered a mystifying, disjunctive narrative, liberally laced with 'real' sex and drug-taking. So while its 11-week shoot and original edit were completed by late 1968, Warners refused to release the film. There ensued 18 months of legal wrangling, during which time the studio again changed hands, both producer Lieberson and co-director Roeg left for other projects, and post-production was removed to Los Angeles where editor Frank Mazzola and composer Jack Nitschze were drafted in to re-package the film.

The film shown in the United States in August 1970 has remained the standard and only surviving version of what was once a longer narrative. Mazzola's staccato montage compressed the early underworld sequences to bring Jagger's character on screen more swiftly, and shortened the more graphic scenes of sex (between Chas and Dana) and violence (the Joey Maddocks fight). Nitschze's soundtrack of eerie electronic pulses also introduced the showcase numbers featuring Jagger in more recognisable performance mode.

For all the apparent compromise and confusion of the film's post-production history, film-making of this originality is only achieved through particularly beneficial circumstances. In this regard we should note the favourable currency of British popular cultural exports which led eager Hollywood studios not only to invest in overseas projects but to risk giving relative autonomy to largely untried production talents. Indeed, by 1968 American investment in British film production had reached an all-time high of £31.3 million (Ballieu and Goodchild 2002: 84). Hollywood studios in Britain became aware of the lucrative potential of the youth market in popular culture and found its lure, for a while, irresistible. In 1967 Warner Brothers had approached the highly bankable Jagger (notwithstanding his recent arrest in a high-profile police drugs raid) to act as their 'youth advisor', an offer which the singer declined (Walker 1986: 416). Nonetheless, this symbolised the majors' interest in this new cultural force. But opportunities in mainstream cinema were available not only because of the studios' willingness to speculate. What was essentially a fragmented British film market (briefly bolstered by American investment) allowed for (and even necessitated) diversity and experimentation. Cultural significance (and briefly power) moved from the mainstream to the margins; the counter-culture came, for a short while, to fill the vacuum at the centre.

One of the claims of the late-1960s' counter-culture which reached its apotheosis in the violent events of 1968, was that personal liberation was a political act. *Performance* remains a radical film in this sense since, in modernist guise, its rehearsal of personal liberation is also mirrored in its formal dissemblance, its disharmony. The film's roughness of texture, its dis-equilibrium, represents a revolt of the world of ideas against the world of objects (so feted in earlier 1960s films). This quality resides not just in the constituent elements of design, performance, photography and editing. We have only to contrast the ordered contents of Chas's dressing-table drawer at the beginning of the film with the subsequent charades of dressing-up, and undressing and cross-dressing, to recognise the frailty of the performance-of-self which constitutes social identity. And the film doesn't shrink from demonstrating liberation as both an act of violence and love, physically disabling as well as spiritually enabling.

From the violent sex Chas metes out to Dana at the beginning of the film, through the shot he fires into Joey Maddocks, the narrative concludes with a single bullet (the ultimate penetration) which dissolves Chas's identity into that of Turner. Liberating sex is posited (pacé Bataille) as death of the self and re-birth, redolent not only of the transcendent mantras of the counter-culture and the polemics of Herbert Marcuse but, moreover, rooted in the spirit of Romanticism.[1] Jon Savage sees the ending of *Performance* with the liberating fusion through death of Chas and Turner as 'satisfying and curiously hopeful'.[2] Yet the final dénouement, in keeping with the moral ambiguity of the film, also posits a darker fate: the violent destruction of the radical but jaded dream that was the counter-culture. Harry's 'Rolls' into which Chas/Turner climbs also symbolises the hegemonic ability of capitalism to absorb, re-package and neutralise dissent.

Politically, 1968 was a watershed and *Performance* internalises within its own radical structure the twin potentialities of liberation and destruction, of radicalism and conformity. By the film's release in 1970, with the war in Vietnam more entrenched than ever, the darkness of *Performance* overshadowed its light. Perhaps its most celebrated line encapsulates the problem of personal identity in the context of the political: 'The only performance that makes it, that really makes it, that makes it all the way, is the one that achieves madness. Right?' (Cammell 2001: 99–100). Herein lies the Nietzschean fable in all its portentous glory.

Notes

1 See Georges Bataille, *Eroticism*, trans. Mary Dalwood, London, Marion Boyars, 1987.
2 Jon Savage, *Sight and Sound*, New Series, Vol. 5, No. 9 (September, 1995), p. 25.

Further Reading

Bill Baillieu and John Goodchild, *The British Film Business*, Chichester, John Wiley, 2002.
Donald Cammell, *Performance*, London, Faber, 2001.
Colin MacCabe, *Performance*, London, BFI, 1998.
Jon Savage, '*Performance*: Interview with Donald Cammell' in Steve Chibnall and Robert Murphy (eds) *British Crime Cinema*, London, Routledge, 1999.
Alexander Walker, *Hollywood, England*, London, Harrap, 1986.

JUSTIN SMITH

A CLOCKWORK ORANGE (1971)

[Production Company: Hawk Films. Director and screenwriter: Stanley Kubrick. Cinematographer: John Alcott. Editor: Bill Butler. Cast: Malcolm McDowell (Alex de Large), Patrick Magee (Mr Alexander), Michael Bates (Chief Guard), Warren Clarke (Dim), Carl Duering (Dr Brodsky), Adrienne Corri (Mrs Alexander).]

In *A Clockwork Orange*'s Britain, the thugs who roam the streets raping, pillaging and murdering at will are at once both the savages from whom the civilised need protection, and the protectors themselves. Alex's psychotic droogs flip from outlaws to guardians of the establishment with the merest whiff of state power.

It is no surprise that the British Board of Film Classification had particular problems passing the film as it seemed a direct attack not only on the civilised values it set itself up to guard, but also on the mechanisms which purported to keep it civilised. As Janet Staiger notes, 'Since the film itself criticised government attempts to control or condition youth behaviour with the proposition that interference by authorities was more immoral than Alex's original behaviour, it might look too self-serving of the Board to question the film' (2003: 38). In the end they were saved the trouble of censoring the film by Kubrick himself who was disturbed by just how potent a cultural force the film turned out to be.

Following the film's UK release in 1971, a spate of supposedly copycat violent occurrences were reported together with a number of threats against Kubrick's own family's personal safety. As a result, Kubrick chose to withdraw the film from distribution in Britain. It remained unseen in the UK from this point until after his death in 1999. It could be that he felt the film spoke so specifically to the youth of the UK that Kubrick chose to withdraw it from this territory alone. Or it could be that he would have withdrawn it globally had he had the power to do so. But the fact remains that the UK is the only country where Kubrick demanded the film be taken out of public circulation. The question is, does this say more about the nature of the film itself or British culture? Either way the two seem inextricably linked.

By the time Kubrick made the film he had long 'gone native'. Born in New York, he had moved to the UK with his family and set up permanent home far from the reaches of all but the most persistent envoys of Hollywood. Perhaps Kubrick's outsider status gave him the necessary distance to carry off such a potent critique of Britain and British cinema. *A Clockwork Orange* is the ultimate antidote to the familiar school of British Social Realism which largely dominated UK art cinema of the time. Kubrick loved to use supposedly low culture to undress high culture. Science fiction and horror are commonly regarded as low-brow genres, looked down upon as 'trashy' by the literary elite. It seems a peculiarly American conceit to use a blend of these disreputable genres to dissect both British culture and the class-fixated school of Social Realism. Kubrick emerged with a visionary critique of the effects of Britain's rigid society, where everyone knows their place, the law serves the powerful and the civilised values this elite dictate form the very foundation of Britain's national identity.

If nineteenth-century Britain were to identify any single value above all others as embodying Britishness, it likely would have been a notion of being civilised. As a result, for Britons, national identity has become almost interchangeable with the idea of being civilised. If this means being considerate, educated and charitable, it also means being right, powerful and in control.

A Clockwork Orange challenges the very meaning of 'civilised' with its carefully orchestrated assault on the establishment. Kubrick has put together a checklist of characteristics of civilised Britain, placing them at the heart of the moral malaise running through his vision of a nation in decline. Classical music from Beethoven, and even more ironically, Purcell's 'Music for the Funeral of Queen Mary' become synonymous not with the genteel drawing rooms of the educated, but with the sadistic erotic fantasies of juveniles. The bowler hat and cane once associated with that bastion of Britishness, the archetypal City Gent, is now turned into a uniform of terror worn by Alex and his droogs. Science and Medicine are now to be found working for the frightened, patronising and deluded government. The British institutional construct of the State is subverted and used as a locus for power, corruption and lies. The irony of the film is that it is this very same corrupt fear which is serving to produce a nation of disaffected amoral and frustrated psychopaths. Perhaps Kubrick meant to indicate that this was also exactly the personality required for Imperial expansion and the subsequent violent 'civilising' of the world.

The striking and much mimicked uniforms of the droogs took the tropes of the City gent and rendered them into something more akin to the identifiers worn by members of any number of contemporary youth subcultures, in itself a very British idea. It comes as little surprise that so many of these subcultures were first produced by the UK. In a grey, impoverished post-war Britain, the youth sought to separate themselves from their parents' 'keep calm and carry on' post-war mentality and asked: 'what has my country done for me?' The answer appeared to be 'not much'. And so the youths sought to distance themselves from their parents' lifestyles and seek out their own more colourful identities often through the rising iconography of pop music. The Teddy-boys, mods, rockers, punks, headbangers – these were all established first in Britain before being exported to the US and beyond. Watching 1960s news footage of the clashes on Brighton Beach between mods, rockers and police, it's easy to see where Antony Burgess and Kubrick might have got their inspiration for Alex and his droogs.

The disintegration of language is a further omnipresent force in the film. The so-called Received Pronunciation (RP) of the BBC newscaster and indeed virtually all public voices aired in the UK up to the 1960s is torn asunder by the droogs' use of a slang called Nadsat. Slang is used ubiquitously by youth subcultures to differentiate themselves from the adults who control their daily lives, as a way of carving out one's own identity and presenting a challenge to social authority.

Nadsat in *A Clockwork Orange* is perhaps the most potent example of Alex's desire to live outside the state-sanctioned social system. Alex has chosen to embrace a way of speaking whose subtext is to say 'I don't want to be a part of the society into which I'm born'. The BBC had long been seen, at home and abroad, as the voice of civilised British values in no small part because of the strongly associated intonations and accents of the dialect used by its reporters and presenters. This RP is also strongly associated with having a formal education, which in turn is often associated with being wealthy and coming from an upper-class background. Alex and his droogs wilfully discard any aspirations to belong to the social class of the power elite by embracing their own dialect, uniform, and criminality. In the same way, Kubrick actively subverts the tropes of so-called civilised values through co-opting Purcell and the bowler hat, producing a peculiarly British critique of all that Britannia stands for. More than that, it's a call for a very British revolution.

A Clockwork Orange sits a little uneasily in this overview of 50 key British films. Is it really a British film or actually a US studio film masquerading as British? After all, few of us would consider *Children of Men* (Alfonso Cuarón, 2006) a British film, even though much of it is shot on the familiar streets of London, any more than we would consider *Our Man In Havana* (Carol Reed, 1959) a Cuban film. But what is it then that makes a film belong to one culture or nation rather than another? Traditionally, because of their high production costs, films are often constructed with a cultural universality in mind. It's a rare film made outside of France, the US or Japan that can cover its production costs from within its domestic market alone. So where does this leave *A Clockwork Orange*? Is it British, American or simply the product of a global industrial process rather than the expression of any single nation's cultural identity?

A Clockwork Orange has a largely British cast, crew and setting and is adapted from a British author's novel. But it is directed by Stanley Kubrick, arguably the most significant of all American directors. Kubrick found finance for the film through Warner Brothers at the very heart of Hollywood. The US studios were actively seeking to fund their very own art-movies in order to compete with the raft of films from Europe which had lately been sweeping up awards, critical praise, and above all dollars around the globe. Using American money to fund what seems on the surface like a very British picture might have been the industrial equivalent of building a cultural Trojan Horse. Britain has long been perceived as a kind of cultural beachhead between Europe and the US thanks largely to its common language. Warner Brothers could easily have conceived of using *A Clockwork Orange* to colonise the European art-house market from within. With their more challenging and adult approach to subject matter, films like *The Conformist* (Bernardo Bertolucci, 1970), *Alphaville* (Jean-Luc Godard, 1965) and *Belle de Jour* (Luis Buñuel, 1967) were selling tickets almost as fast as they were breaking taboos. It's likely that Hollywood wanted a piece of this action and thought that by producing something abroad, which tackled potentially controversial themes, it could beat the Europeans at their own game while keeping the international box-office receipts in-country. Looking at *A Clockwork Orange*'s national identity this way opens up an intriguing argument for the film as a kind of US imperialist indoctrination of the UK in much the same manner as the film's anti-hero, Alex, finds himself brainwashed by state power. The cultural and industrial muscle of Hollywood equates easily with the financial and ethical authority of the British state as depicted in Kubrick's film.

However, *A Clockwork Orange* can hardly be labelled a US film simply because of its US director and funding. It is very hard to imagine the film functioning as successfully if located in any other country in the world besides Britain. It is this exploration of the iconography of the UK which confirms *A Clockwork Orange*'s cultural identity as truly British. There is something inherently British in the way the material addresses social flux in a timeline which could begin with a past depicted in *If . . .* (Lindsay Anderson, 1968), continuing through the disaffected present found in *Trainspotting* (Danny Boyle, 1995) and arriving at the dystopian future in which *A Clockwork Orange* is set. Kubrick uses an idea of Britain, a memory of Empire, casting its eye over the past of this once powerful British Imperial Civilisation and presenting us with a vision of an atrophied future where the savage and civilised have become one.

Perhaps this film is, in a perverse way, Kubrick's paean to Britain. It seems somehow a fitting tribute to the artistry of *A Clockwork Orange* that it resonated so powerfully with British youth culture while simultaneously galvanising the outraged attention of Middle England's moral Right. 'Of all the films that [Kubrick] made in Great Britain, [*Barry Lyndon* and *A Clockwork Orange*] are, paradoxically, the only ones whose cultural background is truly English' (Ciment 2005: 411). What other film in the history of UK cinema has been re-released nation-wide 30 years after its original debut in over 250 cinemas? If there remained any doubt over *A Clockwork Orange*'s national identity, this should triumphantly confirm its position as a key work of and for British cinema.

Further Reading

Michel Ciment, 'A Clockwork Orange' in Alison Castle (ed.) *The Stanley Kubrick Archives*, London, Taschen, 2005.

Janet Staiger, 'The Cultural Productions of *A Clockwork Orange*' in Stuart Y. McDougal (ed.) *Stanley Kubrick's 'A Clockwork Orange'*, Cambridge, Cambridge University Press, 2003.

SIMON WARD

GET CARTER (1971)

[Production Company: Metro-Goldwyn-Mayer British Studios. Director: Mike Hodges. Screenwriter: Hodges. Cinematographer: Wolfgang Suschitzky. Music: Roy Budd. Editor: John Trumper. Cast: Michael Caine (Jack Carter), Ian Hendry (Eric), Britt Ekland (Anna), John Osborne (Kinnear), Tony Beckley (Peter), George Sewell (Con), Geraldine Moffat (Glenda), Bryan Mosley (Brumby), Rosemarie Dunham (Edna), Petra Markham (Doreen).]

The word 'cult' in film terms is synonymous with director Mike Hodges's debut 1971 feature *Get Carter*; a film that in its short life-time has gone from being a critical disaster to *Total Film's* greatest British movie. From its eerily haunting theme music, through its

harsh realism and brutal characterisation, to its postmodernist plun-
dering of British film history (long before postmodernism was de
rigueur), *Get Carter* has affected successive generations of film fans,
eventually persuading critics of its worth.

Set in a decaying Newcastle-upon-Tyne at the end of the 'Swinging
Sixties' the story deals with gangster, Jack Carter (Michael Caine, in a
role forever associated with him), returning to the north to bury his
brother, uncovering the murderous truth of his demise, and taking
calculated, violent revenge. Amidst this Hodges paints pictures of a
world of change, where progress is as unstoppable as Jack Carter, and
as equally brutal and unconcerned for those swept aside. *Get Carter*
signifies an end to the 'Swinging Sixties', and an end to the 'old' in
all its contexts, and yet the dawn of the new that it heralds is tainted,
decadent, deviant, and ultimately deserving of the same emotionless
dispatch that Hodges's protagonist finds at the end of the film.

Decay is on screen from the pre-title sequence in crime 'boss'
Gerald Fletcher's flat where the London 'mob' Carter works for sit
around in the lacklustre decadence of a half-hearted orgy, watching
pornographic slides that themselves have a brutal yet detached reality
about them. Masterfully shot by Wolfgang Suschitzky, the characters
are dissected by the frame, reflecting their incompleteness, loss of self,
and cold separation. This is followed by a title sequence where the
immaculately tailored Carter is travelling north by train, and is seen
taking unidentified drops and tablets (undoubtedly 'uppers' and
'downers') and becoming progressively more dishevelled – even the
'honest villains', the folk hero-monsters of the 1960s, have fallen foul
of the pornography and drugs they peddle, slipping into decadence.

This is the decadence of the south, of London, and whenever and
wherever those connected to the London 'mob' appear there is a
degree of ineffectuality, disconnectedness, and of being somehow
'missing'. Nowhere is this shown more clearly than in the gratuitous
(though laden with symbolism) phone sex scene, where Carter and
Fletcher's wife Anna (Brit Eckland) are literally disconnected by some
260 miles. Carter's detached, soulless persona allows him to indulge
in a graphic sexual conversation with his lover, whilst his landlady sits
only feet away from him, her movements in the rocking chair
reflecting growing passions. After the sexual liberation of the 1960s,
what was left? A sensual, erotic scene, rendered seedy and unsatisfy-
ing: a fitting prediction for the 1970s. The scene itself ends with a
degree of ineffectuality, with Gerald Fletcher arriving home to his
wife writhing on a bed, phone pressed to her ear. His only reaction
is, 'What's the matter? You got gut trouble or something?' (Hodges

1999: 25), leaving Anna unfulfilled and Carter disconnected (though with the possibility of reconnection to a different number – Edna, his landlady).

Whilst decadence captures the South, the North is depicted as a place of decay, in the fabric of the industrial yards the film uses as a backdrop, and in the attitudes, aspirations, and morality of the working class that populate the *mise-en-scène*. There is an evident dereliction in the core industries – gone is Harold Wilson's 'Britain ... forged in the white heat of this revolution'[1] of the 1960s, replaced by a harsh, aging industrial landscape, populated by harsh, aging caricatures: flat-capped, toothless, beer-bellied men, and bouffanted, weighty, hardened women.

Aided by an almost documentary realism[2] sections of the action are played out within traditional working-class places: the pub, the races, the bookmakers, the café, the bingo hall, etc. There is irony in the use of a form that was once seen as a force for unifying the nation, to record a society so deeply divided and so evidently in decline. There is similar irony in the socially predictive nature of the film that seems to offer pre-echoes of Thatcherite Britain, of the pervasive drug culture of the 1990s, and of the sexually open 'gangster' culture of the turn of the millennium.

The documentary feel is enhanced by Hodges's use of local Tynesiders to 'flavour' the action. Suschitzky frames much of the action against this local backdrop, often off-centring the principals to emphasise their place within a wider local grouping. When Carter arrives in Newcastle and heads for a pub, it is the reaction of the 'locals' to his request for a beer that not only lends a sense of difference but a clear sense of realism, highlighting a class divide, and a north–south divide that was to set the political and social battleground for the next three decades.

> *Carter*: A pint of bitter.
> *The barman picks up a glass mug and begins to draw the beer. Carter snaps his fingers at him.*
> In a thin glass.
>
> (Hodges 1999: 6)

The documentary look is consciously relaxed when Carter comes into contact with those controlling events around his brother's death (and consequently this part of Carter's life), and either consciously or subconsciously indicates that the Cliff Brumbys and Cyril Kinnears of this world are somehow disconnected from reality, or perhaps cushioned from it by their wealth and position. Their demise however revives a documentary feel, which suggests a post-modern playfulness in form that sets this film apart from most of its predecessors.

Throughout the film there are conscious nods towards the doc-umentary tradition, but none are so foregrounded as the intertextual referencing of the classic pre-war documentary *Spare Time* (Jennings, 1939). The 'northern' *mise-en-scène* of pubs and dancehalls has its antecedence in Humphrey Jennings's seminal work, as can be seen from the scene where Carter and Edna's lovemaking is juxtaposed with shots of a kazoo marching band, 'The Pelaw Hussars', who are reminiscent of the marching band in *Spare Time* (even to the small boy leading/dancing at the front). The intertextual reference is con-firmed at the end of their sequence where the sound of the kazoos can be heard across a Carter/Edna scene and they are playing a refrain from *Spare Time*. The scene itself is one of moral decay, with Carter's illicit liaison being set against the innocence of youthful activity.

Carter's scenes with Edna are indicative of a broader representa-tional theme, as the roles of women in a post-sexual revolution period are explored. Feminism was only just reaching public con-sciousness, and Hodges displays a mix of the familiar and yet different in the women he portrays. All are secondary to the main protagonist, yet all are prominent in the choices that face Carter, choices that lead ultimately to an inevitable end. Whilst reflecting cultural changes and the impact of gender politics, Hodges maintains Carter as a typical noirish anti-hero, whose ultimate downfall has women at its root. Similarly, these proto-feminist women that Hodges places on the screen fulfil the destinies of the femme-fatale, regularly kissed and slapped in an image of the victim, whilst manipulating scenarios to their advantage with little concern for the consequences to others.

Yet Hodges provides a twist in a neat noir conclusion to an analysis of *Get Carter* through two of the principal female characters, Glenda (Geraldine Moffat) and Doreen (Petra Markham). Glenda initially fulfils the role of the archetypal femme-fatale, in working for Cliff Brumby to ensnare Carter. She works through the noir handbook, bringing Carter to the true villain, saving him from adversaries, offering herself sexually to him, and then paying the price in death. However, Glenda is not the traditional manipulator of noir, but instead a woman surviving in the grip of crime, but with no view of the larger picture, and no motive other than the immediate desire to prove her worth to those who have power. Indeed it is Glenda who offers the narrative 'reveal' (in a scene where Caine's acting is demonstrated at its best) through ignorance of Carter's situation, and by absenting herself from the scene, leaving Carter with a key piece of evidence to finally connect the pieces to understand the reason for his brother's murder.

It is in this scene that the reality of Doreen's situation becomes clear and becomes the plot point for the final act of the film. Doreen is Carter's niece, but in an early scene a throw-away line offers a possibility that she is in fact Carter's illegitimate daughter. The morality of Doreen is shown throughout, and she realistically represents the noir 'virgin' whose role (often unsuccessful) is to save the protagonist. The 'reveal' however shows her to be just another 'actress' in one of the porn films that flicker through the plot, and it would seem one that was not necessarily under duress. Is she simply taking the opportunity to make money without concern for consequences that lead to the death of her father, and the death of her revenging uncle/father? If so, she is no longer the noir 'virgin/victim', but is instead a different and emergent character, presaging a profound change in the representation of women on the screen and their societal roles.

Get Carter's central theme of revenge for the blood of family in the face of capitalist and criminal greed was one that resonated with audiences at the time as it was seen as a man 'doing what men do'. To some in a modern, post-Thatcherite audience, this gangster, this killer, is simply representing the disenfranchised fighting society's dominant and controlling forces: a born-again David with Goliath in the sights of his shotgun. To those whose vision of the gangster world comes from the films of Guy Ritchie, Carter has a sense of authenticity, of believability, whilst retaining style and a set of quotable witty one-liners. When he throws Brumby to his death off the multi-storey car park, there is anger, but tempered with a brutal professionalism. Yet the sophistication of his revenge against Kinnear, and less obliquely Fletcher, shows a level of malevolence and manipulation that takes him out of the role of noir protagonist and into that of tragic hero, who must have realised his actions would result in his own death.

Setting the British gangster film bar high indeed, Get Carter was undeniably of its time and yet (for film audiences and censors worldwide) significantly before its time. Its ending shocked and still shocks; having been prepared for and witnessing Carter's successful revenge it seems fundamentally 'unfair' that he has only moments to savour it, and more so that he is dispatched so callously from afar at the point he is renouncing his past life. It is at this moment, and moments like this throughout the film, where audiences are taken out of a cosy 'narrative reality' and faced with events that are all too 'real', that they either 'get' *Get Carter* or struggle with it until it comes round again, calculated, relentless, and unstoppable.

Notes

1 Speech at Labour Party Conference, Scarborough, 1st October 1963.
2 Wolfgang Suschitzky began his career as a photographer and cut his cinematic teeth working with Paul Rotha. His camera operator was Dusty Miller, later responsible for the gritty London look in TV's *The Sweeney* and *Minder*.

Further Reading

Michael Caine, *What's It All About?* London, Arrow, 1993.
Ali Catterall and Simon Wells, *Your Face Here: British Cult Movies Since the Sixties*, London, Fourth Estate, 2001.
Steve Chibnall, *Get Carter: The British Film Guide 6*, London, Tauris, 2003.
Steve Chibnall and Robert Murphy (eds) *British Crime Cinema*, London, Routledge, 1999.
Get Carter: the original site (http://www.btinternet.com/~mark.dear/carter-index.htm).
Get Carter Tour (http://www.aouq09.dsl.pipex.com/getcarter).
Mike Hodges, *Get Carter: The Screenplay*, Eye, ScreenPress, 1999.

FREDDIE GAFFNEY

THE WICKER MAN (1973)

[Production Company: British Lion Film Corporation. Director: Robin Hardy. Screenwriter: Anthony Shaffer. Cinematographer: Harry Waxman. Music: Paul Giovanni. Editor: Eric Boyd-Perkins. Art Director: Seamus Flannery. Cast: Edward Woodward (Sergeant Howie), Christopher Lee (Lord Summerisle), Britt Ekland (Willow), Diane Cilento (Miss Rose), Ingrid Pitt (Librarian), Lindsay Kemp (Alder MacGregor).]

Although celebrated by *Cinéfantastique* as 'The *Citizen Kane* of horror movies', *The Wicker Man* has only one genuine moment of terror, in the final dénouement (Bartholomew 1977: 4). In many ways it is not really a horror film at all. Moreover, it has had a che-quered history and very nearly disappeared without trace. So this tribute is evidence at least of the canonical status which certain, once debased, texts later enjoy amongst a cognoscenti (of loyal fans, devoted critics and now scholars too). More recently, that process of elevation for *The Wicker Man* reached new heights when it received that most dubious of accolades: a terrible Hollywood remake (Neil LaBute, 2006).

So if it is not really a horror film, what kind of film is *The Wicker Man*? For the most part it is a curious mixture of detective story and folk musical. And the fact that it is an amalgam of many genres makes for its idiosyncratic charm. As Eco suggests, a cult film must first 'provide a completely furnished world so that its fans can quote characters and episodes as if they were aspects of the fan's private sectarian world'. But furthermore, in order for a fan to engage with it, it must be possible 'to break, dislocate, unhinge it' (Eco 1987: 198). We need to enquire how a film which can be so fruitfully disassembled was put together in the first place.

Christopher Lee (who plays the laird of the remote Scottish island, Summerisle) was central to *The Wicker Man* project from the outset. In the late 1960s, weary of Count Dracula, he had approached the playwright Anthony Shaffer who promised to 'write him an intelligent horror film' (Brown 2000: 14); drawing inspiration from David Pinner's 1967 novel *Ritual*, concerning a police investigation of a child's death and occult witchcraft practices in a remote Cornish village, Shaffer began work on an original screenplay. A more fruitful source was J. G. Frazer's Victorian cod-anthropological study, *The Golden Bough*, which provides much of the symbolic iconography and ritual practice of Summerisle. Shaffer encouraged his friend Robin Hardy, recuperating after a mild heart attack, to research the 'old religion' with a view to constructing a story about the nature of sacrifice.

Meanwhile, the financially beleaguered independent producer British Lion had been bought by property tycoon John Bentley, who appointed Canadian Peter Snell as head of production. Keen to avert union fears of peremptory asset-stripping at Shepperton Studios, Bentley charged Snell to instigate some new projects. Snell met with Shaffer, Hardy and Lee and persuaded the studio to film *The Wicker Man* script. But there were strings attached to the modestly budgeted enterprise (£420,000). It had to be an all-location shoot, and it had to begin immediately. Not only was the production team thus assembled with unseemly haste and without proper location planning, but they faced the challenge of re-creating a blossoming Scottish May-time in a wet, cold autumn in 1972.

What the ensuing conflicts recorded by Bartholomew and Brown demonstrate (beyond their contribution to the film's cult notoriety) is how creative tensions in the collaborative process produce certain kinds of results on screen. They show an assemblage of individual creative contributions not properly synthesised by a singular vision, sometimes working against one another, pulling the film in different directions. This last point is a tendency noted by early reviewers and is partly a product also of the editing process.

During post-production British Lion again changed hands and Peter Snell was sacked. *The Wicker Man*, edited by Eric Boyd-Perkins, was released in an 84-minute version and put out as a B-feature on the same bill as Nicolas Roeg's *Don't Look Now* (1973). It previewed in London's Victoria Metropole in December 1973, before its official opening on 21 January 1974 at the Odeon Haymarket (Brown 2000: 113–114).

Most reviewers recognised the film's concept and damned its execution, praised the script and the calibre of the actors, but deemed the whole less than a sum of its parts. The *Financial Times* was not alone in its claim that the film's 'fascinating ingredients do not quite blend'.[1] The *Sunday Telegraph* said the film lacked the balanced 'inter-relation of the ordinary and the extraordinary that marks the best fantasy fiction'.[2] Such negative reactions not only reflect the common difficulty in locating the movie within established generic conventions, they point to the very lack of narrative cohesion which gives the film its cult appeal.

Meanwhile, at a preview screening, Christopher Lee suggested much of the original footage was missing; the ensuing investigation, which has passed into legend, reached the unlikely conclusion that the outtakes had been disposed of near Shepperton in the foundations of the M3 motorway. Lee has subsequently developed an elaborate conspiracy theory which charges the studio with deliberately suppressing much of his finest screen performance, and swears to this day that somewhere the original film exists.

Later a print of a longer (102-minute) cut, originally sent to veteran American independent producer Roger Corman with a view to US distribution, was rediscovered, and New Orleans film buffs Stirling Smith and John Simon launched a campaign with Hardy and Lee, to get this version restored and released. It was eventually shown some 20 years after its first theatrical release, on US cable television in 1993.

The complicated history of the film's different versions begged a definitive 'Director's Cut' that Hardy was only too pleased to endorse. Such flamboyant marketing ploys are designed to appeal to the film buff, the cultist and the collector – to re-brand a past product with classic status. It is significant that the DVD edition of *The Wicker*

Man (released in 2002) offers both the 84-minute and the 102-minute edits. Important to cult fans is the existence, side-by-side, of different versions that can be compared, replayed, debated and dissected.

Aside from the loss of the opening mainland scenes (102-minute cut) which serve to establish Sergeant Howie's dour, spotless Christian copper (Edward Woodward), the other major narrative change in the shorter (84-minute) version is the conflation of the two nights Howie spends on Summerisle into one, and the excision of the initiation rite of Ash Buchanan (Richard Wren). The three-day term Howie endures the islanders' Pagan practices in the longer version, building towards his May Day sacrifice, carries a weight of religious symbolism the shorter version loses. And the ritual offering of a virgin youth to the landlord's daughter Willow MacGregor (Britt Ekland) establishes her as the Siren Howie must resist during the second night. Furthermore, in the 84-minute version we are denied the introduction of Lord Summerisle (Christopher Lee) who brings the boy to Willow's window, with his elegy to fecundity and the promise of tomorrow's 'somewhat more serious offering'. Howie's initiation into Pagan practices is as strongly rooted in its procreation creed as it is in its death rituals. No accident then that his final 'sacrifice' in the cage of the Wicker Man's abdomen, should symbolise a return to the womb for this man who has, on religious principle, thwarted his own entry into the phallic community. The symbolic androgyny of this defining moment is plain: fatal incarceration within a male womb. It marks both the culmination of the profound anxiety about earthly sexual difference which is conspicuous throughout the film, and the spiritual transcendence (in Christian orthodoxy) to a realm in which sexual difference doesn't matter.

There are many self-conscious elements in the narrative which seem at first to jar, but (particularly on repeated viewing) have a resonance that propels them into cult appeal. These manifest themselves in several ways: symbolic reference, acting styles and body language, the use of music and the juxtaposition of certain camera shots. But together they conjure a sort of dissonance which might be termed *the spirit of play*.

This playful subterfuge begins from the moment Howie sets foot on the island and is met with denial by the harbour-master's inscrutable cronies, and continues with postmistress May Morrison's (Irene Sunters) resistance to the idea that her daughter is missing – she has a daughter, not Rowan, but Myrtle (Jennifer Martin), whom she introduces.

The bar-room drinking song that evening disrupts the impetus of Howie's investigation just as he has intruded upon their bawdy entertainment. There is a distinctive slap-stick style about this musical interlude, involving the whole company in an obviously rehearsed set-piece which impinges radically, if playfully, in the diegesis, and wrests power from Howie's serious purpose. Later, as the hapless Sergeant takes the air before retiring, he witnesses couples openly engaged in sex on the village green. This sequence is shot in a stylised slow motion which conveys the drowsy, hypnotic sexual power which has descended upon the villagers with nightfall.

The initiation of Ash Buchanan introduces Christopher Lee's Lord Summerisle whose body language is curiously stiff throughout, as if he were wearing a corset. There is something strange about the way he holds himself: the lower back, neck and shoulders. He is, we might say, a living totem: his physical power (and thus his political status amongst the islanders) is expressed symbolically (rather than actively) in this rigid, muscular, constrained posture. There is something sensually alluring and gratifying in his physical symmetry and command. Indeed, his whole body resonates with phallic power.

By contrast, Howie's waning authority is echoed in the literal stripping of his body: first, as a sexually tormented figure sweating in his pyjamas at Willow's potent dance, then in the donning of the Fool's costume stolen from Alder MacGregor (Lindsay Kemp), and finally in being attired in a plain, messianic shift at the moment of sacrifice.

The discovery of a hare in the coffin of Rowan Morrison (Geraldine Cowper) is captured in close-up with an accompanying musical twang from the Celtic harp. This is another repeated technique in narrative italicising – almost cartoon-style – which is overdone throughout. Similarly, there are visual gags such as the lingering close-up on the organ stop 'flute d'amour' at Lord Summerisle's castle which confound narrative verisimilitude. The body of web-based fan commentary on the film provides ample evidence that it is precisely such self-conscious, jarring discords (in camerawork and sound) which the cultist adores and, on repeated viewing, anticipates with relish.

Cult films tread these cracks in the paths of narrative engagement in the way they subvert codes of cinematic realism. In so doing, they become celebrated and cherished, as much for their hyperbolic flaws as their visual excesses. Such textual incongruities open up narrative spaces for that fan intervention so peculiar to cult films. They rehearse playful rituals which fans appropriate, re-enact and invest with meaningful pleasures beyond the realm of the text itself. *The Wicker Man*, then, offers the believer the raw materials of religious, sexual and political transgression within the safe, fairytale world of vicarious play.

Acknowledgement

A longer version of this work appears in Jonathan Murray, Lesley Stevenson, Stephen Harper, and Benjamin Franks (eds) *Constructing 'The Wicker Man': Film and Cultural Studies Perspectives*, Dumfries, University of Glasgow Crichton Publications, 2005.

Notes

1 Nigel Andrews, 'Holiday Fodder', *Financial Times*, 14 December 1973.
2 Margaret Hinxman, 'Sting in the Tail of the Year', *Sunday Telegraph*, 23 December 1973.

Further reading

David Bartholomew, 'The Wicker Man', *Cinéfantastique,* Vol. 6, No. 3, Winter, 1977.
Allan Brown, *Inside 'The Wicker Man': The Morbid Ingenuities*. London, Sidgwick and Jackson, 2000.
Ali Catterall and Simon Wells, *Your Face Here: British Cult Movies Since the Sixties*, London, Fourth Estate, 2001.
Umberto Eco, *Faith in Fakes: Essays*, trans. W. Weaver, London, Secker and Warburg, 1987.
Mark Jancovich, Antonio Lazaro Reboll, Julian Stringer and Andy Willis (eds), *Defining Cult Movies: The Cultural Politics of Oppositional Taste*, Manchester, Manchester University Press, 2003.

JUSTIN SMITH

PRESSURE (1975)

[Production Company: BFI Production. Director: Horace Ové. Screenwriters: Horace Ové, Samuel Selvon. Cinematographer: Mike Davis. Music: Boy Wonder. Editor: Alan J. Cumner-Price. Cast: Herbert Norville (Anthony 'Tony' Watson), Oscar James (Colin), Frank Singuineau (Lucas), Lucita Lijertwood (Bopsie), Sheila Scott-Wilkinson (Sister Louise), June Page (Sheila).]

Pressure was Britain's first full-length feature by a black director and the first to deal so explicitly with issues of race. Plotting the struggles faced by British-born black youth growing up in London in the early 1970s, it explores the themes of discrimination and the search for identity with anger and sincerity. It has been consistently hailed by critics as a 'transitional' film, a work that merits acclaim as 'a critique of British multiculturalism and institutionalised race relations' (Pines

2001: 180). While it relies on some familiar metaphors of culture clash, it also draws on a diverse range of cinematic influences in its examination of what it was like to be young, black and British at a time of intense social change.[1] It was the first British film to use reggae music so prominently as a film soundtrack, and thus to embed into the spectatorial experience a black art form that already had a profound effect on Britain.[2] Its influence on independent British film-making has been remarkable, and its politicised use of cinema to explore problems of racism and integration remains relevant today.

Horace Ové, born in Trinidad and with mixed African-American and Indian heritage, felt culturally well placed in telling this story about the struggles of three generations of a Trinidadian family living in Notting Hill. He wrote the screenplay with Sam Selvon, a Caribbean author, and together they researched life on the streets of West London, as well as drawing on their own experiences. Unlike the family portrayed in *Pressure*, however, Ové did not come to the UK with the first wave of so-called 'Windrush' West Indian immigrants in 1948, but arrived in 1960 with a desire to become a film-maker. Already an enthusiastic fan of the 'subtle, subliminal ways' (Johnston 2005: 20) used by Hollywood cinema to influence audiences, he found work as an extra on the set of *Cleopatra* and moved to Rome with the production, remaining there for four years at a time when Fellini and his like were producing some of their greatest works. His lack of Italian brought him back to London in the mid-1960s to study film more seriously and to begin to make films about subjects that inspired him personally.

Pressure recounts the story of a black school-leaver, English-born Tony (powerfully played by non-professional actor Herbert Norville) 'struggling to make sense of the casual racism and contradictory values around him' (Johnston 2005: 20). Its core message about culture clash between white British society and non-white immigrants (here, mainly Afro-Caribbean), and the trauma inflicted by racist abuse of different forms remains relevant today as a hard-hitting portrait of the second-generation immigrant experience. It is a character-driven film that examines black-British identity formation via the coming-of-age story of its protagonist and the revelation of his shock at realising that his different skin colour really does matter. This comes despite having grown up amongst white friends, holding British citizenship and having gained a normal education like his friends. The film introduces him as an ordinary young man who, like many school-leavers, is looking for his first job. Unlike most of those he has grown up with, however, the difficulties in finding that first job are compounded by the negative associations made by dominant white British society with the colour of his skin. Torn between the choices and attitudes offered to him as models by his conformist, conservative West Indian parents and his militant older brother, Tony occupies a liminal in-between space, culturally and psychologically. Moreover, the discomfiting portrayal of his journey of self-discovery thus effectively conveys the broader social frustrations of growing up in a situation of racial tension.

The plot focuses on the key moments at this turning point in Anthony's life. On leaving the protective environment of school, he suffers a series of acts of direct discrimination and feels increasingly insulted and patronised. All this comes in stark contrast to the way his white school friends treat him as one of them, and forces him to learn that he is perceived as an outsider regardless of his place of birth. As he searches for a sense of belonging, he ends up with those black friends who seek purpose through engaging in hostile action against the police.

Tony's situation and approach to life contrast profoundly with those of his parents, Lucas and Bopsie, representatives of the immigrants from the Windrush generation. It is made clear by their simple lifestyle and references to a higher social status back in Trinidad that they have had to make great sacrifices in order simply to be tolerated by dominant white British culture. Proud matriarch Bopsie, the least willing to accept that she will never fully integrate, covers up her naturally afro-curly hair by wearing a cheap wig that slips off when she confronts her youngest son about his increasingly erratic behaviour. The opening close-up high-angle image of sizzling fried eggs and bacon reinforces her absolute insistence that even in the kitchen she will pursue the pretence of having created an English lifestyle. She thus rejects the traditional West Indian food openly enjoyed by her older son as if it represents failure and betrayal, despite the fact that her husband sells such products in their shop downstairs. Moreover, she cleans the houses and offices of white people and urges Tony to consider any sort of paid employment, however humiliating this might seem for a bright young man with dreams of success. At first he appears willing to go along with her dream for him to enjoy a quiet, decent life, polishing off his English breakfast without question and taking on a job as a hospital porter after rejection elsewhere. However, he soon rebels when even his most humble attempts to find his place in society are dashed by the ignorance and prejudice of others.

The most obvious contrast, established during the breakfast sequence, is between Tony and his older brother Colin who is openly and aggressively hostile to what he perceives as a clear situation of exclusion of the black community by white colonial oppressors. He rejects his mother's food and ignores her pleas for him to stay out of trouble. He drifts in and out of the house, finding comfort only in his position as one of the outspoken leading members of the Black Power group. Tony finds his brother's lifestyle and politics distasteful and disrespectful at first, and is angry at Colin's hostility towards his white friends. But the younger man's bitter disappointment at being rejected or shunned in a variety of social situations leads him to think again. Through identification with Tony, the spectator is encouraged to consider Colin's attitude as understandable, if not totally acceptable, and Tony oscillates for most of the film between the choice of passive conformity of his parents and the path of violent confrontation chosen by his brother, ultimately remaining in limbo.

In different ways, Tony's cultural background puts him at odds with his white friends from school, and places him at a disadvantage when it comes to job applications even when his intelligence is not in question. While the various antagonisms between him and family members seem familiar to him, he is at first far less aware of the conflict provoked by his different skin colour in social situations. Nevertheless, his white friends are portrayed sympathetically, and the film is remarkable partly because it refuses to bow to any easy black–white dichotomy. Tony and his friends are not at any point portrayed as polar opposites, but as young friends who struggle to understand why skin colour matters. They support Tony as much as they can and are framed together in many shots, but by failing to appreciate the difficulties he faces because of his darker skin colour when trying to get a job or walk a girl home, they are also forced to face up to their own social ignorance. The film thus suggests that the struggle for change should involve white as well as black members of society, and that racial tolerance should be the goal for the sake of harmony and prosperity generally.

Ové was well aware that the themes and approach of his debut feature were likely to upset. He struggled to harness institutional support as *Pressure* was regarded as a risky project, financially and politically. Eventually, the British Film Institute gave some funding, but the organisation was cautious about the project and Ové had to draw on considerable back-up from his (black and white) film-maker friends from the National Film and Television School where he had been a student. He realised that gaining the appropriate permissions for location shooting would be tricky, so decided not to bother and filmed in places, such as supermarkets and high streets, where everyday people went about their everyday business, capturing them without their knowledge and thus adding to the sense of authenticity and urgency of his work. Distribution of the film was also very difficult. The official British film industry was unsure how to market it without making it appear difficult and controversial, and hence unappealing in a commercial sense.[3]

When it was finally released on a limited circuit the film was much praised by those critics and audiences who were able to see it. However, Ové continued to experience difficulty with getting support for a longer or wider release via festivals or commercial circuits. Almost inevitably, the film was uncomfortable for the British establishment with its blunt revelations of social inequality and injustice. It also caused embarrassment for those who had experienced the Windrush migrant directly: the sight of Bopsie, dishevelled and distraught with her skirt above her knees and the dreams of success she had for her younger son in tatters, proved to be too painful a reminder of a recent traumatic and humiliating period of transition.

The final image of black political protest is, as Pines points out, 'deliberately pessimistic in tone, accurately reflecting the general sense of despair over the "failure" of race relations politics that was felt within black communities by the mid-1970s' (2001: 180). The film's final message nevertheless offers a defiant cry for marginalised individuals and communities to join together to fight for their identity and their rights to be recognised and respected by mainstream society. Ové's debut served to expose the fact that immigrant life is a struggle, and that whatever approach to protest is taken – whether compromise and negotiation or hostility and violence – is likely to be long and painful.

Notes

1 Ové's cinematic style was largely influenced by his time spent in Italy: from neo-realism (authenticity achieved through use of non-professional actors and location shooting) to surrealism (as seen in the dream/hallucination sequence that holds echoes of the work of Fellini). The fractured, fragmentary editing style of the protest scenes is further reminiscent of New Wave approaches.

2 Ové's American documentary, *Reggae* (1971), was described by Jim Pines as being 'thoroughly in the black film ethos, making a poignant statement about the black experience' (2001: 117).

3 A similar problem of marketing was experienced much later by the producers of *East is East* (Damien O'Donnell, 1999), whose film was promoted as a British comedy even though it dealt quite seriously with issues of culture clash, prejudice and racism.

Further Reading

Manthia Diawara, 'Power and Territory: The Emergence of Black British Film Collectives' in Lester Friedman (ed.) *British Cinema and Thatcherism*, London, UCL Press, 1993.

Sheila Johnston, 'Filmmakers on Film: Horace Ové on Steven Spielberg's *War of the Worlds*', *Daily Telegraph*, 17 September 2005.

Sarita Malik, *Representing Black Britain: Black and Asian Images on Television*, London, Sage, 2002.

Jim Pines, 'Black Films in White Britain' in Margaret Dickinson (ed.) *Rogue Reels: Oppositional Film in Britain, 1945–90*, London, BFI, 1999.

Jim Pines 'British Cinema and Black Representation' in Robert Murphy (ed.) *The British Cinema Book*, 2nd edn, London, BFI, 2001.

SARAH BARROW

JUBILEE (1978)

[Production Company: Megalovision. Director: Derek Jarman. Screenwriter: Jarman. Cinematographer: Peter Middleton. Music: Brian Eno. Editor: Nick Barnard. Cast: Jenny Runacre (Elizabeth I and Bod), Nell Campbell (Crabs), Toyah Wilcox (Mad), Jordan (Amyl Nitrite), Hermine Demorrane (Chaos), Ian Charleson (Angel), Karl Johnson (Sphinx).]

> Jarman is a troublesome case and appears to relish his role as a thorn in the official flesh of the British cinema ... He is no less troublesome to the avant-garde.[1]

The cinema which dominates our world consists mainly of fictional narratives; it often features established star performers, and fits within or extends established genres. Most of its films last between two and three hours, some are part of a series and through the past hundred years of their history these 'feature' films have often been adapted from novels, plays, short stories and comic books.

This is important, for it reminds us that when cinema was created it quickly adopted many of the devices of theatre and literature to guide its development. Because this commitment to narrative seems somewhat 'natural' we rarely ask why it developed in the first place and in particular why it developed so quickly in a medium – film – which was, in the early 1900s, almost wholly a visual medium with the possibility of a musical accompaniment. Why was this new medium with no facility for words beyond its disruptive inter-titles so swift to adopt the techniques and conventions of literature and theatre and why has it remained preoccupied with narrative, character-centred fiction?

Despite the dominance of narrative fiction there are alternative approaches which reach back many decades including montage, surrealism, abstraction or the search for an 'authentic' documentary realism. These possibilities have continued to interest film- (and now of course, digital video-) makers and their influence can often be seen superficially in pop videos, movie trailers, television advertising and the general 'flow' of moving images throughout our lives. However, it is wrong to consider these 'alternatives' as a single coherent opposition to 'Hollywood'-style fiction.

One of the characteristics of modernist, avant-garde practice in all the arts has been a tendency for practitioners to seek comfort in groups of like-minded artists, proclaiming to the world through manifestos and critical writing their commitment to a particular approach to aesthetic production and their (often vehement) rejection of other kinds of work. In the world of experimental film many of those who pursued a kind of pure abstraction rejected the narrative references of surrealism. The surrealists in turn proclaimed a preference for popular cinema over the bourgeois pretensions of the 1920s avant-garde.

Occasionally a film-maker would emerge with so specific a vision and approach that he or she did not fit easily into any such groups. Derek Jarman was such a film-maker for he seemed to produce work with a powerful visual style, an imaginative use of sound and music and yet an interest in character, narrative and both contemporary and historical documentation. His work seemed to discover and draw upon the range of film practices where other artists would commit to a more limited approach. This multi-dimensional vision might have seen him acclaimed as one of the more remarkable film-makers of the recent past; yet in fact Jarman's films, including *Jubilee*, often upset many of the people they might have most impressed.

Jarman was born in the London suburbs in 1942. From public school he went through art college, studying painting at the Slade and mixing with some of the leading British 'Pop' painters of the 1960s. He worked as a designer for the Royal Ballet, the Royal Opera House and on Ken Russell's films *The Devils* and *Savage Messiah*, before making 8 mm films while continuing to paint. In 1972 he published his first book of poems and four years later released his first feature film *Sebastiane*.

Jarman's second feature film *Jubilee* was released in 1978. It might be described as a punk film, a film about punk or an avant-garde film of its period. Any of these claims would invite criticism which would reveal much about the place of Jarman in British film history. In retrospect, punks have been highly critical of the film, suggesting that while it was made at the time of punk it does not 'represent' what happened in any authentic way. Meanwhile, as *Jubilee* began showing on the mainstream circuit the British avant-garde regarded this as 'selling out'.

This is typical of the reading of Jarman as the outsider, the man who never found a place in any group other than his own, despite his prolific and sociable creativity. As Michael O'Pray has suggested: 'Jarman is an awkward case in the great art tradition: neither a Wardour Street nor an avant-garde film-maker, nor a recognised painter' (O'Pray 1994: 20).

This diversity is intriguing and perhaps explains why Jarman was attracted to punk in his film. O'Pray added that Jarman contributed significantly 'across a wide spectrum of art' but in some respects it is the negatives in O'Pray's statement which are most interesting in that they force us to think imaginatively about how we might summarise clearly the enterprise and contribution of Jarman to British cultural life. We may be able to say what he was not, but can we say what he was?

Jubilee adds to the complexity of any analysis since it is in one sense the major contemporary British punk film, yet it is not greatly admired by many key figures in the British punk scene of the late 1970s. For example, Colegrave and Sullivan recorded how in *Jubilee*: 'Derek Jarman produced his own fittingly anarchic and sensationalist view of punk . . . with plenty of unscary violence, unerotic sex and an uninteresting storyline' (Colegrave and Sullivan 2001: 291).

In the same publication, Sullivan also suggested that the film was 'a badly-acted, over arty and gratuitously violent pile of rubbish' (ibid: 317). He suggests that Don Letts's contemporary 'documentary' *Punk Rock Movie* was always more 'relevant' as a 'testament to the era'.

This raises a fascinating question about the extent to which any film which appears to represent a particular era or set of historical events should be judged against such 'realist' criteria. Was *Jubilee* intended to be a punk 'documentary' and even if it were, might it now function as a film in its own right without being obliged to represent British Punk circa 1977? If we accept Hebdige's (1979: 62–70) identification of Punk as one of the key British subcultures of the period between the 1950s and 1980, then it is interesting to ask to what extent any of the other groups he identified including teddy boys, beatniks, rockers, mods or skinheads were represented effectively in contemporary feature films. The answer, of course, is very little. One key reason is that feature films, unlike recordings, magazines, news stories and even television documentaries take too long to emerge from inception to circulation. In addition there is a romantic view that 'authentic' subcultures always exist underground so that by the time they emerge to be represented in film their essential features have been diluted. This may be an issue for any readings of *Jubilee* by those who claim to have been there 'at the time'. So, *Jubilee* may be better considered as a fictional and somewhat experimental work of cinema in its own right.

Nonetheless even if *Jubilee* fails to satisfy the demands of contemporary punks, it may offer us insights into a certain 'sense' of how punk impacted more broadly upon British life in the second half of the 1970s and this might in turn present ideas about how the film is a punk film even if it is not an 'authentic' film about punk. This is particularly because in certain respects both punk and *Jubilee* resisted popular dichotomies between mass culture and the avant-garde. Both brought together an uneasy collision of aesthetics and anger, convention and chaos, protest and posturing. In punk this occurred through a stylistic merging of proletarian rock and art school invention – in *Jubilee*, through an uneasy mix of experiment, personal vision and narrative conventions.

Punk may be seen as a matter of contradiction, extending beyond the first innocent rebelliousness of previous subcultural groups. It emerged in the 1970s, the decade of high cultural theory, alongside the early public formulations of postmodernism and in a period of significant expansion in higher education when, nonetheless Britain celebrated tradition with a fervour for flags and 1940s-style street parties. It grew from disenchantment with 1960s idealism and is driven by frustration and competing opposites. It was always, as Hebdige puts it, sliding 'between poverty and elegance' (ibid: 66), it used the signs of Empire in a knowing irony, it is angry and oppositional yet caught up in the signs of opposition and unable to make any real difference outside the world of youth culture and consumption.

If *Jubilee* is unsatisfactory to the central players in punk it can nonetheless be seen to embody and even describe these contradictions while pursuing a fairly British literary yet visual experimental film aesthetic. By the summers of punk, Jarman was in his mid-thirties – too old to be an 'authentic' punk although like Malcolm McLaren and Vivienne Westwood a plausible influence. Rowland Wymer (2005) for example tells us that Jarman began the film with an interest in Jordan, who worked in McLaren and Westwood's shop – she had already appeared in his film *Sebastiane* – and Jarman had also shot some early footage of the Sex Pistols performing in London.

This interest in Jordan develops through the film into a depiction of the young punk women as dominant and more decisive than their male counterparts, a point which the openly gay Jarman emphasises through his representation of Britain's two Queen Elizabeths.

However, Tracy Biga (1996) points out that the male and female characters in *Jubilee* seemed to have exchanged sexual and social roles – almost anticipating the dominance of a female British prime minister in the decade following the film's release. She notes that the men's lovemaking

> consists of soulful kisses and long looks in a tastefully under-decorated bedroom and outdoors. The women's names – Bod, Crabs, Mad and Amyl Nitrate – suggest their more graphic, nitty-gritty approach to sex ... The women's ambition to enter the media society fuels their destructive rampages.
>
> (Biga 1996: 21)

Despite these contemporary representations, one of *Jubilee*'s central characters is the first Queen Elizabeth who, accompanied by the philosopher John Dee, travels from the past to encounter the dis-satisfactions of the second Queen Elizabeth's Jubilee year in a Britain struggling with economic and political problems. This link with history is characteristic of much of Jarman's work for he may be seen as the artistic innovator with a deep love of the history and traditions of his culture, yet he simultaneously produces a film of anti-establishment, sacrilegious, sexual and violent images. In *Jubilee*, the visitors from three centuries earlier are dismayed by the lack of optimism they find in their country's anarchic future and they ask fearfully of the whereabouts of God.

Jarman's film-making is highly individual – as independent aesthetically as it was economically. Ultimately it may be that the impossibility of locating Jarman clearly within any apparently coherent group, movement or dominant aesthetic leaves him as an awkward figure within British cultural history. Wymer has pointed out that the ambiguities in *Jubilee* do not merely distance Jarman from the 'simple-minded punk aggression', they also help 'to expose contradictions within punk itself' (Wymer 2005: 59). We might see Jarman's whole approach to film-making as spreading that same sense of uncertainty – thereby explaining why he has remained a somewhat marginalised figure despite considerable critical interest. Perhaps we are generally more comfortable with stories that resemble other stories. If so, neither Jarman nor his films offer us that comfort.

Note

1 Simon Field, 'The Garden of Earthly Delights', *The Face*, 21 January 1993, p. 62.

Further Reading

Tracy Biga, 'The Principle of Non-narration in the Films of Derek Jarman' in Chris Lippard (ed.) *By Angels Driven: the Films of Derek Jarman*, Trowbridge, Flicks Books, 1996.

Stephen Colegrave and Chris Sullivan, *Punk London*, London, Cassell, 2001.

Dick Hebdige, *Subculture: the Meaning of Style*, London, Routledge, 1979.

Chris Lippard (ed.) *By Angels Driven: the Films of Derek Jarman*, Trowbridge, Flicks Books, 1996.

Michael O'Pray, 'If You Want to Make Films', *Art into Film: Sight and Sound Supplement*, July 1994, pp. 20–22.

Rowland Wymer, 'Anarchy in the UK: *Jubilee* (1978)' in *Derek Jarman*, Manchester, Manchester University Press, 2005.

DAVE ALLEN

MY BEAUTIFUL LAUNDRETTE (1985)

[Production Company: Channel Four Films/Working Title Films/SAF Productions. Director: Stephen Frears. Screenwriter: Hanif Kureishi. Cinematographer: Oliver Stapleton. Editor: Mick Audsley. Music: Ludus Tonalis. Cast: Saeed Jaffrey (Nasa), Roshan Seth (Papa), Daniel Day Lewis (Jonny), Gordon Warnecke (Omar), Derrick Branche (Salim), Shirley Anne Field (Rachel), Rita Wolf (Tania).]

My Beautiful Laundrette is indisputably one of the most important British films of the 1980s. It took risks, asked questions, and broke boundaries. The first boundary it broke was that between film and television. Filmed for Channel 4 in 16 mm for the extremely modest sum of £600,000, it created such a sensation at the 1985 Edinburgh Film Festival that it was decided to release it as a feature film. This was contrary to director Stephen Frears's intentions; he had tailored the film for a television audience and liked the idea that it would be seen once by a sizeable audience and prove an instant talking point, rather in the manner of a trailblazing drama such as Ken Loach's *Cathy Come Home* (1966). If it had been proposed as a feature film in the first place, he seriously doubted whether it would ever have been made: after all, he reasoned, who on earth would pay to see a film about a gay Pakistani opening a laundry in a run-down area of London? In fact, the film not only crossed media boundaries but geographical and cultural ones as well. When it opened in America, Pauline Kael, the influential critic of the *New Yorker* magazine, praised its freshness and it was to earn an Oscar nomination for its writer, Hanif Kureishi.[1]

The freshness comes from the style and particularly the perspective. This is a look at Margaret Thatcher's Britain from the immigrant's point of view. It is a country seen as characterised by racism, inequality, gender prejudice and entrepreneurial greed, but the particular viewpoint gives an unexpected twist to this, reversing expectations and stereotypes. The beneficiaries of this materialist, conservative spirit are shown to be upwardly mobile Pakistanis, making the most of the commercial opportunities available and, in the process, upending the power structures of old colonialism. They are now the ones with money, property and jobs, and it is the young white racists with time on their hands who are the new underclass – sidelined, homeless, angry and unemployed. A further irony is that, at the centre of this capitalist success story, in which a young Pakistani, Omar (Gordon Warnecke) is bankrolled by his uncle Nasser (Saeed Jaffrey) so that he can open a new laundrette, is a gay, interracial love affair – something not on the Thatcherite agenda. Omar loves Johnny (Daniel Day Lewis), a former National Front activist now trying to shed his violent and racist past, and wants to involve him in his venture.

At the time of making the film, Kureishi said he was reading a lot of George Orwell essays claiming how decent and tolerant the British were: this did not exactly square with Kureishi's experience as an Asian in England. His screenplay courageously explores some of the tensions and contradictions of immigrant life in a so-called multiracial society, where, as Nasser's associate, Salim (Derrick Branche) says, you are nothing without money and where the sense of home and belonging is always elusive. Born in London of a Pakistani father and a white mother, Kureishi felt that the characters of Omar and Johnny represented two aspects of himself, and the film was his attempt to bring them together in harmony amidst all the frictions. He knew that his portrayal of the Asian community might cause offence. He shows them as ruthless landlords, drug dealers, purveyors of porn, but, as he insisted, he never shows them as victims: there is a real vibrancy to the characterisation and great variety too. There is not only generational conflict between parents and children, but also ideological difference between the same generations. Nasser's dynamic, rampant commercialism ('There's no question of race in the enterprise culture', he tells Omar) is in stark contrast to the passive idealism of Omar's father (Roshan Seth), whose political journalism has forced him into exile from his home country and who believes that college not commerce is the key to his son's future. Women are domesticated and secondary in this society, though in Nasser's daughter, Tania (Rita Wolf), there are stirrings of rebellion and a reluctance to accept female subservience as the status quo.

These are serious themes and the film will build to a powerful climax when the tensions erupt into violence. Nevertheless, Kureishi and Frears seem well aware of the George Bernard Shaw maxim: 'If you want to tell people the truth, you'd better make them laugh, or they'll kill you'. Unlike other British films of the 1980s with a political axe to grind, the tone is satirical more than polemical. The mood is often lightened with some deft comedy, as in the scene where a drugs delivery turns out to be hidden in a man's venerable grey beard, or in the very name of the laundrette, 'Powders', a sly hint at how the operation is being financed. There is even a touch of surrealism, when Nasser's wife casts a spell on his mistress, Rachel (Shirley Anne Field) in an attempt to break up the relationship. It works too: as Rachel reasonably explains to Nasser, she cannot continue with a romance that causes her to come out in a hideous rash and where her furniture starts moving.

This occasional element of play is niftily negotiated by Stephen Frears's direction, which nudges the material away from realism and towards family melodrama. It also has its virtuosic moments, as in an extraordinary shot towards the end of the film, far more elaborate than one would expect in your usual television feature, when the camera cranes from the laundrette up and over the roof to disclose the gang of white racists readying themselves for trouble. Frears was just making use of a giant crane that had been mistakenly delivered one day, but it is a shot that gives a spectacular new dimension to the story, heightening the tension and lifting it off the streets. Like his mentors Karel Reisz and Lindsay Anderson, for whom he worked as an assistant on *Morgan – A Suitable Case for Treatment* (1966) and *If . . .* (1968), Frears had absorbed their gift of presenting familiar things in an unfamiliar way. Like them, his base is broadly realistic, but it is realism with a kink; and although he claims the secret of a good film is in the script, he has a visual flair that brings good writing to life. *My Beautiful Laundrette* turned out to be his breakthrough film: it was on the strength of it that he was offered the direction of *Dangerous Liaisons* (1988), which proved a big Hollywood success. Curiously, the theme of 'dangerous liaisons' was to prove a leitmotif in a number of Frears's films, however strenuously he might disavow the auteur theory: apart from Omar and Johnny in *Laundrette*, where the danger of discovery is one of the film's principal sources of tension, there is Joe Orton and his murderous gay partner in *Prick Up Your Ears* (1987), the precarious friendship at the heart of *Dirty Pretty Things* (2002), even Tony Blair and Gordon Brown in *The Deal* (2003). This in itself is no guarantee of interest or quality, of course, but the recurrence of this pattern might partially explain why the script for *Laundrette* excited him more than any he had read for years, because it combined a favoured narrative and character pattern with a trenchant political critique with which he fundamentally agreed.

Early on in the film, Omar is invited to a party at Nasser's house and is ushered into his uncle's room. There is a striking point-of-view shot as he pushes gently on the door and it opens quite slowly, as if to mark an entry into a whole new world. In some ways, the shot symbolises Frears's approach too. He not only likes outsider-heroes, but he enjoys coming into films himself as an outsider. Unlike many directors who prefer making films about what they know, Frears likes making films about things he initially knows nothing about, thus becoming a tourist in other people's universe and seeing their world afresh. The appeal of *Laundrette* for him was precisely its unusual perspective. Yet, buried within its structure, there is a kind of familiarity to it, which Frears, as an affectionate historian of British cinema, might subconsciously have recognised.[2] It has some similarity to the Ealing comedy, *The Man in the White Suit* (1951), made by one of Frears's favourite directors, Alexander Mackendrick, notably in its focus on a hero whose inventiveness arouses the envy and ire of a vengeful mob.

Even more strongly, it follows the narrative paradigm of Charles Dickens's *Great Expectations*, famously adapted for the screen in 1946 by David Lean and which Frears describes in his documentary as a 'wonderful film'. For example, as the young man rising out of his station in life on a tide of criminal money, Omar is clearly the equivalent of Dickens's Pip; as his best friend, who started by fighting him but who is now his devoted business partner, Johnny is obviously Herbert Pocket; Omar's principled but ineffectual father, who visits the laundrette but feels out of place in his son's new world, recalls Joe Gargery. And the film's Miss Havisham, the hero's supposed bene-factress but who is actually contaminating his soul? Why, Margaret Thatcher, of course. In a decade when the Conservative government explicitly extolled the virtues of what it called 'Victorian values', the work of Dickens (often critical of institutions, the law, injustice) became an important counter-symbol of Victorianism in artistic productions like, for example, the Royal Shakespeare Company's legendary version of *Nicholas Nickleby* in 1982, the BBC's eloquently bleak TV serialisation of *Bleak House* in 1985, and Christine Edzard's melancholy two-part film of *Little Dorrit* in 1987. *My Beautiful Laundrette* was a particularly imaginative (possibly unconscious) addition to this trend, a wholly individual work in its own right but worthy of the 'Dickensian' epithet by virtue of the audacity of its symbolism, the range of its characterisation, its satirical rage. Dickens would undoubtedly have loved the central symbol of the laundrette, this new curiosity shop that becomes a focal point of 'English' enterprise and envy and where the tensions of the main characters finally converge and explode.

At the end nothing has been resolved. In retaliation at Salim's deliberate injuring of one of their members, the white gang has beaten him nearly to death; they also assault Johnny and vandalise the laundrette. In a tender coda, Omar and Johnny lovingly tend each other's wounds, leaving an audience to ponder their future and also leaving us to ponder the social wounds the film has exposed. In the spirit of its remit to cater for minority tastes, Channel 4 helped to fund a number of offbeat and challenging British films during this period: among them, *Another Time, Another Place* (Michael Radford, 1983), *The Ploughman's Lunch* (Richard Eyre, 1983), *Another Country* (Marek Kanievska, 1984), *Letter to Brezhnev* (Chris Bernard, 1985), *Dance with a Stranger* (Mike Newell, 1985), and *High Hopes* (Mike Leigh, 1988). Hugely entertaining, finely acted and socially resonant, *My Beautiful Laundrette* was also the product of this fruitful relationship and one of its finest examples. It remains the artistic yardstick by which the cinematic representation of multi-cultural Britain is measured.

Notes

1 The eventual winner of the Screenwriting Oscar was to be Woody Allen.
2 Frears's affection for history was revealed in his 1994 documentary for Channel 4, *Typically British: A Personal History of British Film*.

Further reading

Lester D. Friedman (ed.) *Fires Were Started: British Cinema and Thatcherism, 2nd edition*, London, Wallflower Press, 2006.

Christine Geraghty, *My Beautiful Laundrette*, London, I.B.Tauris, 2005.

Hanif Kureishi, 'Scenes from a Marriage', *Monthly Film Bulletin*, November 1985, p. 333.

Neil Sinyard, 'Dickensian Themes in Modern British Film', *The Dickensian*, Summer 1989, pp. 108–117.

NEIL SINYARD

THE COOK, THE THIEF, HIS WIFE & HER LOVER (1989)

[Production Company: Allarts Cook. Director and screenwriter: Peter Greenaway. Cinematographer: Sacha Vierny. Music: Michael Nyman. Editor: John Wilson. Cast: Michael Gambon (Albert Spica), Helen Mirren (Georgina Spica), Richard Bohringer (Richard Borst), Alan Howard (Michael), Tim Roth (Mitchel), Ciaran Hands (Cory), Gary Olsen (Spangler).]

Peter Greenaway's films have always divided their audiences and critical response. But *The Cook, The Thief, His Wife & Her Lover* deserves 'classic British' status because, of all his films, it did capture something of its time, and even entered the broader culture, thanks to some courageous performances, Michael Nyman's timely 'minimalist baroque' score, and a very strange title. Greenaway intended *The Cook* as a savage satire, in the tradition of Jonathan Swift, 'on the current British political situation. Since this is a movie about consumer society, it's about greed – a society's, a man's' (Smith 1990: 55). But as with all Greenaway films, *The Cook* is at the same time a rejection of the conventions of mass popular, feature-film cinema– 'Hollywood' – and is concocted according to its director's own distinctive recipe. This is therefore a very ambitious project: can Greenaway's highly individual aesthetic simultaneously deliver a savage social critique?

By the end of 1990 the Berlin Wall had fallen, apartheid was rapidly crumbling in South Africa, and Saddam Hussein had invaded Kuwait. The world we currently know was taking shape. Within this longer perspective, *The Cook* now seems a retrospective, even claustrophobic film, addressing a domestic agenda in peculiarly British terms, in spite of its director's declared preference for European film style. The object of Greenaway's satirical attack was 'Thatcherism', or more precisely, the perceived consequences for British society of Margaret Thatcher's three Conservative administrations, first elected a decade earlier in 1979.

Thatcherism, partnered more grandly on the world-stage by 'Reaganomics', broke with the post-Second World War consensus on the economic regulation of the state. The brisk new agenda demanded: privatisation of formerly state-owned industries, utilities and assets to enforce competitive efficiency; reshaping of labour markets and trade-union law, again in the interests of a freer market; promotion of the entrepreneur economy in order to break the supposed 'dependency culture', and finally, an assault on the privileges and protective practices of the established, professional classes and their institutions – legal, medical and scholastic. These radical interventions delivered greater prosperity to more than half the population, producing what the American economist, J. K. Galbraith, termed 'the culture of contentment': that is, unparalleled affluence for a significant proportion of the electorate, who therefore became politically quiescent. However, on some calculations, at least one-third of the UK population became, in real terms, poorer than they had been in the late 1970s. The abandonment of the one-nation consensus of the post-war period therefore produced a significantly divided society, with increasing social 'exclusion' and levels of disorder and crime that seemed inexorably to rise. The impact of globalisation in the 1990s internationalised and intensified all of these trends and their consequent tensions.

The Cook strips away the armatures of society and social cohesion. The world beyond Richard Borg's restaurant, 'Le Hollandais', is portrayed as no more than an icy blue parking lot that services a rank of restaurants and eateries; dog packs scavenge the bins. The only effective law enforcement seems to be concerned with food hygiene – the police and officials who try to empty two putrifying delivery vans. Spica's 'associate', Harris, does worry about the consequences of their murder of Georgina's lover, 'the modest man' Michael: 'I'm saying the book-keeper's going to get us into trouble – and he wasn't worth it' (Greenaway 1989: 80). But crime and outrage seem to bring no real consequences for anyone within the privileged sanctuary of the restaurant.

Greenaway is a great explainer of his own work; so good, in fact, that you might wonder whether his very helpful commentaries actually betray an unspoken lack of confidence in the power of his films to speak for themselves. He is, for example, very clear about his formalist, anti-realist position as a film-maker:

> Every time you watch a Greenaway movie, you know you are definitely and absolutely *only watching a movie*. It's not a slice of life, and not a window on the world. It's by no means an exemplum of anything 'natural' or 'real'.
>
> (Smith 1990: 59)

Statements such as these come straight out of high Modernist, early twentieth-century aesthetics, and to that extent are perfectly traditional, in their own way. Even the title can be read as a critical perspective on cinema: just three names would read better in terms of conventional expectations: *The Thief, His Wife and Her Lover*. As an audience, we would know what to expect as we settled in our seats. But then there is also *The Cook*, a contriver of menus, surely a figure for the Director himself, yet someone hailing from Provence, France, rather than Newport, Wales. The disconcerting title is an example of Greenaway working against classical film narrative expectations, and just as *A Zed and Two Noughts* (1985) and *Drowning By Numbers* (1988) were structured by the alphabet and number counts, *The Cook* is zoned by colour: blue for exterior reality, green for the creative kitchen, red for the excessive eating floor, white for the rest rooms.

Peter Greenaway's alienating, formalist practice is evident right from the opening credits sequence. A steadily rising crane shot of scaffolding beneath the floor of the sound stage on which the action is being filmed demonstrates a purely Brechtian manner by 'baring the device', that is, by foregrounding the artifice of film in general, and this film in particular. Scarlet-clad flunkies pull back curtains to reveal the theatrical *mise-en-scène*, where two delivery vans, one for meat, one for sea food, symmetrically frame the action. The opulent restaurant itself is redolent of consumer excesses of the late 1980s. Two of the decade's style gurus were on hand to advise: Jean Paul Gaultier designed costumes for the waiters and waitresses, and Giorgio Locatelli of the Savoy Hotel, London, created fantasy food for display. Albert Spica's table is itself a vulgarian spectacle, dominated by a massive reproduction of Dutchman Frans Hals's 1614 painting, 'The Banquet of the Officers of the St George Civic Guard Company'. Spica and his retinue are dressed in the same costumes as Hals's officers, who were, Greenaway explains, 'a gang of people all dressed up with nowhere to go' (Denham 1993: 26).

The film begins with a steadily rising crane shot, and some of its most beautiful and startling moments derive from horizontal tracking shots that run parallel to the action, or 'picture plane' of the film. For example, the camera takes in the pre-modern, artisan bustle of the kitchen then ghosts through a wall to reveal the contemporary spectacle of the restaurant itself. Most disconcerting of all, we – courtesy of the lens – follow Georgina via a service corridor into the ladies' toilet, at which point her dress miraculously changes from scarlet to white. Is this a clinical purity that vainly hopes to disguise the messy 'end-process' of all eating and drinking? The film is as much about appetite as greed, and the vulnerability of the body in desire, an ancient agenda that may finally upstage the transient politics of the 1980s. Greenaway defends his strict camera regime:

> When [my] camera moves, it moves in a very, very subjective, inorganic way. Which again is very much against the general premise of American moviemaking [which is] ... psychodrama realism ... This wretched psychodrama permeates the whole of American culture.
>
> (Smith 1990: 59–60)

An obvious objection here would be to argue that Albert Spica is by any standards a pretty 'psychodramatic' creation, the figure in whom Greenaway wanted

> to create deliberately, almost in a technical way, a character of great evil, who had no redeeming features. Not like a Machiavelli or a Richard III, who have charisma, which is attractive. I had to create a man who *had* to be mediocre. And there's a way that all my heroes are mediocre people.
>
> (Smith 1990: 58)

But the great paradox of Brechtian estrangement theory, in film as in theatre, is that we *must* be interested in the characters at some level, however banal, 'modest' or monstrous they are. Brecht's intention with his 'alienation-effects' was to make us interested in his characters in a *different*, more critical and reflective way. Like Brecht, Greenaway hopes to encourage his audience to maintain a questioning distance on the spectacle they are watching, rather than simply falling in love with the star, and being swept up in the seductive manner of Hollywood classical narrative film. Yet there are a number of undeniably powerful, humanly engaging performances in *The Cook*, given by actors who courageously committed themselves to Greenaway's unsettling vision: Michael Gambon's Spica, Helen Mirren's Georgina, and Tim Roth's Mitchell, as well as many by the supporting cast. Greenaway has said that he would rather spend time working with his cinematographer – the late, prodigiously gifted Sacha Vierny – than with his actors, and the actors may therefore take a kind of revenge, by delivering truly vivid performances which work against the coldness of their director's declared intentions for his vision of cinema. (Directors are a shamelessly calculating breed, so this might also be a part of Greenaway's grand strategy.)

For example: is Gambon's Spica a completely repulsive creation? Is there not a kind of monstrous pathos about this thief, as when he breaks down, shouting, 'Kids, who needs kids?' His horrifying assault shortly after on young Pup is perhaps partly an attack on what he wants so badly, but cannot have. Again, his dependence on Georgina is total, as we see in the final scene when he begs her to come back to him: 'I've – to tell the truth – been miserable' (Greenaway 1989: 90). Spica is a sociopath because, in Freudian terms, his unconscious drives dominate his behaviour. He is the unsocialised baby that remains within all of us. His simultaneous dependence on, and violence towards Georgina is a perfect example of the paradoxical emotions of the unconscious. There is no greater 'psychodrama' than this, one which is even more disturbingly shown by David Lynch, one of the few American directors whom Greenaway can admire, in *Blue Velvet*, made just three years earlier, where Dennis Hopper's Frank Booth makes an atrociously ambivalent assault – if there can be such a thing – on Isabella Rossellini's Dorothy Vallens.

If Greenaway's attempt to make his audience attend to films more thoughtfully is flawed by the unfortunate presence of compelling actors, there are also questions about the nature of his critique of Reagano-Thatcherite politics. If *The Cook* is a metaphorical film, as the director claims, what exactly could the figure of Spica stand for, in terms of an attack on the consequences of Thatcherism? Spica as a graceless monster, 'unleashed' from the working class by the new economic regime, is as much a victim of the new values as anyone else. Alan Howard's antiquarian book-dealer may be read as a member of the professional middle class that felt itself to be increasingly marginalised in the 'new times'. The true villains of the piece are surely somewhere else, forever off-screen. Helen Mirren's splendid Georgina surely escapes from the framework of social critique altogether and, predictably, signifies the consequences of sexuality and desire on the ageing, vulnerable body. For Georgina's magnificent revenge the film gleefully takes on the conventions of renaissance tragedy and bears comparison with the grotesque finale of *Titus Andronicus*, Shakespeare's most 'transgressive' play, for which see Julie Taymor's *Titus* (1999).

Further Reading

Laura Denham, *The Films of Peter Greenaway*, London, Minerva Press, 1993.

Peter Greenaway, *The Cook, the Thief, His Wife and Her Lover*, Paris, Dis Voir, 1989 (petergreenaway.co.uk).

Gavin Smith, 'Food for Thought', interview with Peter Greenaway, *Film Comment* Vol. 26, No. 3, 1990, 54–61.

Michael Walsh, 'Allegories of Thatcherism: the Films of Peter Greenaway' in Lester Freidman (ed.) *British Cinema and Thatcherism*, London, UCL Press, 1990.

Nigel Wheale, 'Televising Hell: Tom Phillips and Peter Greenaway's *TV Dante*' in Wheale, *The Postmodern Arts*, London, Routledge, 1995.

NIGEL WHEALE

THE CRYING GAME (1992)

[Production Company: Palace Pictures. Director and screenwriter: Neil Jordan. Cinematographer: Ian Wilson. Editor: Kant Pan. Music: Anne Dudley. Cast: Forest Whitaker (Jody), Miranda Richardson (Jude), Stephen Rea (Fergus), Jaye Davidson (Dil).]

'In Neil Jordan's new thriller, nothing is what it seems to be.' So ran the tagline for Miramax's US marketing campaign for *The Crying Game*. It is an appropriate hook for a film best known for its plot twist, a revelation of the kind guaranteed to generate frenzied debate in online forums. The film is indeed keenly concerned with the relations between appearance and reality. Genre, narrative, characters: each element contains unexpected trajectories and outright surprises. What makes *The Crying Game* so fascinating however is that the relationship between seeming and being is not a straightforward one. Appearance is not simply a façade or mask which falls away to reveal a 'real' essence. Instead the film offers the audience a tantalising mesh of unresolved ambiguities, suggesting a more complex configuration of manifest and hidden, secrets and disguise.

From its earliest scenes the film places an emphasis on role-playing and dressing up, demonstrating at the outset the power of costume and performance. The fairground seduction scene shows Jude playing the role of a sexually available woman in order to ensnare Jody. She looks the part, dressed in figure-hugging pale denim, gold hoop earrings and bright pink lipstick, making it easy for the spectator, like Jody, to believe in her as a sexy young blonde simply enjoying some male company at the fair. Only the mysterious shot-reverse shot revealing a sombre exchange of glances between Jude and Fergus suggests that the situation might not be what it seems. Jude's masquerade in this scene is highlighted by the contrast in the sequences following Jody's capture, where she is dressed in a strikingly different style. Her hair loose, her frame engulfed by a big, baggy jumper and no make-up: this, we are given to believe, is the 'real' Jude, a serious, single-minded member of the Irish Republican Army, concerned only with her cause. Taken on their own, these early scenes seem to suggest a relatively straightforward process of disguise, deception and revelation, aimed both at the unsuspecting Jody and the equally unaware spectator – a process that will be mirrored later by Dil's seduction of Fergus. Jude dresses up in order to catch a British soldier and then, her mission accomplished, removes her costume to show us who she really is. As the film progresses however, and on subsequent viewings, the opening scenes come to seem more ambiguous. For one thing, as we become aware of Jody's homosexuality, we realise that he too is 'dressing-up' as a straight man, trying out being with a girl as though trying on an alternative costume. This is emphasised when he says, 'never pissed holding a girl's hand, Jude [...] and you know what? It's nice'. This dressing-up game is complicated further still by Dil's cross-dressing, so that Jody is able to 'pass' as heterosexual when showing her photo to Fergus. In both instances then, Jody is also in a sense dressing up in the clothing worn by Jude and Dil. In other words it is not only our own clothes that we use to construct an identity, relationships are also a form of drag.

The second event which renders Jude's dressing up in the opening scenes more complicated and interesting is her subsequent transformation in the second part of the film, where she reappears in a completely different version of femininity. With a slick dark brown bob, black leather gloves and 1940s-style suit straight out of *film noir*, this stylised, almost campily cinematic image leads us to question the existence of one 'real' Jude behind her various masks. The scene where her new look is revealed foregrounds the constructed nature of her image, whilst at the same time playfully blurring the gender lines along which that construction is supposed to lie. She emerges from a dark corner in Fergus's room, emphasising both her transformation and its sinister implications for the narrative: Fergus's shady past has caught up with him. A sequence of shots allows us to absorb fully the new sharp contours of her hair and clothes from Fergus's point of view, half-concealed at first by the shadows, then moving forward to let us take in her whole figure. 'What do you think of the hair?' she asks him, her hand gesture and head movements drawing attention to its new style. 'I was sick of being a blond,' she continues, 'needed a tougher look if you know what I mean.' Her words emphasise the performative quality of her image. It is not just that a new role requires new attire but that the clothing creates the role: she becomes a 'tougher' version of Jude by dressing up as a *femme fatale*. The choice of word is significant, because in her version of drag, Jude is 'toughening up', rather than seeking the softer feminine role that Dil performs, the damsel in distress who needs Fergus's protection. The contrast is underscored by Jude's reference to Dil as the 'wee black chick'. Between Jude's and Dil's different, yet equally constructed, versions of female glamour, the performance of femininity in the film troubles the connections between sex and gender, revealing all femininity to be a form of masquerade.[1] Not only this but 'femininity' is itself shown to be fluid and unstable, not easily distinguishable from its 'masculine' opposite through the usual binary divisions of active/ passive, strong/weak, hard/soft and so forth, since Jude and Dil shore up these qualities in such different ways. The sense of gender ambiguity is reinforced by the later scenes in the film, where Fergus attempts to undo Dil's drag and turn her back into a boy, cutting her hair short and dressing her up in Jody's cricket whites. Swamped by Jody's ample clothes and with a fragility of demeanour brought about by the distressing confusion of the situation, it is arguably in these scenes that she looks most conventionally girlish, and it is impossible to escape the impression that she is dressing up as a boy, rather than returning to her 'proper' gender role. 'You want to make me like him,' Dil says as Fergus cuts her hair. Even drag is not what it seems in *The Crying Game*.

The film's proliferation of transformative dressing up combines with the ambiguous relationships elaborated in the narrative to undermine the idea of identity as something fixed and determinate. This fits with Judith Butler's argument that drag exposes the mimetic performativity of all gender identity. Since the very concept of an 'original' depends upon the possibility of imitation, the idea of its precedence over the copy is flawed. 'There is no originary or primary gender that drag imitates,' she suggests, 'but *gender is a kind of imitation for which there is no original*' (1991: 21). If ever a film illuminated Butler's subtle philosophical deconstruction of identity politics it is surely this one. However, the characters' discussions of 'nature' appear to undercut Butler's idea of 'the real as nothing other than the effects of *drag*' (1991: 29). Jody's assertion that, 'there are two kinds of people: those who give and those who take', illustrated with the fable of the scorpion and the frog, sets up a theme that runs throughout the film. Actions are explained in terms of a natural essence or destiny, 'because it's in my nature' as Mr Scorpion says. Recurrent references to 'natural' roles are sprinkled across the dialogue. 'You were made for this', Jude tells Fergus after the rehearsal assassination, while Dil says wistfully, 'Can't help what I am'. In fact this acts as a red herring that only serves to reinforce the fluid conception of identity in the film, for the opposition between 'givers' and 'takers' asserted by Jody is far from clear. Fergus is the most striking example of the way even this binary collapses in the film: does he seek out Dil purely out of kindness and empathy, 'giving' Jody his dying wish, or is it partly to prove that he can 'take' what Jody had, getting one over the man who gave him the slip, teased and outsmarted him? Or, even more confusingly, is he not also 'taking' Jody by means of the feminine figure of Dil, since his potential homosexual attraction to Jody is repeatedly hinted at, though overtly denied in what he says? The interplay of compassion, aggression and desire is a highly complex one, the only certainty being that they are thoroughly intertwined.

The Crying Game cleverly undoes our assumptions about outsides and insides and how they relate. The 'twist', although offering us a moment of revelation, cannot, as we have seen, be read as a straightforward exposure of Dil's 'real' sex. This is not to say that she is in fact biologically female but rather, like all identities, hers is neither definitively one thing nor the other but depends on what she's wearing, who she's with. 'She's not a girl, Col,' says Fergus to the bartender. 'Whatever you say,' he replies. Interior and exterior are constituted through a permeable membrane rather than a rigid divide. This is explored visually in the film through the motifs of masks, veils and shadows, each of which both obscures and reveals. The first of these is the black hostage hood forced upon Jody to keep him from seeing the IRA volunteers' faces. It is not a mask for Jody to hide behind, but rather a disguise for his captors; in this it already inverts the usual structure of the mask. What is more, despite its opacity the hood becomes the locus for the developing bond between Fergus and his prisoner as it is variously lifted, removed and replaced. Instead of separating the two men, it draws them close, allowing Jody to get under Fergus's skin. This function is taken up by the veiling effects created by the swathes of fabric that adorn Dil's apartment, which play with the distance and closeness between her and Fergus. In the scene where Fergus discovers Dil's male anatomy their passionate embrace is shot through the haze of the semi-transparent curtains around the bed. As Dil moves off to the bathroom, the camera tracks along the bed, finally moving up to peer at Fergus through the parting in the curtains, and rests on him lying on the bed in anticipation. The unveiling, it is suggested, is as much of Fergus's identity as Dil's. The veil plays with the spectator's desire to look and know, always hinting at the possibility of a final revelation that is undermined in subsequent scenes and in the film's ambiguous ending. Shadows, a significant element in the film's visual repertoire, also evoke the viewer's desire to see by both showing and hiding the human form. In the scene where Fergus watches Dil take Dave home, a low-angle shot of her window displays her and Dave's silhouettes like shadow puppets, while Fergus watches from the lower left-hand corner of the frame, mirroring the spectator's gaze.

As we watch *The Crying Game*, the layers of drag and dressing up, masks, veils and shadows create an endless strip-tease. While moments of narrative climax, such as the 'discovery' of Dil's sex, offer us the satisfaction of knowledge, this is only fleeting, for another layer of possibility is always waiting for us underneath. While the focus in this discussion has been on the ambiguities of gender and sexuality, part of the film's fascination is that political and racial identities are equally interrogated and shown to be caught up in the same system of performance. A compelling and tantalising game of hide and seek, *The Crying Game* plays with our desire to know 'the secrets of the human heart' while cleverly suggesting they were there on our sleeves all along.

Note

1 For a full discussion of this concept, see Joan Riviere's seminal paper, 'Womanliness as a Masquerade', *International Journal of Psychoanalysis* 10, 1929, 303–313.

Further Reading

Judith Butler, 'Imitation and Gender Insubordination', in Diana Fuss (ed.) *Inside/out: Lesbian Theories, Gay Theories*, New York and London, Routledge, 1991, pp. 13–31.
Jane Giles, *The Crying Game*, London, BFI, 1997.
Neil Jordan, *The Crying Game*, London, Vintage, 1993.

ISABELLE MCNEILL

GADAEL LENIN/LEAVING LENIN (1992)

[Production Company: Gaucho and S4C. Director and screenwriter: Endaf Emlyn. Cinematographer: Ray Orton. Editor: Chris Lawrence. Music: John E.R. Hardy. Cast: Sharon Morgan (Eileen), Wyn Bowen Harries [Mostyn], Ifan Huw Dafydd (Mervyn), Steffan Trevor (Spike), Shelley Rees (Sharon).]

Gadael Lenin/Leaving Lenin is a Welsh language film which successfully retains its national specificity, traverses geographical boundaries and achieves international appeal. It won the audience award for the most popular British feature at the 1993 London Film Festival and established Endaf Emlyn as one of the most important Welsh directors to work in his indigenous language.

Set in post-communist Russia, Emlyn's plot, co-scripted by Sion Eirian, involves a group of teachers and their sixth-form students on an art trip to Russia. The teachers become separated from the students when their train divides and, facing dilemmas of marital breakdown, artistic ambitions and political disillusionment, they journey towards the students who are meanwhile exploring Russian art and their own sexual identities in St Petersburg.

Produced in 1992, it was a time of expansion for Welsh cinema through S4C's (Welsh Channel 4) support for film production in the 1980s and the development of Sgrin, the Media Agency for Wales, in 1997 increasing English-medium film productions to extend audiences for Welsh cinema (Woodward 2006: 2). Emlyn's earlier films reflect this shift with *Stormydd Awst/Storms of August* (1987), the first Welsh language feature to be distributed on 35 mm in cinemas, and *Un Nos Ola Leaud/One Full Moon* (1991) which 'transcended national boundaries – and demonstrated how a Welsh screen identity and culture might be forged through the 1990s' (Berry 1996: 412).

The Welsh language is important in defining national identity on screen but English subtitles aurally inscribe Anglo/Welsh tensions into an imperialist dichotomy. While noting this duality, Woodward extends it to a trinity of Welsh, English and British identities, evident in Welsh films of the 1980s and 1990s such as *Hedd Wynn* (Paul Turner, 1992) in which a Welsh poet from North Wales is killed in the First World War and posthumously awarded the bardic prize for poetry; *Milwr Bychan/Welsh Soldier* (Karl Francis, 1986), exploring the dilemma of a Welsh soldier fighting a British war in Northern Ireland who uses Welsh to defy his superiors, and *Gadael Lenin*, which adds an international dimension to linguistic tensions with its Russian setting. If Welsh and English languages are a site for struggle in these films, the tension between Welsh, English and Russian in *Gadael Lenin* extends linguistic borders by asserting Welsh alongside two major imperialist languages, thus strengthening Welsh identity further (Woodward 2006: 3–5).

The thematic concerns of the breakdown of communism in 1990s Russia in *Gadael Lenin* can also be read in terms of the 1980–90s British experience of Margaret Thatcher's policies of privatisation, dismantling of large-scale manufacturing industries and her stand against the unions in the 1984/5 Miners strike. The direct experiences of the miners' dispute were addressed in Karl Francis's *Ms Rhymny Valley* (1985), and in the independent co-operative Chapter's documentary on the pit closures, *The Case for Coal* (1984).[1] Thatcher's victory in 1985 and her political legacy had devastating social effects in the 1990s as mass unemployment, casualisation of labour and a rise in drug culture shattered traditional communities across the UK. Welsh films such as *Twin Town* (Kevin Allen, 1997) and *House of America* (Marc Evans, 1997) explored the social and cultural legacy of unemployment in a post-industrial Wales within a disenfranchised youth culture and are posited against satirical stereotypes of rugby players and Welsh male voice choirs.

The Thatcher years also created a breakdown in traditional family relations as the position of men as breadwinners shifted through mass unemployment, and women's traditional place at home was challenged. During the miners' strike, Welsh, Scottish and English miners' wives travelled across the UK to picket working miners and experienced collective politicisation and empowerment by speaking in public. This change found its cultural and gender repercussions explored in 1980–90s British films such as *Letter to Brezhnev* (Chris Bernard, 1985) and *Rita, Sue and Bob Too* (Alan Clarke, 1986), in which women move into the street and the clubs while unemployment relegates men to the home space (Hill 2001: 252).

Cook sees such work as 'transgressing boundaries – between national and international, home and abroad ... All of them are about travelling – through time, to new shores – in a restless search for fulfilment which can only be imagined never realised' (Cook and Dodd 2000: xiv). Justine King, who explores films of the 1980s which focus on female subjectivity and offer charismatic or transgressive representations of women who challenge boundaries of conventional femininity, identifies a common motif of escape – such as travel abroad or education out of the class structure – not to be read as escapism but rather in terms of 'movement through a liminal space, a realm of possibility' (1996: 220). This enables women to remove themselves from their cultural positioning in the narrative and to 'undergo a redefining and re-empowering transformation of identity or rite of passage' (1996: 220). Once this threshold has been crossed the male protagonists have to redefine themselves through her space rather than punish the woman for her pleasurable transgression as was conventionally the case in cinema.

Gadael Lenin can be read as symptomatic of these cultural and cinematic shifts with its narrative journey, away from South Wales to St Petersburg, offering a space within which to re-define gender boundaries, and providing rites of passage for those trapped within the restrictive cinematic stereotypes of the Welsh homeland. For example, art teacher Eileen's (Morgan) journey leads her back to St. Petersburg to reassess herself as an artist and teacher in relation to her husband Mostyn (Harries) and her colleague/past lover Mervyn (Daffyd). While Mostyn has both inspired and dominated her intellectually with his Marxist idealism, Mervyn represents the typical Welsh macho ideal of a rugby-playing heavy drinker, competing against her husband for sexual favour. Both patronise her in different ways and Eileen is overshadowed by their competitiveness. Woodward sees this as confirming a tradition of cinematic representations of Welsh men and women, from John Ford's *How Green was my Valley* (1941) onwards, showing that Welsh women have been portrayed as overshadowed by rugby-playing, beer-drinking male voice choirs (Woodward 2006: 10). *Gadael Lenin*, however, critically re-frames these gender stereotypes through travel away from home to new shores.

The shift occurs for Eileen when the train splits, metaphorically releasing her from her quasi-parental role over the students. She gradually rejects both her husband Mostyn's carping over the changes in Russian culture and her old flame. 'Things are different now,' she tells Mervyn, rejecting his advances. In the morning, she hitches a lift on her own with a Russian photographer travelling to St Petersburg who shares her experiences of marriage breakdown and the need to make a living selling posies to fund her artistic life. This inspires Eileen to reassess her own position as wife, teacher, artist. 'I feel like a young girl running away,' she confesses.

Once in St Petersburg, Eileen confidently leads her students around the Russian art galleries, challenged by her gifted art student Spike (Trevor). He questions Eileen's charade of playing at 'being artists for a week every year' on the school trip. It's not enough for him to go back to Maes Ifor School and live a lie. His courage is a painful reminder of her position, reiterated by Petr Vodkin's painting *Fantasy*, which Eileen interprets as, 'The dream we gave our life to was a lie'. This suggests an awakening to new possibilities, reinforced as she takes the lead over Mervyn and Mostyn in the final scene at the railway station, leaving Lenin to redefine her identity.

Nevertheless, this shift is contextualised by changes in both Mervyn and Mostyn, indicative of a crisis of masculinity. They both lose the signs of their male authority. Mervyn's demise is articulated through costume, as he becomes more dishevelled, losing his chic jacket and sunglasses, and finally dons a dingy black overcoat to keep warm. Mostyn's crisis is represented as youth against the rise of capitalism in a post-Communist Russia and the breakdown of his Marxist ideology which had impressed Eileen in his youth. In the opening shot, he admires Lenin's statue and delights that his hero is in his rightful place; the almost identical closing shot is offered in silence, indicating Mostyn's political disillusionment and the loss of his influence over Eileen – also echoed in the invidious privatisation of 1990s' post-Thatcher Britain. But Mostyn and Mervyn's shift is also a positive one, redirecting them from conventional masculine competitiveness, towards more feminised mutual support. In a rare moment of emotional intimacy Mostyn shares his fears over Eileen with Mervyn: 'What do I have to offer her? Nothing: old dreams gone sour'.

The students follow a different trajectory in their rites of passage when the train splits. Spike is forced to confront his homosexuality without guilt by Sacha (Ivan Shvedoff), a Russian artist who challenges authoritarian approaches to art and sexuality. In a carnivalesque and anarchic moment in the film, Sacha invites Spike to party on the bridge. Drawing on his new-found courage to challenge conventional constructions of male sexuality, Spike crosses the bridge both literally and symbolically. His gay identity is publicly asserted the next morning when he and Sacha embrace at the station.

For student Sharon (Shelley Rees), meanwhile this new space enables her, like Eileen, to challenge male constructions of femininity. When her boyfriend Charlie (Richard Harrington) attempts to seduce her in the hotel, he alludes to her reputation as a girl who sleeps around, drawing on hackneyed patriarchal values of the madonna/whore. She finally refuses him, and his conventional notions of female sexuality, and claims her right to say no on her own terms. Later, she defiantly states 'Cupid won't catch me. I'm going to do as I please from now on'.

One of the strengths of *Gadael Lenin* is its approach to the theme of border-crossing across the generational divide using the device of the school trip with its community demands and quasi familial relationships to authenticate the plot. Emlyn's previous experience of directing S4C youth programmes excels here in the refreshingly plausible representation of young people's experiences, cross-cut with the adults' separate journey. The film doesn't offer radical social change or a post-modernist stylistic aesthetic; rather it explores more cautiously manageable signs of new direction for individual characters within the larger changes of the social framework. Eileen doesn't find a new life in St Petersburg; Spike does. For him the decision is easy, full of youthful integrity. In a powerfully moving closure, a lingering shot on Eileen intensifies her inner regrets, the façade she has maintained and the courage needed to change things. All her fears, contradictions, questions and anxieties are exceptionally captured beyond the dialogue in Sharon Morgan's eloquent facial gestures in this closing frame, leaving us to ponder on Eileen's future and how decisions become more difficult, more contradictory, with time.

The result is an engaging journey for the characters, a story of warmth, youthful idealism, adult regrets, transformation, individual and artistic aspirations and Welsh and Russian community spirit, set against a 1990s landscape of cultural and political breakdown, disillusionment and alienation both in Britain and abroad.

Note

1 Chapter also contributed to the agit-prop Miner's Campaign Video Tapes and Ken Loach's television documentary *Which Side are You On?* (1984), indicating the cross-border impact of the strike and its representation across national platforms.

Further Reading

David Berry, *Wales and Cinema: The First Hundred Years*, London, University of Wales Press, 1996.

Pam Cook and Philip Dodd (eds) *Women and Film: A Sight and Sound Reader*, London, Scarlet Press, 2000.

Tony Curtiss, *Wales the Imagined Nation*, Bridgend, Poetry Wales, 1986.

John Hill, 'From New Wave to "Brit-Grit": Continuity and Difference in Working Class Realism', in Justine Ashby and Andrew Higson (eds) *British Cinema, Past and Present*, London, Routledge, 2001, pp. 249–260.

Justine King, 'Crossing Thresholds: The Contemporary British Woman's Film' in Andrew Higson (ed.) *Dissolving Views: Key Writings on British Cinema*, London, Cassell, 1996, pp. 216–231.

Kate Woodward, 'Traditions and Transformations: Film in Wales during the 1990s', *North American Journal of Welsh Studies*, Vol. 6.1, 2006, pp. 216–231.

TRISH SHEIL

ORLANDO (1992)

[Production Company: Adventure Pictures. Director and screen-writer: Sally Potter. Cinematographer: Aleksei Rodionov. Editor: Hervé Schneid. Music: David Motion and Sally Potter. Cast: Tilda Swinton (Orlando), Quentin Crisp (Queen Elizabeth I), Jimmy Somerville (Falsetto/Angel).]

Whenever one is tempted to bemoan a certain tendency in British cinema to create lavish, well-crafted but ultimately rather futile period drama, one should remember the eccentric and clever counter-example of *Orlando*. From a distance it could almost be mistaken for something less interesting than it really is. Like many films in the 'heritage' genre flourishing across Europe in the 1980s and 1990s, *Orlando* is based on a canonical literary text, a contrivance often used in cinema as a convenient, exportable emblem of artistic merit. What is more, like a typical literary heritage film, much of *Orlando* is set in a grand English stately home, where a sumptuous array of props and costumes allows the audience's gaze to revel in a recreated historical scene, nostalgically transporting us to lost, aristocratic worlds of leisure and luxury. As *Orlando* shows us, however, appearances can be deceptive. In fact Potter's film subverts both genre and gender in an unusual and complex narrative journey. The visual splendour of the *mise-en-scène* is no mere eye candy, rather it is integral to a cinematic exploration of the interweaving threads of social identity, sexuality and time.

All literary adaptations into film pose certain challenges. Moving from words to an audiovisual medium entails a shift to a very different kind of sign, a transposition from description to showing. However Virginia Woolf's novel *Orlando: A Biography* (1928) has a further layer of difficulty, for it is a written text itself obsessively concerned with questions of writing. Potter's film responds to this in a variety of ways, not least by making radical changes to the plot, but the central underpinning of the approach is a delicate sense of the relations between words and images. In her introduction to the published screenplay of the film, Potter describes how, despite the book's fascination with literature she felt instinctively that the image was a vital part of its textual fabric. This instinct, Potter found, 'was affirmed in Virginia Woolf's diaries where she writes of her attempt with *Orlando* to "exteriorise consciousness" [. . .] she set out to find images rather than abstract literary monologues to describe the secret machinery of the mind' (1994: ix). This suggests that the move from description to showing in the transition from writing to film is already at issue within Woolf's literary aims, and Potter harnesses this by using cinematic technique to explore precisely what is at stake in our exterior images.

Like Woolf's protagonist, the filmic Orlando is a writer and a lover of literature, but Orlando's role as an obsessive reader is mostly stripped away in the film, creating space for an emphasis on theatricality and performance. This offers a more directly visual way of exploring the complex relations between inside and outside evoked in Woolf's diary. The external world as Orlando experiences it is conjured for the viewer through a series of highly controlled colour palettes in the mise-en-scène and lighting: rich gold, orange and crimson for the Elizabethan banquet, chalky white with smudges of brown-black for the frozen winter under King James, or lush green and velvety blue clouded with mist for the romance of the Victorian era. In each setting Orlando both fits in and sticks out; despite his elaborate costumes he – and then she – fails to produce the complete and acceptable performance demanded by the surrounding social environment. Youth, nobleman, ambassador, soldier, lady, woman: each is revealed as a role shaped from the outside, always at odds with the fluid and mysterious interiority of the individual. Tilda Swinton's remarkable presence as Orlando is crucial here, capturing as she does a gauche innocence that jars slightly with the visual harmony of the scene. While her androgynous look doubtless makes it easier for the viewer to accept her as both male and female, more significant is a certain blankness in her gaze, both expressive and unreadable, that enables her to convey a character at once uniquely individual and yet subject to continual inscription by the discourses of each age. This is reinforced by her third-person voiceover at the opening and close of the film, which draws attention to the way words combine with the visual symbolism of fashion and environment to situate the individual. 'There can be no doubt about his sex – despite the feminine appearance that every young man of the time aspires to', pronounces the voiceover, picking up the ironic 'no doubt' from Woolf's text in order to emphasise the way sex and identity are generated through expectation and description.

This understanding of identity resonates with the theories of Judith Butler, who has argued that sex is constituted through socially regulated performance. For Butler, sexual difference 'is never simply a function of material differences which are not in some way marked and formed by discursive practices' (1990: 1). Performance is at issue in the film not only in the ways described above, where within the diegesis we are shown the imposing exteriors of class, fashion and milieu all demanding a certain enactment of identity, but also in the performance of the actors of the film themselves. The casting, in particular, of Swinton, Quentin Crisp and Jimmy Somerville creates, as casting often does, an extra layer of signification, as recognisable figures from a cultural context outside the film evoke a host of potential associations in the viewer's mind. Swinton is often described as Derek Jarman's muse, and was very much associated in the 1980s and early 1990s with his avant-garde, painterly and queer aesthetic in films such as *Caravaggio* (1986) and *The Garden* (1990).[1] Her screen persona is therefore well suited to the portrayal of a character possessed of what the Archduke Harry calls 'ambiguous sexuality'. The

sense of Swinton as an edgy actress herself present in the film, highlighted by recurrent moments where she looks at or addresses the
camera directly, contributes to a more blurred and complex evocation
of gender performance. For rather than presenting us with a character who simply changes sex during the course of a 400-year life-
time, Orlando's sex oscillates before our eyes as we see both actress
and youth. Orlando's desire for the boyishly exotic Sasha (Charlotte
Valandrey) contains within it a lesbian relationship. Similarly, when
Orlando, now become a woman, discovers sex with Shelmerdine
(played by Billy Zane who bears a hint of resemblance to Valandrey),
her history as a man resurfaces in gestures and glances. More explicitly queer casting gives us Quentin Crisp as Queen Elizabeth I and
pop star Jimmy Somerville as an Elizabethan falsetto as well as the
singing angel caught on video camera by Orlando's daughter. An
ageing virgin queen who desires Orlando for his youth and a singer/
angel: both roles are sexually indeterminate, neither gay nor straight,
nor even straightforwardly male or female. So while both Crisp and
Somerville are gay icons whose sexuality forms part of their public
personae, their performances here suggest a fluidity of identity and
sexuality at work in between the inner and outer worlds of the film.
In this way the film can be seen as a site of contestation of the
performative naturalisation of sex and sexuality described by Butler.

Despite the sexual oscillations suggested by Swinton's performance,
the journey from Elizabethan youth to modern woman remains a
vital progression in the film. *Orlando* has a classical narrative structure
in which the protagonist encounters obstacles, learns lessons and
becomes wiser (thought not, in this case, older). Orlando's experiences
of love and sex, her travels to Constantinople and her encounters in
English society are portrayed cumulatively rather than as detached
episodes. The vision of the angel shared with her daughter at the end
of the film suggests a culminating moment of redemption, understanding and freedom. Orlando's voiceover tells us, 'she's no longer
trapped by destiny [...] since she let go of the past, she found her
life was beginning', and this suggestion of a reconciliation of temporality and sex is reinforced in the lyrics of the angel's song: 'Neither a
woman nor a man / we are joined, we are one / with a human face
[...] I'm being born and I am dying'. This ending also provides a
moment of reflection on the question of adaptation, evoking a journey
in women's artistic production as well as the more central journey of
identity. Orlando having handed in the final draft of her novel, her
daughter's playful experimentation with a video camera gestures
towards future forms of representation. The chaotic, light-infused

images of grass, treetops and sky – not to mention the ability to make angels visible – suggest new artistic possibilities. In changing Orlando's child's sex to a girl, Potter forces her to let go of her grand house and class-burdened past; she also hints at a genealogy of women's art, in which the film-maker picks up where the writer left off. Adaptation itself becomes a theme, as women are seen to adapt to different historical constraints and the different forms of artistic expression available to them.

The trajectory of the narrative suggests a linear, progressive vision of history, in which individuals of the present moment – women or men – really do have greater freedom of movement, identity and expression than the stiff, power-laden structures of past epochs allowed. However parallel to the historical succession is an equally striking thematic structure, in which the historical sequences embody ideas: death, love, poetry, politics, society and birth. This suggests an alternative mapping of Orlando's life, through concepts and experiences that are timeless as well as historically contingent. There is a non-linear temporality in the film that provides a playful counterpart to the classical progression of the narrative. Potter explains that she never thought of *Orlando* as a 'historical film': 'I always thought of it as a film about now that happened to go through 400 years'.[2] The film's music, composed by Potter herself with David Motion, reflects this in its fusion of contemporary pop sounds, such as electric guitar, with motifs that gesture to the music of each period. A strong visual alternation between movement and stasis mirrors the way Orlando both moves through time and stays still, her features and gaze remaining the same. In a particularly memorable scene Orlando runs through a topiary maze in eighteenth-century costume, the image cross-cutting between mobile point of view shots and shots from just behind as though we were chasing her. The editing accelerates and by interspersing shots that give the impression she is just out of our sight, Orlando can then emerge in a Victorian crinoline; a time span of a hundred years is crossed. Creative use of fades to black and white contributes to the feeling of time as fluid and erratic. The fade to black (or white) is a filmic convention often used to indicate the passing of time but in *Orlando* its use is subtly subverted. For example, after Shelmerdine rides off romantically into the mist, we see a medium close-up of Orlando in heavy rain. After the fade to black we expect a lapse of time to have moved us into a new scene, but instead there is a close-up of Orlando in the same Victorian costume, though the rain has now stopped. The roar of an aeroplane passing overhead therefore acts as a dramatic intrusion of the twentieth century into the nineteenth; for a brief moment the two eras co-exist.

This wry toying with the conventions of the medium allows the overt reconciliation of past and future at the end of the film to arise out of subtle discontinuities throughout, disrupting the overall linearity of the narrative. As with sex and sexuality in the film, time's flow is imagined somewhere in between the poles of sameness and difference, stasis and mutability. But the fluidities of sex, time and identity are evoked within a recognisable story, and lightened by quirky humour. *Orlando* may be far removed from a typical period drama or literary adaptation but it was nonetheless a global commercial success, a striking example of conventional cinema undone from within.

Notes

1 See for example David Ehrenstein and Sally Potter, 'Out of the Wilderness: An Interview with Sally Potter', *Film Quarterly*, Vol. 47, No. 1, 1993, p. 2.
2 Director's commentary on the 2 Disc Special Edition DVD, Artifical Eye, 2003.

Further reading

Judith Butler, *Gender Trouble*, London and New York, Routledge, 1990.
Sally Potter, *Orlando: Sally Potter*, London, Faber & Faber, 1994.

ISABELLE MCNEILL

BHAJI ON THE BEACH (1993)

[Production Company: UMBI Productions. Director: Gurinder Chadha. Screenwriters: Gurinder Chadha and Meera Syal. Cinematographer: John Kenway. Editor: Oral Norrie Ottey. Music: John Altman. Cast: Kim Vithana (Jinder), Jimmi Harkishin (Ranjit), Sarita Khajuria (Hashida), Lalita Ahmed (Asha), Mo Sesay (Oliver), Shaheen Khan (Simi).]

In an interview for a report commissioned by the BFI on British films with black themes, Gurinder Chadha revealed that: 'It was after I saw *My Beautiful Laundrette* that I decided that I wanted to direct. I thought wow! This is something I could do [...] it is a great way of telling our stories' (Arnold and Wambu 1999: 38). Indeed, she drew on many of the issues and themes explored in Frears's work, and was influenced by some of its stylistic innovations, and created a film that marked another new turning point for British cinema. Chadha was one of only two black women to make and release a film in Britain in the 1990s. Concerning the surprise commercial success of *Bhaji on the Beach*, Karen Alexander has suggested that '[w]hat engaged critics and audiences alike was the opportunity of seeing and hearing from a section of the community so often constructed as silent' (2000: 112). To do this, Chadha drew not only on the specific strategies of *My Beautiful Laundrette* (realism, surrealism and rich symbolism), but also on the models of narrative structure, characterisation and humour of classical melodrama, as well as on the theatricality of the traditions of popular Indian cinema.

Chadha's debut feature followed *Laundrette* in exploring what it means to be Asian and British, but from a more overtly comic perspective and from a female point of view (Street 1997: 107). It follows a group of British Asian women from Birmingham on a day trip to Blackpool to see the lights and enjoy a break from routine. It is soon made clear that despite the cultural unity of the group, each character is dealing with a different personal dilemma that is in some way connected to the tensions of living in Britain. Whether discussing the clash between Indian traditions and modern values, or the racial prejudice that exists within Britain, the insights offered are often provocative. Older characters are shown trying to preserve their traditional cultural identity, while the younger ones appear anxious to be accepted by and become a genuine part of British life. The narrative relies upon the successful interweaving of these individual tales, developing a multiple-diegesis model that allows for a fuller understanding of the network of social relations and diverse cultural identities. The multiplicity of British Asian female identities is revealed via three generations of Asian women in Britain, and the film deals with 'questions of feminine destiny and identity ... lived out in the complex post-colonial hybridity of contemporary Britain' (Arnold and Wambu 1999: 36).

The opening title sequence reveals a row of small shops that provide goods mainly for the local Asian community, interspersed with visual signs of hostility towards that community in the form of abusive graffiti on the shutters of some of the shops. Cultural identity is embedded into the soundtrack as music and Punjabi voices are heard from the radios blaring in each shop. The tone of the film then switches to fantasy, at the end of which reality is returned by the accidental smashing of a tray as the character suffering the nightmarish vision stumbles and falls. Thus, the film's preoccupations with tension and conflict suffered on a private and personal level, interlocking with a specific cultural and social context, are neatly and powerfully introduced.

Chadha set out to make an entertaining film that dealt with the two most taboo topics for the Asian community in Britain: African-Caribbean and Asian relationships, and domestic violence. Debates about these issues are developed via focus on a differentiated group of culturally connected people, who share a journey away from the primary site of conflict for a single day during which the various dramas are played out under the microscopic gaze of the rest of the group. During their day-trip to Blackpool, the various women each come to slightly new understandings of their situation and those of the other characters.

Jinder, for example, has already left her violent husband and taken their five-year-old son to a refuge for Asian women, but is unsure what to do next. She is shown struggling to cope with the stigma of separation and potential divorce (labelled 'the English curse' by the older generation), struggling to decide whether to put family duty above personal safety and happiness, and whether to return to her husband. Meanwhile he is shown battling to cope with the emasculated position of having been deserted by his wife, in a society that he feels has already marked him out as ethnically and racially inferior. Sensitive character development is helped by careful framing; close-ups of Jinder, Ranjit and their boy aid our grasp of their dilemma, while distancing of the camera from the final physical struggle encourages the viewer to consider both sides, empathise more greatly with Jinder, but ultimately to remain as outside observers of their plight. The approach to characterisation and engagement of audience sympathies in general is complex: heterogeneity within cultures is acknowledged and shown as complicated to deal with, especially for those who regard the values of unity and family loyalty as superior to all others. The film thus denies that identity can be reduced to straightforward polarities of good/bad, and refuses an essentialist position of victim/oppressor.

The general themes of destiny and choice for (British) Asian women, and the specific issues of inter-racial relationships, inter-generational struggle, are all embodied by the dilemma faced by student Hashida who discovers that she is pregnant by Oliver, who is black. Stuck in an unthinkable position for a young Asian woman, she is treated with disgust by the older members of the group who are concerned with holding onto a distinctive sense of their own cultural and racial identity. They will not accept the 'mixed' nature of the relationship and the inevitable hybrid that will be produced by such a union, a child that will have difficulty fitting into British, Asian or Caribbean culture. Sexuality is used as a metaphor for cultural relations, and the film thus suggests that 'the most intimate acts are [...]

implicated in a complex set of social determinations' (Brunsdon 2000: 166). Hashida is under enormous parental pressure to go to medical school although her natural yearning is to be an artist, and scenes early on in the family home emphasise the generation clash that has emerged. Her parents are desperate to climb the social ladder, and need their daughter to follow the route of education and career as proof to their white neighbours that they are worthy of their respect. Again, this situation arouses sympathy since they genuinely appear to want what is best for their daughter, and is more complex in that it relates the difficulties to issues of class as well as race. Meanwhile, Oliver faces pressure from a black college friend who would rather he stuck to his own culture, arguing that: 'Black don't mean not white any more. Forget the melting pot and respect the differences. You try fusion and you get *con*fusion!' The friend recognises ethnic difference as being far broader and more complex than a simple black/white dichotomy and forces Oliver to think hard about the future of his relationship with Hashida.

Although white characters are kept on the periphery of the narrative, at several moments during the film the Asian women become the erotic subjects of the white male gaze. Teenage sisters Madhu (Renu Kochar) and Ladhu (Nisha Nayar), relishing a day of liberation from parental constraint, are only really interested in checking out the local talent, and find themselves attracting the attention of two white boys, one of whom comments on the exotic nature of their looks: 'You're all golden, like the top of a sesame seed bap'. More uncomfortably, Simi, the leader of the group and the most vociferous in terms of her feminist beliefs, and Jinder are the subject of verbal and physical abuse at the service station when they react negatively to the sexualised taunts of the same men who had earlier displayed their backsides to them from their van. Later on, timid and traumatised Asha finds herself being shown the sights of Blackpool by a charming pantomime performer, Ambrose Waddington (Peter Cellier) who admires her 'exquisite' beauty, and is fascinated by what he perceives as her culture's strong and pure sense of tradition. He instantly idealises and stereotypes her, and situates her romantically in a nostalgic past that shows no understanding of her contemporary predicament.

Indeed, the scenes focusing on Asha are perhaps the most disturbing and most representative of the general dilemma experienced by the women in the film. Chadha inserts extra-diegetic hallucinatory sequences in the theatrical style of Indian popular cinema (Bollywood) to dramatise the anxiety Asha feels about her position in society. Her low self-esteem appears to stem from a loss of individual and cultural identity. She no longer knows who she is or where she belongs, having spent all her life being told how to behave according to a set of cultural rules which are now being questioned and challenged by the younger generations, as well as by Rekha (Souad Faress), a visitor from Bombay who wears western style dress and declares that they are all living in the past.

The location of Blackpool is used as a complex site where personal desires and social tensions are worked out away from the domestic spaces where those conflicts have been allowed to develop. The reality of the seaside town is less important than its value as an imaginary space with ambivalent symbolic value. It is presented as a place for tacky consumer culture, even compared by Rekha to modern-day Bombay. Moreover, the diversity offered by the people, colours, surreal performances and even snake charmers are highlighted to show Blackpool as a potential site of cultural merging. It is thus transformed, on the one hand, into a post-modern space where new forms of social connection become possible. On the other hand, any veneer of social change is easily disrupted by incidents such as the racist sneers and abuse directed at the older women as they try to enjoy a cup of tea in a local café.

With its charming blend of the melodramatic with the political, this film highlights the notion of diversity within an ethnic group that tends to be stereotyped and homogenised by the dominant white British culture, and which is rarely given a voice with which to explore such differences. Unusually, the Asian women are placed at the core of the action while the white characters remain largely one-dimensional and on the margin, in a reversal of the conventional core versus periphery opposition of (post)-colonial relations. It shows the frustrated attempts by the younger women to become accepted by, and integrated into, white British society, and emphasises the distance that remains between white, Asian and African Caribbean communities. The film thus reflects a British society of the early 1990s in which issues of cultural diversity and hybridity were still wrapped up in hostility and racist discourse. In this context, Chadha's film joins the diverse cinematic representations of Britishness. As she declared at the time: 'What I'm trying to say is that Britain isn't one thing or another. It isn't just *Howard's End* or *My Beautiful Laundrette*. There are endless possibilities about what it can be – and is – already' (Street 1997: 107).

Further Reading

Karen Alexander, 'Black British Cinema in the '90s: Going, Going, Gone' in Robert Murphy (ed.) *British Cinema of the '90s*, London, BFI, 2000, pp. 109–114.

Kevin Arnold and Onyekachi Wambu, *A Fuller Picture: The Commercial Impact of Six British films with Black Themes in the 1990s*, London, BFI, 1999.

Charlotte Brunsdon, 'Not Having it all: Women and Film in the 1990s' in Robert Murphy (ed.) *British Film of the 90s*, London, BFI, 2000, pp. 167–177.

Sarah Street, *British National Cinema*, London, BFI, 1997.

SARAH BARROW

THE REMAINS OF THE DAY (1993)

[Production Company: Merchant Ivory Productions and Columbia Pictures. Director: James Ivory. Producer: Ismael Merchant. Screenwriter: Ruth Prawer Jhabvala (from novel by Kazuo Ishiguro). Cinematographer: Tony Pierce-Roberts. Music: Richard Robbins. Editor: Andrew Marcus. Cast: Anthony Hopkins (James Stevens), Emma Thompson (Mary Kenton), James Fox (Lord Darlington), Peter Vaughan (William Stevens).]

The films of Ismael Merchant and James Ivory tend to provoke strong reactions. Their work provides some of the most iconic moments of 'British' cinema – the couple sitting at the window in Florence, Stevens physically recoiling from the (actually desired) advances of Miss Kenton – as well as some of the most popular films. However, some audiences and critics find Merchant Ivory films all but unwatchable; the period style and themes of restraint provoke frustration rather than admiration.

The Remains of the Day seems to be a quintessentially English – rather than British – film, but there is very little which is English in terms of funding, creative production or distribution of the film. It was produced and distributed by a Hollywood studio (Columbia), directed by James Ivory (an American) from a novel by the Japanese-British author Kazuo Ishiguro. In one way this is just another move in a game called 'What is a British film?' and therefore not particularly illuminating. It is also problematic to suggest that only people with British passports can make British films. It does, though, emphasise one of the main criticisms made about Merchant Ivory films, that they are a Hollywood simulacra of British cinema, a fake vision of an England based on a false memory. For those who are critical of these films this representation of a lost England operates ideologically, placing the values and structures of England's colonial past, over those of the present. This criticism of Merchant Ivory films is particularly based on the visual style – the civilised beauty of the costume drama – where the look of the film is deemed to obscure any social or political analysis of the period. This criticism has also gained credence due to the reported comments of Ismael Merchant which seemed to confirm an attitude of snobbery about contemporary British society detected in the films:

> What made a person civilised in the past was reading, writing and the art of conversation ... Who is England being inherited by? The lower class, not by the upper class. The ruling class is the lower classes – who talk about making money in the City and football.[1]

Those who enjoy Merchant Ivory films and those who don't are, however, united in identifying the reasons for the films' success. The disagreement between the groups comes more from the interpretation and meaning given to the pleasures available to the audience. In the context of this debate *Remains of the Day* has been read as both an indictment of the hypocrisy of the British class system and as a celebration of it. Responses to the film can be further complicated by the fact that for some that celebration is to be valued; a corrective to a perceived collective shame about England's colonial history.

With the success of *Room With a View* (Ivory, 1985), followed by *Maurice* (Ivory, 1987), *Howard's End* (Ivory, 1992) and *The Remains of the Day* the term Merchant Ivory (often assumed to be one person – Ivory directs, Merchant produces) gained a meaning beyond the literal identification of the producer and the director of the film. This isn't simply the result of an adherence to auteur theory as there are Merchant Ivory films which aren't 'Merchant Ivory' films, e.g. *Slaves of New York* (1989), *Le Divorce* (2003). Rather, Merchant Ivory became a brand, selling a particular type of film style – and Englishness – to a mass audience. The components of the Merchant Ivory brand, which had been apparent since the late 1970s (*Heat and Dust*, *The Bostonians* and *The Europeans*) but which only became successfully marketed in the mid-1980s, can be identified fairly clearly. A Merchant Ivory film will be a literary adaptation (E. M. Forster and Henry James are particularly popular), set in the past with great attention to period detail in setting, architecture and costume. The settings also tend to be signifiers of upper-class life (great country houses, landscaped acres) as well as high culture (Oxford, Cambridge, Rome, Florence, literary salons, classical concerts). The films are made with great technical skill in a visual style which emphasises the classical and harmonious – smooth camerawork, a predominance of mid-shots, an emphasis on meaning created by the mise-en-scène rather than by the juxtaposition of shots. British actors (rather than film stars) dominate, often appearing in more than one film, creating the feel of a repertory company (Emma Thompson, Helena Bonham Carter, Greta Scacchi, Anthony Hopkins, Judi Dench, Maggie Smith). While the description of the films as beautifully shot costume dramas may suggest that the brand is a conservative one appealing to middle England, it is also true that the films deal with themes of repression, whether due to class, nationality, gender or sexuality.

The Merchant Ivory film aesthetic has the backing of Hollywood money (as producer and/or distributor) but signifies something different from, and better than, mere commercial films. This awareness of cultural status is apparent in the differing responses of audiences and critics. These are characterised by the interplay of elitist views, all of which rely upon signifying the superiority of their own tastes. Hipsky (1994) explains the appeal of the films to American audiences as based on this aspect of the brand. To Anglophile Americans, he argues, Merchant Ivory is a signifier of serious, artistic film-making and the term operates as a shibboleth – a password – connoting membership of an elite club. Several critics have made explicit reference to the film-makers as a brand. Sheldon Hall (2006) summarises the dominant critical view:

> *Merchant Ivory* now tends to be regarded as the cinematic equivalent of Crabtree and Evelyn or Fortnum and Mason: a provider of tasteful, exquisitely crafted, up market fare, but slightly dull and very definitely bourgeois.[2]

In his critical review of *The Remains of the Day*, Hipsky (1994) supports his argument that this is a snobbish film obsessed with appearances, by comparing its audience with people who shop at Ralph Lauren, an American brand which uses references to an (idealised) English country style in its clothes.[3] The interpretation of the brand also reveals levels of snobbery; there is an implied – sometimes explicit – disdain for the group of people who mistakenly see Merchant Ivory as high culture. This 'mistake' is based on the fact that the films are literary adaptations and include references to high culture; Greek mythology, poetry, painting, philosophy etc. Evident in critical responses to Merchant Ivory is a desire to embarrass those audiences who confuse such middle-brow films with the real thing of high culture. This condescension is particularly notable when the subject is an American audience's reaction to the films.

This doesn't necessarily mean that the criticisms of *Remains of the Day* aren't valid. Does the appeal to the vanity of the audience (through their recognition of high culture references) engender the same false feeling of superiority over others found in the hierarchical structures – apparently criticised – in the film? Is the Merchant Ivory brand based on a deception? While seeming to criticise the hierarchy of class it congratulates the audience on their similarity to the upper classes – belonging above rather than below stairs.

Remains of the Day opens with a neo–classical (an artistic movement defined by a yearning for an earlier period) drawing of Darlington Hall. This establishes the weight of the past on the present – further emphasised by the use of flashback – as well as the dominant role the house plays in the film. The setting of the Hall becomes a microcosm of England, creating a symbolic world in which the characters become representations of particular groups and ideas (the different classes, English and US national identity, appeasement, Nazism) rather than individuals. As the camera pulls back to reveal the green of the English countryside, it also emphasises the isolation of the house and, we soon realise, that of Lord Darlington and Stevens. The film opens in the late 1950s and it is clear that the England represented by the image of the stately home is now gone; the remaining treasures from the house are being auctioned off and an American is now the owner of the Hall. Whether this is a cause for sadness or celebration is not apparent. This ambivalence is at the centre of the film and is personified by Stevens who sometimes seems to understand the danger of his master's views but who ultimately states his own position, 'I am his butler', as reason not to question them.

Such conflicting viewpoints are evident in the film's investigation of the redundancy and loss of a particular way of life. The contrasting representation of the US – in the guise of the US ambassador, Jack Lewis – as modern, democratic and professional (Lewis tells Darlington's gathering that the era of the 'well meaning amateur' is over) is in direct contrast to that of Lord Darlington and his allies from Old Europe. Their attitude to Lewis is to underestimate him and his country by sneering at what they understand professionalism to mean – greed, power and ungentlemanly behaviour.[4] American culture disrupts the hierarchy of the English class system, but in the character of Lewis it also seeks to emulate it, Lewis becomes Darlington's replacement. (This ambivalence could also explain the appeal of the film to an Anglophile American audience.)

The visual style of the film is undoubtedly linked to one of the main themes – the effect of the hierarchical society on the working class. Stevens is not merely repressed in his inability to express his desires. His position means he must be invisible; his aim is to efface himself, to become, as far as possible a part of Darlington (the Hall and the man being indivisible). The dominant style of the film is a visual representation of this idea. The precise composition repeatedly emphasises the position of the servants at Darlington Hall as they are closely framed by doors and narrow, endless passageways. The emphasis is always on the need for invisibility; servants seem to appear and disappear through the elaborately decorated walls of the house, the doors camouflaged to aid the pretence that the aristocracy is served by invisible forces. That these images of restraint and denial are also visually pleasing highlights the problem of reading *Remains of the Day* as an attack on English society. Any attempt in the film at a political analysis is undermined by the beautiful, harmonious style.[5]

Notes

1 Quoted in 'Bookmakers are the icons of the modern age', Terence Blacker, *The Independent*, 7 November 2000.
2 Sheldon Hall in Robert Murphy (ed.) *Directors in British and Irish Cinema: A Reference Guide*, London, BFI, 2006.
3 Anthony Lane, 'Remains of the Day' in *Nobody's Perfect*, London, Random House, 2003.
4 This representation of the relationship between England and the US is also found in an earlier British film, *Chariots of Fire* (Hudson, 1981), which contrasts the amateur ethos of the English establishment with that of the professionalism of the US athletics team.
5 This analysis of the film form of Merchant Ivory should be placed in the context of film studies theory. Since Truffaut published 'A Certain Tendency in French Cinema' (1954) with its attack on the cinema of quality, a style which valued the literary over the visual, it has become critical orthodoxy (as is the case in other arts subjects) to value the experimental, the foregrounding of film language, over content in cinema. One of the reasons for the antagonism towards Merchant Ivory could well be their resistance to this type of film-making, their perusal of what is pejoratively referred to as 'civilised space' which is assumed to privilege the status quo over any disruption or revolution.

Further Reading

Martin A. Hipsky, 'Anglophilia: Why Does America Watch Merchant-Ivory Movies?', *Journal of Popular Film and Television*, 1994, pp. 98–102.
Robert Emmet Long, *The Films of Merchant Ivory*, New York, Abrams, 1991/97.

John Pym, *The Wandering Company: Twenty-One Years of Merchant Ivory Films*, London and New York, BFI/Museum of Modern Art, 1983.
John Pym, *Merchant Ivory's English Landscapes*, New York, Abrams, 1994.

SARAH CASEY BENYAHIA

LONDON (1994)

[Production Company: BFI Productions/Koninck Studios. Director, cinematographer and writer: Patrick Keiller. Editor and sound design: Larry Sider. Cast: Paul Scofield (narrator).]

Patrick Keiller's debut feature defies the normal categorisation of cinema. Part visual essay, part chronicle, part pilgrimage, and part haunting homage to a sprawling capital city and its people, *London* (1994) is neither documentary nor fiction but transcends both modes of cinematic expression. It tracks the imaginary journey of its unseen protagonist, Robinson, accompanied by the invisible narrator (voiced by Paul Scofield), around London at a time of great social, political and cultural turmoil for the capital city, and at a time of profound personal distress for at least one of its characters. It makes reference throughout to sources of inspiration from English Romanticism and earlier literary flâneurs as they seek to rediscover a spirit of humanity and conviviality within a metropolis which appears on the surface to have been all but destroyed by international finance and the demands of commerce. As such, this film is not only interesting for its experimentation in form, and its contribution to the further blurring of boundaries between avant-garde and art cinema, but also as a highly policitised exploration of 'capitalism, class, and history' (Dave 2000: 339) that sets out to reveal the reasons for the decline of this city and those who inhabit it.

The work of architect-turned-director Patrick Keiller is often compared to that of other cinema poets such as Peter Greenaway and Chris Marker, both references underlining the innovative, elegant and enigmatic intentions of Keiller's work. The latter perhaps also pointed to the photographic, essay-like approach of *London* in particular which holds echoes of Marker's seminal *La Jetée* (1962 France). However, when Keiller first approached the BFI for support for a feature-length project, he had only a few critically well-received short films behind him and just a rough draft of the script in place.[1] As Claire Smith acknowledges, this was a huge gamble on the part of both film-maker and backer, tempered perhaps only slightly 'by the fact that it would be a kind of documentary, produced on a low budget (£180,000)' (Smith 2000: 149).

London clearly draws on Keiller's fascination for such avant-garde movements as European surrealism and Russian formalism, in particular in the way both groups shared the desire of 'refining creative methods to transform our experience of everyday life' (Dave 2000: 340). In his earlier work, he revealed an interest in using image and sound to record events that were important on a personal and private level as well as on a more public scale. He experimented with the documentary form, and deliberately broke the conventions of authenticity by creating poignant land and cityscapes, usually in silence, and later adding carefully constructed soundtracks that combined scripted voice-overs with fragments of music from a range of sources.

While Keiller resisted the convention of scripting his first feature fully in advance, and opened up a space for a different kind of relationship between subject and camera, he nevertheless had the clear intention of exploring London in the early 1990s as a place of conflict and contradiction, as a place where people felt neglected by society. He does so on the one hand through the juxtaposition of the imagery itself, and through the occasional deliberate dissonance between image and sound, and on the other through the decision to focus and comment upon key political and social events that transformed the life of the city in 1992. Images of contemporary events such as the relentless IRA bombing campaign, royal ceremonies, the crash and gradual recovery of the London Stock Exchange, the election of the fourth term of the Conservative government are presented and reflected upon via the deadpan, satiric commentary of the unseen, but apparently all-seeing Narrator. Intercut with these grander events are classically proportioned images of squalor and decay – buildings left to rot away and people left to fend for themselves, on the streets, in poor housing, on houseboats on the outskirts of the city. Much of this is set to the melancholic music of Beethoven, interspersed with more quirky upbeat sounds of Brahms' Alto Rhapsody. Other impressionistic sounds which have been added to the score to enhance the sense of contemporary urban place and human existence include on-location recordings of singing by schoolchildren, church congregations, and carnival gatherings.

Many of the images are in fact static camera shots, held in a fixed position for several long, uncomfortable seconds, forcing us to gaze at the 'lost' spaces of industrial sites and supermarket car parks: images of bridges across the Thames abound, signalling the criss-crossing pattern of the route taken by the two characters as they travel around the suburbs and into the heart of the financial City itself. In fact, the film begins with a perfectly framed Tower Bridge in all its splendour, marking the location as one of the world's most familiar landmarks. As the bridge is raised to allow a cruise ship to pass through, so the narrative begins with the announcement of the arrival of the Narrator in London along the Thames having completed work as a cruise ship photographer. It is assumed that the ship we see is the one from which the Narrator embarks when in fact it is probably just used as a device to trigger the story of his journey through the city.

For all its formal complexity, the film's narrative structure is quite simple: the Narrator returns to London after a seven-year absence and stays with his old friend Robinson, an eccentric academic prone to depression and nostalgic ranting. Robinson enlists his friend to accompany him on a series of short trips round London, exploring its problems and in search of its inner character. They do so with a blend of affection and despair at the way some things have changed, perhaps irrevocably and in most cases – according to them – for the worse. Their first journey is a kind of pilgrimage to the sources of English Romanticism, including the Gothic Villa of Horace Walpole, modelled in part on Westminster Abbey. Their second takes in the haunts of writers such as Apollinaire and Poe, and also includes a trip to observe the unveiling of yet another war memorial by the Queen Mother, an event that is slightly disrupted by jeering from sections of the crowd.[2] The third and final excursion is inspired by a desire to locate the house where French poets Rimbaud and Verlaine once lived together, prompting much controversy at the time. They find in its place the telephone exchange tower and despair at the cultural and artistic decline of this once great city. As Susan Doll suggests, Robinson 'searches for a modern-day café society of bohemian artists and intellectuals that he can relate to, but he realises he will not find it in London proper – which has become a towering financial centre' (2006: 10).

As the characters travel from Vauxhall, where Robinson lives on a busy road, to other areas of South London and beyond, so the Narrator also reflects on matters of art and poetry, literature and photography, sociology and economics, shifting almost effortlessly from one topic to another in the manner of the free association techniques of the Surrealists of the 1920s and 1930s. Through his sardonic commentary, it is made clear that 1992 marks a traumatic year for the city of London, with a government that seems interested only in financial success, an insurgent campaign that threatens to bring the city to its knees, and a royal family that seems cocooned by the pomp of its rituals and oblivious to the poverty and squalor suffered by many of the people on its doorstep. The Narrator begins by describing London, and by extension England, thus:

> Dirty Old Blighty. Undereducated, economically backward, bizarre. A catalogue of modern miseries. With its fake traditions, its Irish war, its militarism and secrecy, its silly old judges. Its hatred of intellectuals, its ill health and bad food. Its sexual repression. Its hypocrisy and racism. And its indolence. It's so exotic. So, homemade.

It's without doubt a bleak picture, but one which spurs Robinson and his friend to go in search of some spark of hope and optimism that might lead them to believe in change and a fresh type of development that will create a more inclusive and less self-destructive society.

As they meander in search of signs of life in places like Strawberry Hill, Richmond Park, Stoke Newington, Brixton and Elephant and Castle, a passion for flâneurs, writers and explorers of the past is quickly revealed. As Danny Birchall points out, they seem to be 'obsessed with late nineteenth century French poets and eighteenth century Romantic English writers' (2003: 1), the former group (like Robinson) being literary exiles in London at some point in their lives. On visiting Leicester Square, for example, they notice the monuments and placards which everywhere record the existence and presence of such influential people in their midst, now almost concealed by signs of consumerism, entertainment and general detritus. Even in Vauxhall, the starting point for their excursions, reference is made to the destruction of the beautiful gardens that once were there but which made way for housing and other development triggered by the introduction of the railway line and light industry in the 1840s. The gateposts that remain as dislocated signs of survival of that heritage 'speak' to them at the start of the film of time, people and events from the aristocratic past, but turn silent as the Narrator returns, unable to provide the answers he seeks.

Rather than remain depressed by this, however, they deliberately seek out places where humanity seems now to be thriving, and which Robinson might use as a base for his writing: amidst the crowds of Brent Cross Shopping centre, the arcades of Brixton Market, on Routemaster buses, even amongst the huddled groups of street homeless. At the end of the journey, back in Vauxhall at the end of the year, things may have changed for the worse with some seemingly bizarre traffic policies and reference to the need for steel shutters to fend off the constant break-ins, but the film closes with an image of the local butcher's shop preparing for business, with its shutters raised and lights glowing. Via this unflinching tour of the city by its key characters, *London* connects a whole range of disparate phenomena in an attempt to make sense of both the chaos and the splendour of modernity, and in so doing to reclaim a sense of the past.

Notes

1 Those 16 mm shorts included *Stonebridge Park* (1981), *Norwood* (1983), *The End* (1986), *Valtos* (1987) and *The Clouds* (1989). Before that Keiller had begun to develop his unique approach while a postgraduate student at the Royal College of Art's Department of Environmental Media, through slide presentations that created fictional narratives with architectural photography.

2 The statue referred to is a memorial to 'Bomber' Harris, the airman who led the wartime raids on Dresden, once a hero, now considered by many a mass murderer. A parallel questioning of the past is suggested by the image of flames blazing on Bonfire Night and reference to Guy Fawkes, remembered mainly as a conspirator but by a few as a hero who attempted to do away with the government. The association here with the discontent with the government of John Major is further reinforced by images of protest and strikes and announcements of mass unemployment.

Further Reading

Danny Birchall, '*London* (1994)', www.screenonline.org.uk/film/id/497617/index.html, 2003–6, accessed 2 February 2007.

Paul Dave, 'Representations of Capitalism, History and Nation in the Work of Patrick Keiller', in Justine Ashby and Andrew Higson (eds) *British Cinema, Past and Present*, London & New York, Routledge, pp. 339–351.

Susan Doll, 'A Guide to Robinson's *London*', Facets' DVD notes, 2006.

Claire Smith, 'Travelling Light: New Art Cinema in the 90s', in Robert Murphy (ed.) *British Cinema of the 90s*, London, BFI, 2000, pp. 145–155.

SARAH BARROW

LAND AND FREEDOM (1995)

[Production Company: Parallax Pictures. Director: Ken Loach. Screenwriter: Jim Allen. Cinematographer: Barry Ackroyd. Music: George Fenton. Editor: Jonathan Morris. Cast: Ian Hart (David Carr), Rosana Pastor (Blanca), Iciar Bollain (Maite), Suzanne Maddock (Kim), Angela Clarke (Kitty), Eoin McCarthy (Coogan), Tom Gilroy (Lawrence), Marc Martinez (Juan Vidal).]

Placed at the centre of *Land and Freedom* there is a scene that is at the thematic heart of this film. Not only does it crystallise the understanding of the Spanish Civil War expressed in the film but it also embodies the essence of Ken Loach's approach to film-making. In the middle of the war, with the power exerted by landowners and the Church over ordinary people's lives seemingly broken, the inhabitants of a small rural area gather to debate the future of their community. In the commandeered grand house of the local aristocratic landlord, declared to be 'the house of the people', they discuss whether the land around their village should now be owned and farmed in a collective way. With them and welcomed to take part in the discussion are a group of international socialists who are in Spain to defend that country's fledgling democracy. The dialogue-driven scene in which an array of characters stand and put forward their views lasts 12 minutes and defies our expectations of mainstream cinema. Loach allows the debate to run its course: the issues under discussion were at the heart of the Spanish Civil War and so must have their place at the heart of the film. Furthermore, the ideas rehearsed here are central to Loach's ideology; he has absolute faith in ordinary people's ability to organise their collective lives in a co-operative fashion, and his film-making displays this same faith in his audience.

At this point the film is a drama of ideas, but it is the reality of ordinary people's lives that gives expression to those ideas. For Loach his film-making must simply and unobtrusively tell a story, allowing the voices of 'real' people to be heard in the expectation that an audience will recognise the truthfulness of those voices. If we have been brought up on Hollywood film-making this can be experienced as 'boring' film-making in which 'nothing happens'; there is no action, just people in a room talking (although this downplays the fluid intimacy of the cinematography that positions us in the midst of the debate). If we are studio executives we 'know' this will turn audiences off; the key participants are not even characters with whom the audience has previously identified and acquired some vested interest in what they have to say; and rather than highlighting the views of central characters the functional editing merely seems to give equal weight to each point of view. But for Loach (and Jim Allen, the scriptwriter) this is the most moving material possible, this is about people taking control of their lives, demonstrating their ability to effectively employ democratic processes.

For the engaged reader this seemingly static scene involving a prolonged period in a single location is full of drama: one group of people have left their homes to travel to an unknown country to fight and die for their beliefs while most of the others have probably not travelled beyond the nearest local market town and yet together they are thoughtfully debating the possibilities for a more just way of life. Each character comes across as an individual and yet each is focused on discussing a single issue; what we are shown is newborn socialist democracy in action. Such a political process is not easy and Loach doesn't shy away from this; the debate always seems liable to end in disagreement – this is the reality of such fledgling political processes and was certainly the reality of left-wing alliances during the Spanish Civil War. If we empathetically understand this scene, how it has been made and why it has been included, we understand the film as a whole (and we also, incidentally, understand Loach's career).

To do full justice to *Land and Freedom* we need to know a little about the Spanish Civil War and the political debates raised by that event. However, we should also be aware of more recent political events in Britain and the rest of Europe, and be prepared to consider how Loach might be seeking to locate his film within the context of an economically rundown mid-1990s Britain (and Europe) within which attacks on ethnic minorities were increasing. As discussion of the scene above suggests we could also usefully consider Loach's approach to film-making in relation to what he might be attempting to achieve in that process. So, when the film opens in a stairwell containing right-wing graffiti and continues with handheld camera-work that gives a strong sense of the confined space of an old person's flat we are immediately presented with a sense of the importance for Loach of political context and a realist film-making style.

The Spanish Civil War (1936–1939) resulted in around 600,000 deaths, thousands of them before General Franco's firing squads during and just after the war. It was a conflict between Left and Right that mirrored the political battle going on all over Europe during the 1920s and 1930s. One of the arguments put forward in this film is that if democratic governments and those who believe in democracy are not prepared to fight fascism wherever it emerges then it is allowed to gain strength; for Loach this is as true for Europe in the 1990s as in the 1930s. The viewer is offered the possibility of positioning themselves alongside the granddaughter, Kim, as a member of a later generation learning lessons about the past and coming to realise the absolute relevance to the present of an older generation's experience.

In 1931, five years before the Civil War, the Spanish monarchy was replaced by a parliamentary democracy. Liberals, socialists and Republicans promising reforms to benefit workers and peasants alike began to challenge the power of landowners, the Church and the army. In 1936 the Popular Front, a coalition of left Republicans, Socialists and Communists, won the elections and rightwing groups feared a complete social revolution. In July, the army (eventually under General Franco) attempted a military coup, but trades unions and political parties which believed in the new democracy formed militias and resisted. *Land and Freedom* offers a reassessment of this historical moment, essentially suggesting Stalinists within the left-wing coalition of the Popular Front brought about the defeat of a potential full-blown revolution.

The film employs a classic narrative structure involving a journey told in flashback. David (Ian Hart), a young unemployed communist from Liverpool leaves his girlfriend, Kitty, and travels to Spain in autumn 1936 to join those defending the reforms.[1] While there he falls in love with Blanca (Rosanna Pastor), an anarchist. We accompany David not only as he travels through Spain but also as he develops his understanding of the politics of the period. Within the narrative there is a two-dimensional love story: there are David's letters sent home to Kitty while he experiences a growing love for Blanca, but there is also the love of a granddaughter for a grandfather. This is a familiar pattern for the political film to follow: one of the most famous Hollywood romances, *Casablanca* (Curtiz, 1942), is essentially a plea for democracies (in particular the United States) to become involved in fighting the fascism of Hitler's Germany.[2]

It is clearly a common narrative device to begin a story in the present and then use flashback to show something that has happened in the past, but for Loach this is not simply a film about the adventures of one man in the 1930s. For Loach history is only important for its relevance to the present, for the ways in which it enables us to reflect upon the contemporary world. It is important that as a member of the younger generation Kim should be enabled to see a whole new world of ideas and possibilities through her grandfather's experiences, and that she should discover how much we lose if we do not listen to and learn from previous generations.

Loach and Allen align themselves with the final verdict on the civil war given to David: 'Had we succeeded here – and we could have done – we would have changed the world'. For them the 'we' here is not the Republicans but rather those believing in full-blown, on-going revolutionary change.[3] Loach has said:

> It just grows ever more apparent that there are two classes in society, that their interests are irreconcilable, and that one survives

at the expense of the other ...You walk through the cities, especially the outskirts of cities, and you see people are not having a good time. The underlying observation of what people are experiencing is that things don't have to be this way. There are better ways to live.

(Fuller 1998: 113)

This film presents political arguments regarding the Spanish Civil War that allow for a reassessment of that conflict; demonstrates the ongoing relevance of those arguments to contemporary society; and subsumes all of this within a powerful human drama. Amongst all of the discussion of the politics the subtlety of the film construction can be missed. In addition to the cinematography already mentioned during the critical central debate and during the opening we could also, for example, consider the way Rosana Pastor as Blanca is photographed as she experiences the death of her lover Coogan (Eoin McCarthy). Here Loach's determination to film in sequence is also key; from day to day the actors can see events unfolding but never know what will happen next to their character, so when one of them 'dies' the stress released creates real emotion. We could also consider a series of shots of David against blank white or grey backgrounds in the film as he attempts to understand the truth of the situation in which he finds himself: as he decides to 'confess' his part in Coogan's death to Blanca, as she leaves him in Barcelona, and as he sits with her dead body in her parents' home.

It can be useful to know a little more about the POUM (the Trotskyist Workers' Party of Marxist Unification), the CNT (the anarchist National Confederation of Labour), and the position of other groups involved in the struggle but it is more important to respond to the film-making – the way in which internationalism is expressed through both casting and use of language, or the way in which the subtitle ('A story from the Spanish revolution') gently puts this forward as but one story while also asserting that what was taking place was 'revolution', or the way in which a keyword such as 'companeros' recurs throughout the script.

Notes

1 One text worth reading in conjunction with the film is George Orwell's *Homage to Catalonia* – David's path towards greater understanding of the national and international forces at work in the Spanish Civil War is very similar to that of Orwell.

2 Humphrey Bogart's character, Rick, has been fighting for the Loyalists in Spain and also against Mussolini's troops in Ethiopia.

3 Kim is given a further 'final' verdict on events when at David's funeral she reads from William Morris's poem 'The Day Is Coming', effectively urging both those around the grave and the audience to join the socialist struggle.

Further Reading

Ian Christie, 'As Others See Us: British Film-making and Europe in the 90s' in Robert Murphy (ed.) *British Cinema of the 90s*, London, BFI, 2000.

Graham Fuller (ed.) *Loach on Loach*, London, Faber, 1998.

Jacob Leigh, *The Cinema of Ken Loach*, London, Wallflower, 2002.

George McKnight (ed.) *Agent of Challenge and Defiance: The Films of Ken Loach*, Trowbridge, Flick Books, 1997.

George Orwell, *Homage to Catalonia and Looking Back on the Spanish War*, Harmondsworth, Penguin, 1966.

JOHN WHITE

SECRETS AND LIES (1996)

[Production Company: Thin Man Films. Director and Screenwriter: Mike Leigh. Cinematographer: Dick Pope. Editor: Jon Gregory. Cast: Timothy Spall (Maurice Purley), Brenda Blethyn (Cynthia Rose Purley), Marianne Jean-Baptiste (Hortense Cumberbatch), Phyllis Logan (Monica Purley), Claire Rushbrook (Roxanne Purley).]

When *Secrets and Lies* was awarded the Palme d'Or at Cannes in 1996 it was the latest in a long line of achievements for a director whose career spanned more than 30 years and whose output included work for theatre, television and cinema. Television plays such as *Nuts in May* (1976), *Abigail's Party* (1977), *Grown Ups* (1980) and *Meantime* (1984) were popular with audiences and critically acclaimed. His earlier feature films, including *Bleak Moments* (1971), *High Hopes* (1988), *Life is Sweet* (1990) and *Naked* (1993), had all been enthusiastically received by critics and audiences alike.[1]

By most definitions, Leigh is an auteur director, and his signature style, themes and working practices are apparent in *Secrets and Lies*. Leigh wrote the final screenplay for the film after improvising with actors in the early stages to develop his original concept for the story. The film shows his preoccupations with, as he puts it, 'families, relationships, parents, children, sex, work, surviving, being born and dying' (Coveney 1997: 5). In common with all his films since 1990, *Secrets and Lies* was produced by Thin Man Films, his own company, allowing him maximum artistic freedom. All the hallmarks of a 'Mike Leigh' film are there: a distinctive kind of humour, approach to characterisation, visual style and narrative structure.

Indigenous production in the UK has always taken place in the shadow of Hollywood and the dominance of that industry has meant that British cinema is often synonymous with 'arthouse' screenings, niche audiences and films which attract reverence rather than large audiences. Leigh has expressed his frustration at this situation: 'the idea that [...] any film I have made should be dumped in what are regarded as arthouse cinemas isn't on. I am not concerned with making esoteric, obscure kinds of films' (Malcolm 2002: 1). Nevertheless, his rejection of Hollywood conventions is equally clear, and he describes *Secrets and Lies* as a film that:

> deals with ordinary people in an unsentimentalised, non-sensationalised way – which is code for an un-Hollywood way [...] the fact is there is a great tradition, which exists in Europe and plenty of other places [...] of making films about real life, uncluttered and unfettered and uninterfered with by the kind of disease that you can – broadly speaking – diagnose as Hollywood.
>
> (Miller 1996: 1)

For many directors, the adoption of a British cinematic realism which has its origins in the documentary films of Grierson and Jennings is in itself the ultimate rejection of Hollywood values. However, while the complex narrative structure and flexible audience positioning in *Secrets and Lies* clearly come from a different vision of cinema than the straightforward goal-led narratives, rigid audience positioning and simplistic characterisation of most of mainstream Hollywood, the film also challenges the 'transparency' of this documentary realism.

The opening sequence of the film demonstrates Leigh's approach to narrative structuring. The shots of the funeral and the subsequent shots of Hortense (Marianne Jean-Baptiste) posting the letter to the adoption society seem to serve to set up the 'narrative goal' of the film. However, the intercutting of these with shots of Maurice (Timothy Spall) taking photographs of a bride, Monica (Phyllis Logan), stencilling, Roxanne (Claire Rushbrook), Cynthia (Brenda Blethyn) and Hortense at work, then the montage of Maurice's studio portraits, offers the audience a series of different perspectives on family and work relationships rather than one simplistic view. This paralleling and contrasting of characters and situations is one of the ways in which Leigh creates a dynamic and flexible interaction between audience and film which is creative of meaning rather than reductive. He has said that: 'I work on the assumption that my audience is at least as intelligent as I am, if not more so, which is another reason why I wouldn't last for more than two minutes in Hollywood.'[2]

The sequence resonates with visual and verbal echoes of the film's preoccupation with families, relationships, and misunderstandings. 'I expect he'd have had us up to visit by now if it wasn't for her' says Cynthia, referring to her sister-in-law, when in just the previous scene we have heard Monica suggest that Cynthia and Roxanne are invited over. The film starts with Hortense weeping at her mother's funeral, while Cynthia uses the loss of her 'poor mother' to emotionally blackmail Roxanne while they quarrel; Maurice and Monica lament the loss of contact with their 'surrogate' child, Roxanne; Hortense's siblings quarrel over who is to inherit their mother's house. After this series of glimpses into family life, an ironic, quirky montage of idealised family situations is shown through Maurice's camera lens.

Leigh's structuring technique means that sequences which are redundant in terms of narrative progression are tightly woven into a thematic structure. The sequence introducing Stuart (Ron Cook), the former owner of Maurice's studio, is a good example of this. Stuart presents us with a stark vision of life without family: 'There but for the grace of God' says Maurice, inviting us to reassess the frustrations of family life we have seen so far. The shot of Maurice and Stuart framed either side of a studio portrait of two children ironically contrasts with the other family portraits we have seen and resonates with ideas central to the film. Stuart's discontent with the weather in both Britain and Australia provides a comic manifestation of Leigh's exploration of the relationship between subjective and objective viewpoint. Stuart's distorted vision of his own role in Maurice's success, together with his easy assumption that Maurice has kids, is one of many points in the film where characters create their own distorted vision of their own and others' situations. The audience is implicated into these false assumptions by Leigh's exploitation of the misleading nature of the photographic image.

The sequence starts with Maurice photographing the young woman injured in the car crash for her court case – ironically, this time using the camera to distort the 'truth' in the direction of ugliness rather than the idealised (Hollywood?) version of reality seen in Maurice's previous photographs. Her bitterness and inability to get over the perceived wrong done to her, and the strength of her hatred towards the once loved boyfriend, is an extreme version of a tendency many of the main characters share, where subjective perceptions distort 'truth' yet become a 'reality' which define and limit their lives. The arrangement of the shot, seen first from her unblemished side before revealing the scar, makes the audience literally experience the limitations of seeing things from one side only, a central metaphor in the film, and also the intentional falsity of the photographic image. From one side, she is 'lovely', from the other side an object of pity and repulsion. Unlike the other characters, her scar is on the surface; the 'secrets and lies' which blight the lives of the other characters are harder to perceive.

This challenges the 'transparency' of documentary realism. 'There are a lot of different things going on at a lot of different levels in my films. As far as I am concerned, these are worked out in terms of imagery and metaphor just like any piece of art' (Leigh in Carney and Quart 2000: 146). When surface realism is used in *Secrets and Lies*, its apparent meanings are frequently undercut by conflicting meanings emerging through the narrative structure and symbolism of the film.

The symbolic use of colour and mise-en-scène is not in itself unusual. The use of each character's house as a reflection not only of their social status but of their emotional state (Hortense's flat all-white minimalism; Monica's house cold blues and rigidly ordered) is a common one. What makes it distinctive here is the way in which this intersects with other meaning systems in the film. A central idea in *Secrets and Lies* is vision/seeing. While Maurice's job as a photographer and Hortense's profession are presented realistically and are believable within the context of their characters, they also provide the central metaphoric focus of the film. As a photographer, Maurice seems to be concerned with putting a gloss on the complexity and awkwardness of reality. The montage sequence of photographic vignettes makes it clear that real families not only differ from their photographic representation, but differ in different ways. Hortense's professional goal is to make people see more clearly and it is therefore fitting that it is her narrative agency in the film which brings hidden family truths to light. The sequence showing Hortense with her young client reveal how difficult it is to be clear about what you see; in a different but related way, the wedding sequences and the montage of studio photographs Maurice takes show the unreliability of the photographic image.

This central idea positions the audience to question the very 'realism' of the film's images in ways which can be seen as a critique of the 'transparent' realism of documentary style and the photographic image generally. This idea is also reinforced through seemingly inconsequential 'realist' dialogue which often works to destabilise meanings. When discussing Roxanne, Monica resignedly comments 'Well, she's on the streets now', a deceptive remark which is humorously undercut by the shot of Roxanne in her uniform sweeping the streets. *Secrets and Lies* abounds in conversations where there is a disjunction between surface and underlying meaning and much of the film's humour comes from this discrepancy: from Stuart's consistent contradiction of Monica's relentlessly upbeat comments about his trip to Australia; to Hortense and Cynthia's stumbling attempt at the family barbecue to convince the others that they work at the same factory.

The ways in which these allusive layers of meaning are built up mean that by the climactic birthday party sequence, the film is stylistically different from both Hollywood and the social realist tradition. The sequence shot of the group gathered around the garden table which lasts over six minutes is reminiscent of Maurice's deceptively happy family photos, but because of the way the film has encouraged the spectator to think about these, and about the characters, the irony is clear. All the deceptions and conflicts seething under the surface are recognisable. At the start of the film, Monica seemed a stereotype from the British social realist genre: the shrewish woman who has lost sight of real values under a welter of materialism. This judgement is recast in the light of subsequent revelations.

Leigh's style both adheres to a version of the British realist aesthetic but also interrogates and reveals the superficiality and limitations of photographic realism. The final shot of the garden of Cynthia's terraced house – the archetypal 'gritty realist' icon of working-class life – is juxtaposed with Cynthia's apparent satisfaction with her lot, which acts as a rejection of the pessimism of the social issue film. The motivation behind Leigh's working-class characters is fundamentally different from those in a social realist film. Leigh's interest lies with how individuals live within certain political and social structures. He does not see them as victims nor use them as vehicles to expound an explicitly political viewpoint.[3]

Notes

1 For example, he won Best Director at Cannes for *Naked* and Best Film at the US National Society of Film Critics awards for *Life is Sweet*. See www.pfd.co.uk/clients/leighm [accessed 21/06/06].

2 See *Mike Leigh On His Film Making Techniques* from www.tohubohu.
com/leigh/miketalk [accessed 21/06/06].
3 Since *Secrets and Lies*, Leigh has produced a further four films to date:
Career Girls (1997); *Topsy Turvey* (1999); *All or Nothing* (2002); and *Vera
Drake* (2005), the latter nominated for Best Director and Best Original
Screenplay at the Academy Awards.

Further Reading

Ray Carney and Leonard Quart, *The Films of Mike Leigh*, Cambridge,
Cambridge University Press, 2000.
Michael Coveney, *The World According to Mike Leigh*, London, Harper Collins,
1997.
Derek Malcolm, 'Mike Leigh at the NFT', http://film.guardian.co.uk/
print/452168–101730,00.html, 7 October 2002 [accessed 21/06/06].
Laura Miller, 'Listening to the World', www.salon.com/weekly/inter-
view960916.html, 16 November 1996 [accessed 21/06/06].

JEAN WELSH

THE FULL MONTY (1997)

[Production Company: Redwave Films. Director: Peter Cattaneo.
Screenwriter: Simon Beaufoy. Cinematographer: John de Borman.
Music: Anne Dudley. Editor: David Freeman and Nick More. Cast:
Robert Carlyle (Gaz), Mark Addy (Dave), Tom Wilkinson (Gerald),
William Snape (Nathan), Lesley Sharp (Jean), Emily Woolf (Mandy),
Steve Huison (Lomper), Paul Barber (Horse), Hugo Speer (Guy),
Deirdre Costello (Linda).]

The Full Monty is a British film with the classic 'feel-good' values
of a mainstream Hollywood movie[1]: the city might be rundown,
unemployment rife and men struggling to come to terms with
changing gender roles and marriages at breaking point, but with a
little screen magic the world can seem a wonderful place again. Dave
clearly announces before the final 'full monty' stage-show that this is
'for one night only' and therefore nothing more than a very temporary solution to the working-class male predicament; but the
resolution phase of a film has such special power that for the cinema
audience the ultimate meaning of the film is likely to be a frozen
moment of warm, finely established emotional bonding between
father and son (*Nathan*: They're cheering out there – you did that.
Now get out there and do your stuff), wife and husband (Jean
whooping and smelling Dave's shirt), and even estranged wife and

former husband (Mandy, importantly without Barry, catching Gaz's belt). This is the traditional happy ending appropriate to the genre: it re-establishes order within society, celebrates human resilience and creativity, and reassures the audience that decent human beings in the natural order of things will eventually come to enjoy a good life as of right. To this extent the film is clearly selling the audience a falsely reassuring perspective on the disintegration of the UK's manufacturing industries and on the divided nation created by government policies that the film has seemed to want to address. Yet, at the same time the use of a final freeze frame might be said to reinforce the fact that the future for each of these characters remains uncertain.[2]

It is a feature of comedy that difficult, even intractable, problems are solved in a comforting way but *The Full Monty* takes this to extremes. The bleak hopelessness of Lomper's attempted suicide becomes the occasion of slapstick comedy as Dave bundles him back into the fume-filled car and leads to the repartee of the set-piece discussion on possible suicide methods (set, we might note, in the open space of a green Sheffield hillside with the cold, grey city relegated to the background[3]). It is true that the darkness of Lomper's day-to-day existence is emphasised with increased power by the cut from the light atmosphere and emotional warmth of this scene to the dingy claustrophobia of the house he shares with his invalid mother, but then the mother is never seen again and is conveniently killed off while Lomper finds life is worth living with the arrival of a clichéd, politically correct homosexual love affair. This is uplifting, it is as comedy should be an affirmation of life, and yet it might also be considered a false representation of reality. Screenwriter, Simon Beaufoy, was it seems aware of both the commercial pressure on film-makers and the way in which he was using the genre to enable him to approach social issues: 'It's a way of sugaring the pill – and sadly you now have to use more and more sugar' (Owen 2003: 287).

From the beginning the very real psychological stress of unexpected, long-term unemployment is addressed with humour. In the opening sequence the hustle and bustle, bright colours and chirpy narrator's voice found on the early 1970s promotional film for Sheffield[4] is transformed into the muted greys, cold blues and hollow emptiness of the mid-1990s derelict factory. The moment of change from one to another is startling and the contrast achieved by the edit (employing a stark black screen and simple inter-title, '25 years later') makes a powerful comment on the social consequences of industrial decay, but the audience is prevented from dwelling on the implications of the transition by the arrival of the film's central comedy duo.

In a later scene in the job centre Gaz and Dave (along with the other 'men' there) are clearly shown as having regressed to the status of schoolchildren; here in the factory with Nathan they are also children, 'kids' with too much time on their hands taking part in a bit of trespassing. The audience warms to them because of their comedy antics (Gaz grabbing Dave as the car they are standing on begins to shift in the canal and then nodding to the passer-by, for instance) but also because of the comic timing achieved not only in the delivery of the lines but in the editing (the initial cut from Gaz's 'Shut up, I'm thinking' to the canal scene, for example). The success of the comedy throughout diverts attention from the seriousness of the issues under examination. This is not necessarily a problem; in fact, it is the nature of the particular comic form being used. This is not a biting satire but a gentle celebration of the human ability to make the most of any situation. In a scene such as that with Gaz and Dave on the car in the canal, it is the coming together of the script, the delivery of those lines, the performance and movement of the actors, the framing of the shots (particularly the final long shot along the canal), and the editing (for example, from the passer-by to Gaz and back again) that creates the humour. In other words, the elements of film construction (including, and this is clearly important for the whole film, the music) work to complement each other.

The central characters in this film are men and the key focus is on men's problems within a changing society and yet it seems to appeal as much if not more to a female audience than a male audience. In part this is because the gaze employed is essentially an observational one, looking in on males and their idiosyncratic ways and emotional difficulties. It is not a gaze that objectifies the male body despite the fact that this would be the expected implication of having a film with a plot revolving around men who become strippers. But it is a gaze by which men are placed as it were under a microscope. They themselves are increasingly aware that their former social position is not simply under threat but is no longer tenable (describing themselves, for example, as 'obsolete').

Men are shown to be vulnerable, physically and emotionally deficient rather than strong and able to deal with problems in a traditionally male way. Within the conventional norms of British working-class society men are expected to fulfil certain roles and embody certain values. They should be physically strong, emotionally strong, virile and strongly heterosexual; above all they should work and provide for the family. In this film Dave is fat, out of condition and impotent, Gaz is struggling to show his love for Nathan, Gerald lacks the courage to tell his wife he's lost his job, Horse is worried about the size of his penis, and Lomper and Guy turn out to be gay. Most importantly they are all unemployed ('scrap' as Gaz describes it) and therefore unable to see themselves as 'men'. By contrast, both Jean and Mandy are in work (with Mandy twice adding to Gaz's sense of disempowerment by offering him a job) and Linda reveals strength of character her husband had failed to appreciate when she finally finds out he is unemployed.[5]

In traditional terms, the men are seen to be emasculated by this society. But what the film also shows is the men struggling to re-define their roles in a new society, and indeed succeeding in doing so: Gaz successfully nurtures a developing relationship with Nathan (and, it is suggested by the ending, with Mandy), Dave successfully rekindles his relationship with Jean it seems, Gerald has secured a new job but remains loyal to his mates, and Lomper and Guy are accepted within the male group. Interestingly, the men find the strength to deal with the new situation facing them by drawing on an old source of strength: male camaraderie. Given this strong focus on relationships and emotions, a further way of exploring the film would be to consider it as a male melodrama and this might also be a fruitful area for further consideration of its success with female audiences. Politically, the men survive by re-establishing a sense of community in direct opposition to the self-centred individualism encouraged by Thatcherism.[6]

It is in accepting and being prepared to reveal their vulnerability, literally to expose themselves to the community, that they find their way back to a place and an acceptance within their society. At a political level through its use of comedy this film could be seen as papering over the cracks rather than challenging the defects in society. But at a psychological level it is profound in its recognition of the need to be able to express vulnerability in order to come to terms with it. Because they are prepared to display their vulnerability, the men are rewarded with a one-off pay day but more vitally with a sense of restored personal self-worth and the confidence (it is implied by the 'feel-good' ending) to move forward in their lives. It is through their involvement with the group that the men (who span sexualities, race and generations) are able to regain a sense of self-worth (Murphy 2000: 185) but more importantly it is the strength the group gives them that enables them to reassess their relationships outside of the homosocial sphere. Each character is able to 'come out': Lomper and Guy obviously, Dave in talking openly with Jean, Gaz in expressing his love for his son, and Gerald in re-evaluating what is important in life. Finally, Horse, operating as a metaphor for all of them, is able to expose that part of himself about which he has always felt most vulnerable.

Notes

1 For a short account of the film's success in the United States see Sarah Street's *Transatlantic Crossings: British Feature Films in the United States*, New York and London, Continuum, 2002, pp. 210–211.

2 The final shot of Francois Truffaut's *The Four Hundred Blows* (1959) would be a classic example of the use of a freeze frame at the conclusion of a film. It is also employed at the end of *Flashdance* (Lyne, 1983), a film referenced in *The Full Monty* in which a female welder (or worker in steel) wants to become a ballet dancer.

3 The shot across the bleak city symbolising momentary escape from the entrapment felt by the central characters is a feature of a British New Wave film such as *The Loneliness of the Long Distance Runner* (Richardson, 1962) and points to the underpinning social realist strand of British film-making to be found within *The Full Monty*.

4 *Sheffield – City on the Move* (Coulthard Productions, 1971).

5 Not only are women taking over the role of men in becoming the main breadwinners, they are also seen symbolically invading male spaces such as the working men's club and even the men's toilet!

6 See Monk for a discussion of the film in relation to Blairite policies and the commodification of the underclass that could be said to take place in this and other films from the period.

Further Reading

Nigel Mather, *Tears of Laughter: Comedy Drama in 1990s British Cinema*, Manchester, Manchester University Press, 2006.

Claire Monk, 'Underbelly UK: the 1990s Underclass Film, Masculinity and the Ideologies of the "New" Britain' in Justine Ashby and Andrew Higson (eds) *British Cinema, Past and Present*, London, Routledge, 2000.

Robert Murphy (ed.) *British Cinema of the 90s*, London, BFI, 2000.

Alistair Owen (ed.) *Story and Character: Interviews with British Screenwriters*, London, Bloomsbury, 2003.

JOHN WHITE

RATCATCHER (1999)

[Production Company: Holy Cow Films. Director and screenwriter: Lynne Ramsay. Cinematographer: Alwin Kuchler. Editor: Lucia Zuchetti. Music: Rachel Portman. Cast: William Eadie (James), Tommy Flanagan (Da), Mandy Matthews (Ma), Leanne Mullen (Margaret Anne), John Miller (Kenny), Michelle Stewart (Ellen), Lynne Ramsay Jr. (Anne Marie).]

Something about the gentle, meditative force of Lynne Ramsay's startling debut feature captured the attention of audiences, critics and jury panels alike when it was first released in 1999. And yet on the surface, there is little remarkable or distinctive about it at all. The narrative is simple and sparse, the setting familiar in its focus on the downbeat and the character ensemble likewise in their situation of poverty. In fact, in less assured hands, this film could easily have become yet another derivative piece reminiscent of all those by British directors before Ramsay who had sought to bring the world of the urban marginalised of Britain to the cinema screen. Instead, it is the emotional impact of *Ratcatcher* that sets it apart, and the sheer beauty of its cinematography that makes it extraordinary. Violence and tragedy resonate in every image, while moments of tenderness offer respite and hope by reminding the viewer of the overwhelming power of human love.

With this film, Ramsay was praised for her deft ability to develop intense and harsh situations without slipping into manipulative melodrama. In fact, *Ratcatcher* was considered by critics and audiences to be one of the best British feature film debuts for many years. It opened the Edinburgh Film Festival in 1999 to great acclaim, and won its director a BAFTA award for best newcomer in British cinema 2000.[1] While her tendency to focus on the harshness of working-class lives calls for comparisons with the films of Ken Loach, particularly his trilogy that is also set on Glasgow estates, Ramsay's work has also been likened to that of Scottish film-maker Bill Douglas and Liverpool-born director Terence Davies, for their similarly poetic approach to the notion of growing up amidst poverty and brutality. Like them, she effectively combines the real with the magical, and with *Ratcatcher* powerfully captures a sense of place and a segment of society with a poignant story about growing up.

Ratcatcher is set in a neglected part of Glasgow in the 1970s during the so-called 'Winter of Discontent', when a long strike by dustbin collectors meant that refuse remained on the streets for weeks. As such it is a peculiar take on the period heritage genre which in British cinema has tended to be taken as shorthand for a focus on the upper classes. Here, however, the tight-knit world that is put under scrutiny is that of a loving yet dysfunctional family living in one of the poorest parts of a city often associated in film with social hardship. They struggle against forces that are largely out of their control, and are revealed as being the forgotten victims of a social system that neglects those at the bottom of the pile, or blames them for being where and who they are. This is also, then, a vehemently political film, not in the didactic vein of a work by Loach perhaps, but political nevertheless in that it invites us to witness the most private moments and spaces of the Gillespie family home, and to understand and sympathise with their plight. Merging the poetic with stark realism, Ramsay treats all her characters with compassion, and casts harsh judgement on society for its refusal to do the same.

The film's main character is James Gillespie, a twelve-year-old boy who accidentally pushes a playmate into a polluted canal and leaves him to drown. Immediately breaking the standard conventions of narrative cinema, and blurring the boundaries between victim and aggressor, *Ratcatcher* offers us a character with whom to engage and identify who is marked out from the start as a killer. Keeping his terrible secret to himself, he finds comfort in his friendship with Margaret Anne, a complex, slightly older local girl who also seems to be alone except for a gang of youths whose abuse she tolerates so as at least to feel noticed. The audience is thus placed in a privileged position of knowledge, of sharing James's secret and witnessing Margaret Anne's pain, and this makes the tender scenes between them seem all the more heart-rending. We also learn that James longs, like his mother, to leave the council estate and fantasises about life in one of the new houses in the countryside that he has discovered at the end of a bus line. Like her, he yearns for a different life but has absolutely no idea how to achieve it.

Despite the trance-like beauty of its imagery, *Ratcatcher* is a dark, grim film about guilt and redemption, with the latter coming only through tragedy. Duncan Petrie describes it more specifically as 'an intense and melancholic study of childhood dislocation, confusion and loneliness' (2000: 216). James feels responsible for the accidental drowning of his friend, and is unable to deal with the emotional turmoil that follows, even though no one blames him at all. He also struggles to understand his father's drinking and is unable to articulate his unhappiness even to his beloved mother. Little more actually happens in normal narrative terms, and yet, as Petrie points out, the pleasure of this film comes from the invitation to its audience 'to experience a rich palate of [...] emotions from James's guilt and loneliness to moments of spontaneous bliss when he runs through the open fields' (2000: 216). Ramsay's main achievement is to set up an intense connection between her characters and the film's spectators such that we might understand the meaning of the lives depicted on screen, and share in the tragedy of their unrealised dreams.

Alongside the painful exploration of loss of innocence that marks an abrupt end to childhood, this is also a film about what it means to be a man in such harsh conditions. The idea of traumatised masculinity is seen most clearly in the character of James's father who uses alcohol as a means of escape from a life seemingly without hope. His mood swings rapidly from showing care and compassion for his children, especially his daughters who love him unconditionally, to uncontrolled violence when forced to recognise that he is incapable of providing for his family properly. Unable to articulate his emotional turmoil, to deal with affection, or to ask for help from those around him, he uses his fists instead and causes further misery for those he loves most. Again, only the film's spectator bears witness to his intense sense of grief and powerlessness, a strategy that highlights the tragedy of the situation by foregrounding his isolation.

The mystery and tension of the film is set up by the tone of the opening sequence, during which young Ryan Quinn (Thomas McTaggart), the boy who will die in the following scene, is shown wrapping himself up in his mother's net curtain. He thus unwittingly creates a shroud-like covering, the significance of which only becomes clear as the film progresses. Filmed in ghostly silence and slow motion and from a position that obscures the context completely, the image only makes sense once Ryan's mother (Jackie Quinn) has slapped her son hard (from off-screen) and woken him from his daydream with her sharp rebuke. The frame remains still throughout, so that as Ryan runs off, the audience is left pondering the sight of the gently unravelling curtain material and contemplating the sudden and violent interruption of the boy's game. Such a moment of everyday conflict makes the mother's grief at the loss of her child all the more unbearable since it eschews melodrama and sentimentality completely.

Despite the overriding tone of bleakness, the film does also offer moments of pure joy that provide breaks from misery and emphasise the power of familial love and the importance of physical contact. When James and his sisters dance around the flat with their mum, for example, or when James shares a playful bath with Margaret Anne, such images demonstrate the way respite can be found in the most unlikely places and life can be enjoyed whatever the circumstances. James's child-like escapades at the unfinished housing estate, and his excitement at exploring one of the new homes with its brand new shiny bathroom and views of cornfields provides particular pleasure (for him and the viewer) and a space for him to imagine another sort of family life. As Petrie points out, 'the image framed by the window like a cinema screen [. . .] functions as practically a fantasy of freedom and possibility for the young boy' (2000: 216). The fantasy sequences that depict his dream of family life in this house further allow for blurring of time and space that shows how important the alternative world has become for James and how difficult it would be for him to continue living without hope of change. Even more absurdly surreal are scenes such as those when friend Kenny attaches his pet mouse to a helium balloon and sends it squeaking off into space. And the final closing image of James underwater, accompanied by a minimalist other-worldly soundtrack, is both intensely beautiful with the light shining in from above, and profoundly sad.

Indeed, part of what is remarkable and bold about this feature is that so much is left unsaid, unexplained, or only half explained, right down to its denouement. In this and her subsequent films, Ramsay has been understandably described as 'relentlessly experimental, [. . . bringing] a photographer's eye to the cinematic image: through silence and space within the frame, her films unfold in expanded time, showing rather than telling'.[2] Thus rather than let her characters talk about the binmen strike, she provides visual evidence of the long-running dispute in the form of piles of black, split refuse bags and scenes of the children playing amongst the rotting rubbish, taunting each other with rats. The general social decay is likewise referred to via the sight of dilapidated flats and squalid stairwells which become the space for intense conversations or moments of private grief. Meanwhile, notions of claustrophobia and entrapment are reinforced by extreme facial close-ups, tiled angles and repeated images of tightly framed doorways and window frames that also give the panoptic sense that those who live on such estates are constantly being watched by their neighbours. Use of sound is also remarkable for its intensity: empathetic music is sparsely used and only then at low volume, with haunting Celtic tones contributing to the melancholic tone of the piece. Key diegetic sounds, usually those that relate to water and thus suggestive of the multi-layered fluidity of its characters' lives, are given just as much attention.

Ratcatcher skilfully combines ordinary moments of everyday family life with more elaborately designed extra-diegetic sequences that reveal the inner feelings and thoughts of its young protagonist. It powerfully depicts a key turning point in the life of a boy whose world is torn apart by one terrible act of cowardice, and who is forced by circumstances to be more adult than he really is. The performances elicited from its child actors, notably William Eadie as James and Leanne Mullen as Margaret Anne, make even the tiniest moment, such as when James nervously touches Margaret's bloody knee, intensely memorable. In many ways, *Ratcatcher* is a masterclass in cinematic economy, showing the bare minimum and leaving the rest to the imagination.

Notes

1 Ramsay was already an award winner: *Small Deaths*, her graduation film from the National Film and TV School, won the Cannes Jury Prize in 1996, and one year later she produced two other prize-winning shorts, *Kill the Day* and *Gasman*.
2 'Ramsay, Lynne', http://www.screenonline.org.uk/people/id/552070/ [accessed 25 November 2006].

Further Reading

Harlan Kennedy, 'Ratcatcher', *Film Comment*, Jan./Feb. 2000, pp. 6–9.
Duncan Petrie, 'The New Scottish Cinema: Themes and Issues', *Screening Scotland*, London, BFI, 2000, pp. 191–221.
Liese Spencer, 'What are you Looking at? Interview with Lynne Ramsay', *Sight and Sound*, October 1999, p. 18.
Linda Ruth Williams, 'Escape Artist', *Sight and Sound*, Oct. 2002, pp. 22–25.

SARAH BARROW

WONDERLAND (2000)

[Production Company: Revolution Films. Director: Michael Winterbottom. Screenwriter: Laurence Coriat. Cinematographer: Sean Bobbitt. Editing: Trevor Waite. Music: Michael Nyman. Cast: Shirley Henderson (Debbie), Gina McKee (Nadia), Molly Parker (Molly), Ian Hart (Dan), John Simm (Eddie), Stuart Townsend (Tim).]

Following the lean years of the 1980s, there was something of a revival in British cinema in the 1990s, and in 1996, the number of UK films produced in a year reached a peak.[1] New film-makers emerged with new approaches, Michael Winterbottom being one of these. Michele Carmada, from Kismet films, approached Winterbottom to direct *Wonderland* from a script by French writer, Laurence Coriat, because of his 'sense of aesthetics' and his 'ability to get great performances from actors'.[2] The central performances, the portrayal of emotions and the visual flair validate this confidence, and make it an essential inclusion in this volume.

Wonderland was released in the UK in January 2000. Funded by BBC Films and Polygram Filmed Entertainment, it was moderately budgeted at £4 million. Like most of his oeuvre, it was not particularly successful at the UK Box Office, making £395,498.[3] However it brought critical acclaim, winning the British Independent Film Award for Best British Film and was nominated for a BAFTA and a Golden Palm at Cannes.

One of Britain's most prolific film-makers, *Wonderland* was Winter-bottom's sixth theatrical feature and by 2007 he had made a further six, with three more in production or pre-production. Ambitious and inventive, he first gained recognition in television for the hard-hitting *Love Lies Bleeding* (1993). His TV drama series, *Family* (1995), written by Roddy Doyle, was nominated for a BAFTA and won awards at the Torino International Festival of Young Cinema. It was this project's subject matter that triggered Winterbottom's interest in looking at 'a family that is living separately'.[4]

In *Wonderland,* he brilliantly conveys the difficulties of everyday existence for an extended family as its members struggle to find some connection with other people. A contemporary ensemble piece, the protagonists are all London-based and each character is at a different stage in their life. Nadia (Gina McKee) is single and searching for love through 'Lonely Hearts' telephone introductions; her estranged brother, Darren (Enzo Cilenti), briefly in London for his birthday, is in a happy relationship. Younger sister, Mollie (Molly Parker), and husband, Eddie (John Simm), are expecting their first child. Older sister, Debbie (Shirley Henderson), a single mother, is separated from Dan (Ian Hart), Jack's (Peter Marfleet) father, and enjoying commit-ment-free lovers. Parents, Eileen (Kika Markham) and Bill (Jack Shepherd), co-exist uncomfortably, with Eileen's low mood exacer-bated by the continuous barking of the neighbour's dog. Bill sidesteps the flirtatious advances of lively neighbour Donna (Ellen Thomas), a single mother living with her children including older son, Franklyn (David Fahm). The three sisters dominate the screen, and through them, sharp observations about singledom and single motherhood are powerfully conveyed.

Participation in rituals such as going to the hairdresser, a Bingo session, a football match and a firework display flesh out these char-acters and remind us that people need patterns to their lives. Different family groupings come together for specific reasons. Molly has her hair done by Debbie. Dan collects Jack from ex-partner Debbie's flat. Sisters Molly, Debbie and Nadia meet in the coffee bar where Nadia works. Dan goes to Nadia's home to seek Jack. With Debbie unable to accompany him due to the onset of Molly's labour, Jack has taken himself to the promised firework display while Dan sleeps off a drinking session. Jack, Nadia, Dan and Debbie meet later in the Police Station. Eileen goes to the hospital to see Molly and her new grandchild, the same hospital to which Eddie is taken when he falls off his scooter after circling London all night in panic at impending fatherhood. Eddie and Molly are reunited in their separate wheelchairs in the hospital corridor and the name, Alice, is agreed for their newborn.

The backdrop is London. Serving almost as another character, it determines the quality of their daily lives, and their mode of existence within it helps to define their personalities. St Paul's Cathedral, the red buses and the Post Office tower signal the city known by tourists, but a different version is shown with litter, beggars, coffee shops, and bars full of drinkers. Constant traffic and trains wind their way through the city. The title, *Wonderland*, is partly ironic, describing London itself, as well as the world baby Alice is born into, the reference reminding us that life is often confusing and inexplicable. Cinematographer (and documentary-maker) Sean Bobbitt used a handheld camera shooting on 16 mm and his keen observational approach creates a vibrant and convincing portrait of contemporary city life.

Wonderland reveals what happens to these characters over a long weekend and deliberate links are made between characters through careful juxtaposition of key scenes. Although most have endearing qualities, all the male characters fail the women. Bill cannot meet Eileen's emotional needs. Dan's incompetent fathering enrages Debbie. Eddie takes flight at a crucial time. His moment of departure is cut next to a shot of Dan squeezing his spots in the mirror before he heads out to the pub, leaving Jack 'home alone'. Eddie's rehearsed justification to Molly for quitting his job immediately prior to the birth of their child, performed while leaning on a bridge over the Thames, effectively conveys his confusion.

Dan and Eddie are immature. Like Jack – the child – they leave the spaces they should inhabit, and all three suffer consequences. Jack absconds from Dan's. His passage through the firework display is intercut with Eddie's journey through London. For both there is a sense of being spellbound, in a 'wonderland', achieved through the camerawork on the fireworks, shot after shot of lights across the sky, and on the streets of London where Eddie drives. This impression is heightened by Michael Nyman's intense music. Eddie's scooter spins out of control in the shot immediately before Jack is mugged. Jack's headphones are stolen and Eddie's helmet comes off. Their shared vulnerability is made evident through the intercutting.

Nadia's search for love bookends the film. Over the opening credits, her words utter the profile she thinks single men will want to hear. When we finally see her, she is talking of her involvement with sport – walking, dancing – and, perhaps ironically, we see her blowing cigarette smoke from her mouth, eyes closed and slightly left of frame. The murky coloured background is later distinguished as the wall of the Ladies Room in a bar. A jump cut has her face tilted upwards, awkwardly filling the screen in such a big close up that her face is distorted. She draws on her cigarette. Her movements look gawky as the camera follows her face down and then up again. The next shot shows her at the right side of the frame drawing on her cigarette and then it swings round so that she is at the edge of the frame with smoke covering her face. The editing and the camera movement make evident her discomfort. This is typical of the camerawork throughout the film, as it varies from extreme close-up to movement around and behind the character it presents.

Nadia checks her appearance in the mirror while the voice-over talks of 'meeting someone looking for friendship or well, yeah, and possible romance'. The 'r' of 'romance' is pronounced with 'w' and, in combination with her faltering words and use of the mirror, underlines her self-consciousness and discomfort at the 'Lonely Hearts' route to finding a soul-mate. She extinguishes her cigarette in the basin, which like the earlier smoke camouflage suggests that she is hiding this habit, and so something of her true personality, from her date. As Sarah Street argues, her attire, a 'layered look' (2001: 76), a see-through patterned top with vest showing underneath, also hints that there is more to her than is initially apparent. There follows her embarrassed return through the congested pub for stilted conversation. Nadia invents another toilet visit and walks out into the streets of London where speeded up images followed by slow motion powerfully convey the pace and intensity of city life in a kind of hyper-realism. In combination with Nadia's earlier voice-over followed by the ambient sound of the bar, Nyman's crescendos underline the mood of alienation. This sequence is intercut with scenes showing Nadia's sisters relaxed in their own homes, Debbie in her high-rise flat, and Molly in more affluent surroundings, emphasising the connection but also the difference between the three women.

Nadia abandons three dates. The second is when Dan pretends to be a new 'Lonely Hearts' introduction, and the third is after she has been left in no doubt as to Tim's disinterest in her once intercourse is over. He grabs a beer, switches on the light, serves himself the remains of the supper he had previously cooked for them. He is only again shown in the same frame as Nadia when he restores the cushion she is still leaning on to its pre-intercourse position. Nadia's embarrassment is clear as she dresses hurriedly. The close camerawork emphasises her vulnerability, as do her tears as she heads for home in the rain on a bus dominated by people loudly enjoying themselves.

Her hunched demeanour throughout the film expresses lack of self-esteem. She is forceful only in her role as aunt, when confronted with Dan's ineffectual response to Jack's disappearance.

In the final scene Nadia meets her father beside his unreliable car, and Franklyn (David Fahm), who has previously noticed her in her cafe, joins them, offering Bill his manual. As Nadia and Franklyn walk away side by side, Franklyn's clumsiness as he trips over a drain makes them both relax into laughter. The final shot is from behind as these two walk towards the city, implying that here is someone to whom Nadia might become close without the aid of the dating agency.

This incident, along with the birth of the baby, Mollie and Eddie's reunion, the fatal poisoning of the barking dog, an answering machine communication from estranged Darren to his parents, all seem to suggest solutions to the major issues. These are small triumphs on the larger canvas of ongoing struggle for this city-dwelling family, each experiencing his or her own version of loneliness or alienation.

Winterbottom's films employ a plethora of genres and styles: literary adaptation, drama-documentary and romantic comedy amongst them. For this reason, critics have debated Winterbottom's auteur status. He makes films frequently with the same industry professionals, which means a kind of technical and artistic consistency, despite the range of material, and runs Revolution Films with his main producer, Andrew Eaton, thus ensuring a degree of artistic freedom.

Consistency of outlook is also evident. Loneliness and the experience of the outsider are regular themes in Winterbottom's work, as is a commitment to revealing the injustice of real events. By his own account 'the stories that interest me a lot involve deep emotions at some level'.[5] In *Wonderland* the emotions occur as a result of everyday situations, but are as skilfully explored here as are those experienced by people living in a war zone (*Welcome to Sarajevo*, 1997) by asylum seekers (*In This World*, 2002), or by men wrongfully imprisoned (*The Road to Guantanamo*, 2006).

Notes

1 Eddie Dyja, *BFI Film and Television Handbook*, London, BFI, 2002, p. 23.
2 *Wonderland Production Notes*, Universal Pictures, 1999.
3 Eddie Dyja, *BFI Film and Television Handbook*, London, BFI, 2002, p. 40.
4 *Production Notes*.
5 Nick Roddick, 'The Roddick Interview', 1997 (http://www.filmfestivals, com/cannes97/cintb3.htm).

Further Reading

Xan Brooks, '*Wonderland*', *Sight and Sound*, January 2000, p. 62.
Anthony Kaufman, 'Michael Winterbottom's *Wonderland*', indieWIRE, http://www.indiewire.com/people/int_Winter_Michael_000728.html (accessed 28 July 2000).
Sarah Street, *Dress Codes in Popular Film*, London, Wallflower, 2001.

CATHY POOLE

MY SUMMER OF LOVE (2004)

[Production Companies: Apocalypso Pictures and BBC Films. Director: Pavel Pawlikowski. Screenwriter: Pavel Pawlikowski. Co-writer: Micheal Wynne. Cinematographer: Rysard Lenczewski. Music: Goldfrapp and Will Gregory. Editor: David Charap. Cast: Emily Blunt (Tamsin), Natalie Press (Mona), Paddy Consadine (Phil), Dean Andrews (Ricky), Michelle Byrne (Ricky's wife), Kathryn Sumner (Sadie).]

Pavel Pawlikowski's third feature film, *My Summer of Love*, is a chimera with a rock solid centre, one where what we think we see may turn out to be fake, de-familiarised or fantasised. A coming-of-age story of two teenage girls falling in love, it sets up genre expectations which, like some of its striking visual moments, of schoolgirl hangings, drownings in baths, or a gothic ivy-clad house, are deceptive and unreliable. This is no fast-cut teen thriller, lesbian love killer or country house mystery with a twist: even though its narrative pace is fast, and its editing tight and economic. The lush and leisurely cinematography draws us in, to a self-sufficient dreamy land more evocative of European art house than its Brit-Grit roots might suggest.

Fakes are everywhere in this film; the misrepresentations and de-familiarisations pervade the characters' actions and their surroundings, just as the words 'fake' and 'real' crop up constantly in their dialogue. Main character Mona's very name is not real; as she explains to her counterpart, middle-class Tamsin, her name is Lisa; Mona is her brother Phil's name for her, because she moans. Boarding school escapee Tamsin not only picks up the reference, but off-handedly claims to have 'studied the original', just as she proceeds to study Mona's working-class life. Mona's responses are more intense – the opening credits see her drawing her own version of a Mona Lisa in crayon on her bedroom wallpaper, a 'fake' representation of Tamsin which she then kisses, in the absence of the real thing. It is a moment that presages the multiple crossovers of identity in the film, and a scene that viewers later realise is the only one displaced in time, out of sequence in this otherwise linear realist narrative, a flash forward from towards the end of their relationship to tantalise the viewer.

Similar fakes scatter the landscape; Mona pushes around a scooter with no engine, her newly fundamentalist Christian brother presides over a pub with no beer, now given over to 'born again bingo', while Mona offers Tamsin (and us) virtual voice-over sex as experienced with her married ex-boyfriend Ricky: 'Do you want to be shagged by Ricky? Are you ready?'

Location is a key focus for this fakery; Tamsin describes Ricky's housing estate home as 'like Lego – pretence', it becomes the site for another verbal fantasy of sex, this time with a sour edge, as Tamsin imagines her father's girlfriend ('I bet she's there now, bent over the cooker') followed by the girls' punishment of Ricky by visiting his wife to deliver a fantasised version of his unfaithfulness with Mona, involving 'her abortion of your husband's foetus'. These love revenges put a different light on Tamsin's earlier assertion about their own relationship, gleaned from her school study of Nietzsche, that 'this is what is real'.

From the girls' first meeting, when the perspective of the shots disorientates, as Mona, lying on the grass, opens one eye and gives us a reflection of an upside-down image of Tamsin on horse-back, faking goes hand in hand with a cinematography of de-familiarisation to make all strange. As they begin their mutual mesmerisation intimate close-ups are inter-cut with distancing overhead and travelling shots of the two on the road, suffused by Goldfrapp's haunting alien music.

This impression is heightened in later shots where the landscape itself takes on an alien aspect of emptiness and geometric lines, from the cold light that pervades the setting for Ricky's unceremonious dumping of Mona to the whitely over-lit halo of light from the prayer meeting that reflects back on Mona as she stands behind Phil's dry bar. In contrast, Mona enters the alien greenery of Tamsin's 'fairytale' home like a rescuing prince, magically unlocked doors stand open to a series of corridors like a maze in a folk tale through which she glimpses another life, lit with an ultra real, unaccustomed sumptuousness. 'Now the pub is like a temple,' Mona tells Tamsin, an image echoed in the forest scenes of their lovemaking by religious images for a different transcendence at their favourite rock with water and fire ('A strange cathedral,' as Tamsin remarks).

A recurring image of the girls lying sprawled on the ground, evocative of sex and of death, both draws and warns the audience, presaging the games both play with dying. When Tamsin's outdoor cello playing (significantly Saint-Saëns 'Dying Swan') accompanies a dance by Mona which ends in her falling to the grass, the tone of this, as often, is self-conscious, both a parody of, and an embracing of, intensity, in imitation of their heroine Edith Piaf's 'wonderfully tragic' life. But it also touches real loss and death, reminding us of the china swans Mona has packed away, from the time 'The Swan' pub was 'real', a gift from her mother who died of cancer. The core of Tamsin's deception of Mona, which she builds up over several scenes in mounting detail, is the fantasised death of her sister from anorexia, again represented in bodily and folk lore terms – 'my beautiful sister developed hair all over her body like a werewolf'. Gathering force cumulatively, the multiple faked images take on a more serious edge; as Mona reluctantly begins to inhabit her sister Sadie's clothes, her role as 'other' sister slides into our growing realisation of mixed transferences and identities.

Visually the fantasy and realism mix inextricably: Tamsin stands nude at an ivy-covered window in answer to Phil's knocking, at once precocious teen temptress and imprisoned heroine, while the comic edge to Mona's death-game playing of the faked hanging similarly links illusion and seriousness. As she escapes back to Tamsin it is monumentally self-deluded Phil who gives the prophetic warning 'something's not right with that girl, something drives her'.

It is this particular mix of the fantastic, fantasy and fantasist, of comic re-playing and serious re-visioning that gives the film its ungraspable quality, and poses questions of reliability and truth, which the narrative style deliberately avoids. It also poses an intensity of sexuality and love, recognised and embraced by the girls despite all the pretence around and within their relationship, which spills out into the visual quality. Pawlikowski's achievement is to portray the (self-) deceit inextricably with the clear-sightedness, the consciously comic with the unconscious game-playing, and to suffuse all with an intense underlying reality, the spiritual which he has claimed to find missing in everyday life.[1]

This is partly achieved by the poetic quality of Rysard Lenczewski's cinematography. Richard T. Kelly has remarked that the effect for the viewer is the yielding of 'mundane reality', an impression heightened by 'wistful cutaway shots' taking us back to the location, of 'ominous clouds, smoking chimney stacks, wisps of cigarette smoke rising from the heather'.[2] This aspect is set alongside, and given everyday gravitas, by a more realist aesthetic. Pawlikowski's acclaimed second feature, *Last Resort*, followed the experiences of a Russian asylum-seeker and her son, in a British seaside town shot in grey uniformity, with mise-en-scène and experiences often resembling an East European police state. The lush English greenery of *My Summer of Love* is a negative reverse of this, being both iconic dream and accurate documentary. Pawlikowski, who spent his early years in Poland, became a BBC documentary-maker turned feature film maker[3] claiming as influences European film-makers such as the early Emir Kusturica, but equally citing Ken Loach and 1960s British realist films.[4] He borrows from their methods of improvisation with actors, resulting in dominating and authentic performances from the young leads, relative newcomers Natalie Press and Emily Blunt[5] and pitch-perfect menace from the more experienced Paddy Consadine, a regular on Pawlikowski's team.

The film is based on the novel of the same title by Helen Cross, but Pawlikowski's adaptation exchanges its political and social setting of a Britain of the 1980s riven by the miners strike for his enclosed timeless world of an apparently unending summer. Even so, key elements of the real are kept; the location in Yorkshire and Lancashire is a major element of the film's effects, as are the heavy use of realist methods of ambient lighting, and the mix of observingly distant swooping overheads and tracking with more intimately close, often handheld, cameras. Pawlikowski points out the cross-over, commenting that he has always treated documentary as film, whereas the feature films he has most admired had their roots in neo-realism (Macdonald and Cousins 1998: 389). The effect is striking in the filming of the activities of Phil's religious group; their prayer meetings are tracked round in over-held close-ups which mark their responses with all the detail of a documenting of cult activities, while the cutting between handheld close-ups and swooping overheads during the outdoor gathering to erect a giant cross to cleanse the valley moves the tone between the seriousness of the participants and the girl's mocking undermining of Phil's involvement.

This mix is at its most effective when its shifts work subtly at the level of images which tap deeper into character and narrative. The sequence which begins as an emotional searching through the 'dead' Sadie's room, moves into a quasi-religious making of vows of eternal love over magic mushrooms found, folk-tale like, in a casket, and taken like communion bread. The glowing red transcendent lighting quickly shifts to that of hallucinatory white light, formerly mainly cast over Phil's prayer meetings, and perhaps already hinting at fakery. This shifts again as the mists begin to clear and reveal the girls' dancing transferred and now taking place at ex-shagger Ricky's nightclub singing venue, from which they are forcibly removed. A further move to early morning light reveals an erotic 'Babes in the Woods', where Mona feeds Tamsin breakfast of blackcurrants at their favourite rock while Tamsin typically, breaks the spell first, with 'Blackcurrants are not enough breakfast; I'm cold, I want to go home'. Economically shifting between its realities, almost wordless until Tamsin's come-down, this sequence presages and prepares for the climactic scenes of the ending where Mona is forcibly disenchanted.

This last scene ends inscrutably. Having demonstrated both her passion and her emotional strength in a final fake drowning scene, which takes the viewer through a roller-coaster possible alternative ending, Mona reaches her final vindication alone, walking away Valkyrie-like[6] to the same strains of Edith Piaf which had celebrated their liberation as a couple: we watch her strides strengthen under the camera's last shot of swooping away observation.

Notes

1 *Film Eye* quotes Pawlikowski's remark that 'everything is measured economically or in terms of lifestyle or appearance, and the meaninglessness around promoting that' (*Film Eye*, No. 4, 2004, p. 1).

2 *Sight and Sound* review, Vol. 14, No. 11, November 2004, p. 60 quoted in *Film Eye*, No. 4, 2004, p. 4.

3 See Kevin MacDonald and Mark Cousins, *Imagining Reality: The Faber Book of Documentary*. London, Faber and Faber, 1998.

4 In an interview with David Thompson in *Sight and Sound* he claims British films of the 1960s as influences ('Another England', *Sight and Sound*, Vol. 14, No. 10, October 2004, p. 38).

5 Natalie Press returned to art-house film in *Red Road* (Andrea Arnold, 2006). Emily Blunt has taken a more mainstream route in *The Devil Wears Prada* (David Frankel, 2006).

6 Reviewer Andrew Wright commented that the 'alternately homely and Valkyrie gorgeous' Press seems 'herself unsure of what exactly her character is capable of' (www.thestranger.com/seattle/content?oid = 21465 – accessed 5 April 2007).

Further Reading

Samantha Lay, *British Social Realism: From Documentary to Brit Grit*, London, Wallflower, 2002.

LYNDA TOWNSEND

Index

Related titles from Routledge

Fifty Key American Films
John White and Sabine Haenni

Fifty Key American Films provides a chance to look at fifty of the best American films ever made from a cultural studies perspective. With case studies from the 1930s heyday of cinema right up to the present day, this chronologically ordered volume includes coverage of:

- *Mean Streets*
- *Goodfellas*
- *Hard-boiled*
- *The Doors*
- *Platoon*.

In addition to a raft of well-known examples from the big screen, the careers of America's best known talent, such as Spielberg, Kubrick, Scorsese and Stone are defined and discussed. This is essential reading for anyone interested in film.

978-0-415-77296-9

Available at all good bookshops
For ordering and further information please visit:
www.routledge.com